Adapting Content to Empower English Language Learning Students (ACEES)

Professional Development for Content Area Instructors, Grades 6–12

Margaret A. Rohan

Nova Southeastern University

Boston   Columbus   Indianapolis   New York   San Francisco   Upper Saddle River
Amsterdam   Cape Town   Dubai   London   Madrid   Milan   Munich   Paris   Montreal   Toronto
Delhi   Mexico City   Sao Paulo   Sydney   Hong Kong   Seoul   Singapore   Taipei   Tokyo

For
Kate, Anne, and Sandra

Vice President, Editor-in-Chief: Aurora Martínez Ramos
Development Editor: Barbara Strickland
Editorial Assistant: Meagan French
Director of Marketing: Chris Flynn
Marketing Manager: Amanda Stedke
Production Editor: Mary Beth Finch
Editorial Production Service: DB Publishing Services, Inc.
Manufacturing Buyer: Megan Cochran
Electronic Composition: Schneck-DePippo Graphics
Interior Design: Deborah Schneck
Cover Designer: Linda Knowles

Library of Congress Cataloging-in-Publication Data

Rohan, Margaret A.
  Adapting content to empower English language learning students (ACEES) :
professional development for content area instructors in grades 6–12 / Margaret A. Rohan.
    p. cm.
  Includes bibliographical references and index.
  ISBN-13: 978-0-13-509586-7 (alk. paper)
  ISBN-10: 0-13-509586-7 (alk. paper)
1. English language—Study and teaching—Foreign speakers. 2. Language and languages—Study and teaching. 3. Content area reading—Study and teaching. I. Title.
  PE1128.A2R625 2011
  428.2'4—dc22   2010003398

Printed in the United States of America
10 9 8 7 6 5 4 3 2 1 BRG 14 13 12 11 10

www.pearsonpd.com

ISBN-10: 0-13-509586-7
ISBN-13: 978-0-13-509586-7

Contents

Chapter 1

Creating an Environment for Success   1

Chapter 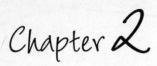2

Equitable Assessment of ELL Students' Performance 23

Chapter 3

Second Language Acquisition 51

Chapter *4*

ELL Students' Reading and Literacy Development 68

Chapter *5*

ELL Students' Writing, Listening, and Speaking English 91

Chapter 6

Math, Science, and Social Studies: Challenges and Adaptations for ELLs 113

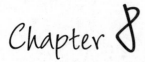

Chapter 7

Peer and Cooperative Learning Structures 152

Chapter 8

Technology, Multiliteracy Instruction, and ELLs 167

Chapter 9

Cross-Cultural Dimensions   180

Chapter 10

Parent–Teacher Communication, Students with Abilities, Professional Collaboration, and Final Thoughts   201

Foreword

To study culture and not include communications and language should be unacceptable in education. Ongoing dialogue and conversation are integral aspects of learning. Instructors' informal dialogues with students as a means of assessment is a tool for enhancing understanding. For content area teachers, expected outcomes and objectives are dependent on the effective use of communication. Clear communication is essential especially when thoughts and ideas of participants differ.

In classrooms all across the United States, teachers and students are failing to communicate effectively because of language barriers. Often, first language English speakers take for granted that English as a second language (ESL) learners fully understand the English language, if they are speaking in a seemingly comprehensible manner. I admit to being guilty of such an assumption. I recall a brief conversation I had with one of my middle school students several years ago. Before the morning bell rang, he and I were engaged in conversation about our exciting weekend. As our discussion was coming to an end, I made the statement, "Today is Monday and boy, do I feel blue." Juan, an ESOL student, replied, "Mrs., you not blue." My response was, "Yes, I am blue. I am just miserable." Juan's facial expression was one of confusion and his body language perplexed as he sort of smiled and went on his way. At that moment, I realized something profound: Although I was conversing with Juan, we were not truly communicating.

Something as simple as the word *blue* in my mind should have been understood by a middle school student. However, Juan was not a typical middle school, American student. He and his family had arrived in the United States a year ago from Guatemala. Before entering school in the United States, he had had very little formal schooling and no experience with the English language. Because Juan was speaking English (basic interpersonal communication, or BIC), I mistakenly assumed that he understood the meaning behind my idiomatic English. In other words, I mistook the student to be CALP (cognitive academic language proficient). For most English-speaking educators, this mistake is too common.

The English language is complex and one of the most difficult languages to acquire. Metaphors, similes, hyperboles, and acronyms, to name a few, as spoken by English speakers, may impede effective communication between two native English speakers. Thus, English language learners are even more likely to be confused during conversations with English speakers. In *Adapting Content to Empower English Language Learning Students*, Dr. Rohan explores solutions to address the discrepancies between language and learning for ESL speakers.

This book may be easily adopted as an everyday reference for educators faced with the challenges of helping second language students to negotiate meaning and unveil the roadblocks on the path to academic performance and success. Fundamental reform is not optional, if we are to maintain a free and optimal education for all students in this country. It is imperative in this environment of high-stakes testing that educators provide comprehensible instruction. In this book, Rohan takes a no-nonsense approach to confronting the cognitive and linguistic demands of both students and educators at the secondary level. She provides clear strategies, tools, and techniques for instructors to implement best practices and encourage transformative perspectives in today's diverse classroom.

Educational leaders must be confident in addressing issues related to cultural language as part of the English language, and they must be prepared to empower students whose second language is English. To do less than this will be detrimental to the improvement and quality of performance by language minority students.

Larthenia Howard, EdD
Author of *Challenging Mediocrity:*
Balancing Diversity and Student Achievement
CEO, The StimuKnowology Institute
www.blogtalkradio.com/dr-empowerment

Preface

Culturally diverse students are empowered or disabled as a direct result of their interactions with educators in schools.

—Jim Cummins

Most teachers would agree that they enter the profession with lofty ideals, noble principles, laudable goals, and boundless optimism—with a sense that they can change the world, one student at a time. With new crops of students arriving in the schools every year and even every semester, teachers have the opportunity, as well as the privilege, to plant the seeds of knowledge and fertilize them through conducting invigorating discussions and experiential activities, ultimately growing unique specimens of young people.

Most teachers would also agree with the educational philosophy that they, as educators, embrace the challenge of educating every child by cultivating his or her intellectual ability, improving the condition of his or her physical being, and stimulating his or her conscience. Teachers would also likely agree that their mission is to equip each student with the skills and knowledge necessary to become a compassionate, thoughtful, responsible, enterprising citizen—someone who achieves personal fulfillment in whatever he or she pursues.

So, how do teachers accomplish all of this in the rapidly changing dynamics of the twenty-first-century classroom? Teachers must retool practice, revise standards, redirect assessment, and reevaluate personal perspectives. This seems a daunting task both for teachers who are entering their thirtieth year and those who are just concluding their first. Even though many instructional approaches have withstood the test of time, many new approaches have been proven more effective than "old school" practices.

Shifts in population patterns and demographics are part of the history and culture of the United States. These shifts influence many aspects of Americans' lives, including public education. Although more than 60 percent of English language learners (ELLs) in grades 6 through 12 reside in five states (California, Texas, New York, Illinois, and Florida), other states have rapidly growing numbers of adolescent ELLs. From 1993 to 2003, for example, North Carolina experienced a 500 percent increase, and Colorado, Indiana, Georgia, Oregon, Nebraska, and Nevada more than doubled their numbers of ELLs (Perkins-Gough, 2007). By the year 2030, nearly 40 percent of all school-age children will be ELLs (Serve Regional Educational Laboratory, 2004).

Complicating the situation is the fact too few teachers know about their students' cultural and linguistic backgrounds or understand the challenges inherent in learning to speak and read standard English. Moreover, there is a long-term shortage of new teachers who are specially trained to work with ELLs. This shortage underscores the importance of training veteran teachers to work more effectively with new populations of ELLs (Ruiz de Velasco, 2005).

The No Child Left Behind (NCLB) Act of 2001 has changed the landscape of public education and emphasized the role of standardized testing in grades K–12. As part of NCLB, ELLs are no longer exempt from content area assessments, and they are held accountable for attaining the same levels of academic proficiency as their native-English-speaking counterparts. The rationale for this legislative directive was to ensure that ELLs would not be overlooked by the academic system, with teachers having few or no academic expectations of them because of their limited English proficiency.

As laudable as this directive is, it has one incredible snare: How is ELLs' mastery of educational standards going to be measured? Clearly, the focal problem in the standardized testing of ELLs is *language*. Students cannot accurately be tested when they are struggling with the language of the test. The travesty here is that much of what is known about second language learners may have been overlooked by NCLB policy makers, and provisions that were made to advance ELLs have actually widened the achievement gap between these students and their native-English-speaking counterparts. Secondary-level ELLs have been particularly vexed by passing the high-stakes standardized test required to earn a standard high school diploma. This test, given in isolation, has become the sole determinant of a student's mastery of standards.

Before the renewal of NCLB, the TESOL (2007) organization made several suggestions:

> For accountability purposes, both the language proficiency assessment and academic assessments should be taken in consideration and weighed according to each student's level of language proficiency. For ELLs at the beginning levels of English language proficiency, more weight should be given to language proficiency assessment results. As a learner becomes more proficient in English, gradually more weight can be given to the academic content assessment results.

What is needed is an array of authentic instructional approaches and assessments that will consider many aspects of ELLs' academic abilities. In the everyday practice of teaching, assessment is what drives instructional and curriculum planning. Given that, teachers must provide instruction that provides comprehensible input by contextualizing lessons. Doing so is absolutely critical for the success of ELLs.

English language learners in the secondary schools face special challenges. The cognitive and linguistic demands of secondary school are considerably greater than those of elementary school. Secondary-level students must be able to understand, integrate, and communicate complex bodies of knowledge and abstract concepts in math, language arts, science, and social studies. In addition, ELLs must learn English while concurrently learning abstract concepts in a language that is not their thinking language. The most obvious challenge for ELLs at the secondary level is to develop their proficiency in academic English quickly enough to succeed in courses and tests that require advanced English skills.

The National Literacy Panel on Language Minority Children and Youth released a long-awaited comprehensive synthesis of research on literacy attainment (August & Shanahan, 2006). It concluded that the instructional approaches to reading and literacy that are effective with native-English-speaking students are not effective with ELLs and that these approaches must be adjusted to have maximum effectiveness for ELLs.

English language learners need a comprehensive, dedicated, standards-aligned English language development (ELD) curriculum, strategies to promote English skills throughout the academic curriculum, and intentionally designed opportunities to use English with peers for both social and academic purposes. A quality ELD program actively develops all the domains of language and addresses varying levels of English fluency. A quality program also develops age- and context-appropriate language, with an emphasis on academic English in the content areas. The optimal program includes opportunities for ELLs to interact with native-English-speaking peers and creates a supportive learning environment for language learning (August & Shanahan, 2006).

A survey of 1,300 secondary teachers of ELLs in California found that their most significant issue was communicating with students (Maxwell-Jolly, Gandara, & Benavidez, 2007). The study also indicated teachers' significant challenge in finding appropriate tools and techniques and learning how to use them. This book, *Adapting Content to Empower English Language Learning Students* (*ACEES*), addresses that challenge, as it provides many techniques and strategies for the teacher's "treasure chest" of instructional tools.

There remains a stark mismatch between what is known about adequate professional development for teachers of ELLs and what is actually delivered in the classroom. Despite the added pressure teachers feel to ensure that information on standardized tests is covered, they need to reach out to ELLs.

The purpose of *ACEES* is to emphasize the importance of developing the ability of all content area teachers to work with linguistically and culturally diverse students using their districts' adopted textbooks. To facilitate instructional approaches that foster ELLs' success, this text was specifically designed for secondary content area instructors. *ACEES* focuses on principles of effective practice and resource material analysis; equitable assessment of ELLs; second language acquisition; reading, writing, and literacy; specific accommodations in math, science, and social studies; instructional technology; and cross-cultural dimensions.

References

Maxwell-Jolly, J., Gandara, P., & Benavidez, L. M. (2007). *Promoting academic literacy among adolescent English language learners*. Report published by University of California, Davis, School of Education, Linguistic Minority Research Institute.

August, D., & Shanahan, T. (Eds.). (2006). Executive summary. *Developing literacy in second-language learners: Report of the National Literacy Panel on Language-Minority Children and Youth*. Mahwah, NJ: Lawrence Erlbaum. Retrieved on September 21, 2008, from www.cal.org/projects/archive/nlpreports/Executive_Summary.pdf

Perkins-Gough, D. (2007). Special report/Focus on adolescent English-language learners. *Educational Leadership, 64*(6).

Ruiz de Velasco, J. (2005). Performance-based school reforms and the federal role in helping schools that serve language-minority students. In A. Valenzuela (Ed.), *Leaving children behind: How "Texas-style" accountability fails Latino youth*. Albany: State University of New York Press.

Serve Regional Educational Laboratory (SERVE). (2004). *English language learners in the southeast: Research, policy, and practice*. Greensboro: University of North Carolina.

Teachers of English to Speakers of Other Languages (TESOL). (2007). Statement of principles and preliminary recommendations for the reauthorization of the elementary and secondary education act. Retrieved December 7, 2007 from www.tesol.org/s_tesol/seccss.asp?CID=32&DID=37

Acknowledgments

The journey involved in writing this book would not be complete without giving thanks and voice to English language learning students and recognizing the important contribution they have made to the world of education.

In addition, special thanks goes to these individuals:

- Linda Pelli, who has been a confidante and friend when it has not been popular

- Suzanne Kromrey, Pat Beonde, Randy Locke, Delores Cooper-Johnson, Chandra Dixon, Norma Maldonado, Pat Griffis, Cathy Tedesco, Roxanne Gary, Doris Saffron, Michael Shawler, Danielle Semprini, Ashley Stover, Heather Higham, and Megan Higgins for their tireless work with ELLs

- Erick Hofstetter, who truly believes all children can succeed

- Sandra Hancock, from the University of Florida, for her support

- Porolle V. Simm for her lesson plan on astronomy

- Robert Kershaw, Carole Wilkinson and Mel Coleman, of Nova Southeastern University, who provided great encouragement

A special note of appreciation goes to Carlos Diaz, of Florida Atlantic University, who developed great relationships with teachers, sharing the gift of the transformative knowledge not only to education but our lives, as well.

I would be remiss in not recognizing the many public school teachers of grades K–12 who have contributed their experience, wisdom, and insights to this area of educational reality. I express great appreciation for their willingness to embrace the wonderful challenges and diversity found in the twenty-first-century classroom.

I appreciate all the feedback and comments that were given by my reviewers: Dr. Eileen Austin, USF Tampa; Mildred E. Berry, Florida Memorial University; Bethany Dannelly, Hampton Roads Academy; Donna C. Horton, Hillcrest Middle School; and Dr. Karen Mae Lafferty, Morehead State University.

Thanks also goes to Sue Freese, my careful copyeditor, and Denise Botelho, my project manager—together they helped to shape this manuscript into its final form.

Without additional words and a lifetime of true friendship, I want to say thank-you to Martha Howland Rose, Mo Martens, Sarah Mosling Warnke, Margaret DiNome Hearndon, and Frances Carter.

Chapter 1

Creating an Environment for Success

You come from a foreign land,

And you do all that you can,

Understand, to understand.

But it's not easy being you

In doing what you want to do,

When your tongue has tied up your hands.

So let me try to explain:

I think more than I say, and I feel more in my way,

But I can't always say what I mean.

—Anonymous student

Secondary school students whose native language is not English face the daunting task of learning the academic curriculum and a new language concurrently. With the increased number of these students across the United States and increased accountability requirements for their performance, schools are under pressure to better serve English language learning (ELL) students.

To create classroom conditions that are particularly supportive of English language learning students (ELLs), teachers learn to amplify and enrich, rather than simplify, the language of the classroom, giving students more opportunities to learn the concepts involved. Instead of presenting the curriculum as a linear progression of concepts, instructors reintroduce key information and ideas at increasingly higher levels of interrelatedness and complexity.

In creating an effective program of instruction, teachers must first recognize who the students are. Doing so means looking beyond the single label "English language learner" to understand the different needs of the individuals who enter the classroom. ELL students differ in many ways, including the languages they speak, the degree of English proficiency they have, the **cultures** they represent, the types of educational experiences they have had, the socioeconomic status they hold, and the experiences they have had coming to the United States (Cho & Reich, 2008; Keefe, 2008).

Because of this diversity, no single ELL program model fits all populations and contexts. English language learners need a cognitively complex, well-articulated, and meaningful standards-based curriculum that is taught at a comprehensible level and in a manner that keeps students engaged in an age-appropriate, grade-level academic curriculum.

Content area teachers should consider three principles when designing lessons for ELL students in **mainstream classes** (FLDOE, 2003):

Principle 1: Increase comprehensibility.

Principle 2: Increase interaction.

Principle 3: Increase higher-order thinking skills.

If teachers integrate these three principles into their lesson plans, they will help ELL students—along with all the other students in their classes—learn content, develop English language proficiency, and meet state standards.

Applying the Three Principles

To increase **comprehensibility**, principle 1, teachers can **contextualize** content delivery, build background knowledge, and provide **language focus lessons**. To increase **interaction**, principle 2, teachers can incorporate **cooperative learning** and peer learning activities, which allow for negotiation of language meaning within that content. These activities can foster both **positive interdependence** and individual accountability. To promote **higher-order thinking skills**, principle 3, teachers can create assignments or sets of questions that cultivate critical thinking.

Increasing Comprehensibility

To provide information in a way that ELLs understand, thereby increasing comprehensibility, classroom teachers must provide extralinguistic cues to meaning. Students can then match words and concepts with their meanings, which are obtained through nonverbal clues (Branch et al., 2008). Some nonverbal clues include demonstrations, pictures, gestures, and **graphic organizers**. Providing background information when presenting new content can also increase comprehensibility. Tasks and content can be broken into smaller components, and comprehension can be checked frequently. With the use of graphic depictions and visual **scaffolding**, such as graphs, charts, content organizers, and illustrations, key concepts can be reinforced.

Doing an application or expansion activity—for instance, creating a semantic map, listening to part of a public radio program, or viewing a segment of video—can be used to motivate students, draw on prior knowledge, and establish a purpose and relevance for learning. Doing so builds the background knowledge students need to comprehend the text. Students' comprehension is also supported through the use of supplementary materials, such as video, a piece of literature, a picture book, a gamelike activity, a Text Quest, any form of realia, or Word Bingo.

Building background and activating prior knowledge are vital in setting the stage for lesson delivery. Consider the following:

> Hocked gems financing him, our man defied the scornful laughter. "Think of it as an egg, not a table," he said. Then, three sturdy sisters sought proof, forging vast calmness, and sometimes over turbulent peaks and valleys, until at last welcome winged creatures appeared, signifying monumental success. (MCSD, 2007)

What do you think this passage describes? Eagles soaring, wagon trains, pioneers struggling over mountains, or gold diggers perhaps?

This passage describes an event you are likely aware of if you grew up and went to school in the United States. If you studied the discovery of the New World and were given a picture of three ships, you may recall the events surrounding Christopher Columbus's sail across the sea. Lights are probably going off in your brain now. If you knew *before* this passage was presented that it had something to do with discovering the New World, then your mind would have been set and ready to absorb more details about this event. Clearly, activating prior knowledge and building background helps to increase students' understanding by linking their experiences to the content and by **bridging** past learning to new concepts.

One way to do this is to have students examine the study questions and summary at the end of the chapter in their textbook before reading the material, thus previewing the content and identifying key concepts. This simple approach can be applied with second language learners by using a strategy called *Teaching the Text Backward* (FLDOE, 2003). Here is the sequence of steps involved in this strategy:

1. Have students complete an activity, such as a *Text Quest*, to become familiar with the content of the chapter.

2. Discuss the material in class by considering the photographs, diagrams, and other graphics within the chapter.

3. Conduct a language focus lesson to explore the content-related vocabulary of the lesson.

4. Go to the end of the chapter, and review the summary and answer some of the study questions.

5. Go to the beginning of the chapter, and read the entire chapter.

Applying this strategy prepares ELL students for their most difficult task: reading the textbook. Reading can also be made more manageable for ELL students by reducing the quantity of material they have to read. This can be achieved using techniques such as group assignments and graphic organizers.

Increasing Interaction

Providing opportunities for peer interaction, principle 2—such as buddies, partners, small groups, and cooperative learning—is especially helpful because the language of peers is generally less complex than that of the teacher. Peer interactions give ELLs chances to actively participate and try out their ideas and language in small group settings.

Cooperative learning situations are low anxiety in nature and thus give ELLs opportunities to develop their English-proficiency skills. Interaction with native speakers of English helps promote second language acquisition, as ELLs negotiate communication. Cooperative learning also greatly increases students' opportunities to interact in the target language, using important content area information. Gamelike activities that cultivate vocabulary—such as the *ABCs of a Topic; Give One, Get One;* and *What's the Script?*—exercise students' critical-thinking and synthesis skills and provide motivation.

In addition to providing gamelike vocabulary activities, following an organized schedule of activities is effective in teaching ELLs. The **schedule of balanced instruction (SBI)** is a working model for timing and conducting activities that maximize what can be accomplished in a 60- or 90-minute class schedule (see Appendix B). By rotating groups and activities, teachers allow for more student-centered learning. Doing so also allows teachers the opportunity to conduct frequent comprehension checks and to talk individually to students when meeting in small groups. With the teacher as moderator, the student-to-student learning that takes place is very beneficial for ELL students. To follow the SBI, teachers must prepare materials and be well organized.

Another helpful approach is to display a list of **cognates**, or words in English that are similar to words in a student's **first language (L1)** (see Appendix D). For example, the English word *paraphrase* is similar to the Spanish word *parafraear*. Teachers may want to enlarge these terms by making a poster to hang on the classroom wall. Identifying cognates validates students' cultures and allows native English speakers the opportunity to learn words in **second language (L2)** translations. Translations of sentences in other languages can be found on these websites: www.google.com/language_tools?hl=en and www.freetranslation.com.

Increasing Higher-Order Thinking Skills

The higher-order thinking skills, as identified in **Bloom's taxonomy** (Churches, 2008; Overbaugh & Schultz, 2009), are analysis, synthesis, and evaluation (see Chapter 2). Increasing these skills is the goal of principle 3 for developing lesson plans for ELL students in mainstream classes. Proficiency in these skills is necessary to achieve a passing score on a **high-stakes test**.

In a science class, students complete projects in small groups. Cutouts depicting famous scientists hang from the ceiling.

One of the easiest ways for content teachers to integrate higher-order thinking skills into their lessons is simply to ask follow-up questions. For example, suppose the class is learning about the solar system. The teacher asks "What's the hottest planet in our solar system?" and a student answers "Mercury." Next, the teacher asks a simple follow-up question, such as "How do you know?" Answering this question requires students to use more complex language and more complex thinking.

Teachers can also develop students' higher-order thinking skills by asking questions that focus on the concepts being taught, not the language used to express them. Here is an example of modifying a typical question for this purpose:

Original question: What is the relationship between the principles of communism and the principles of democracy?

Revised question: How are communism and democracy the same? How are they different?

The revised version of the question is clearly easier to understand and focuses students on the concepts: *communism* and *democracy*. Analyzing and relating the two concepts are higher-order thinking skills. To further clarify the revised question, it could be illustrated with the aid of a Venn diagram or compare/contrast graphic organizer.

Specially Designed Academic Instruction in English (SDAIE)

The **SDAIE** approach emerged in the 1980s to fill the gap between the increased number of ELL students and the disproportional increase in the number of bilingual and ELL-trained teachers. The assumption underlying SDAIE is that if teachers adapt their traditional ways of teaching, ELLs will be given access to the content area curriculum and ultimately be able to participate in the academic discourse without falling behind in subject matter knowledge. Thus, the goal of SDAIE is to provide access to content area knowledge through comprehensible language development, instructional modification, and a supportive affective environment (Rohac, 2000). Teaching must take place in an environment that is rich in mutual respect and based on the belief that ELLs have linguistic resources that teachers can tap to teach content and English language skills.

These assumptions are the backbone of a successful SDAIE lesson. The core pedagogical elements are (1) providing content, (2) creating meaning through making connections, (3) improving comprehensibility, (4) increasing language interactions, (5) using L1, (6) conducting assessment, and (7) providing reflection/critical stance.

Content is the heart of the SDAIE lesson (Rohac, 2000). Thoughtful planning is guided by content standard objectives, specific language objectives, knowledge of learning channels/styles, and selection of materials. Brain-based theory postulates that learners are engaged when the brain is able to create meaning by blending knowledge from previous experiences with that of present experiences. SDAIE provides comprehensible messages and informational delivery in a variety of ways. Opportunities for students to interact with the content are critical for ELLs' academic progress, as it allows these students to collaborate on learning tasks and use English language freely. Assessment in the SDAIE approach is both formal and informal; the latter is used frequently to check for understanding. Reflection is an integral component of SDAIE. Teachers with integrity look back and reflect on their teaching, their practices, and their own learning.

SDAIE is most effective with students who have achieved an intermediate level of English fluency, but it is not appropriate for those with incipient English skills (Rohac, 2000). This type of program requires a certain level of English proficiency—a level beyond most newcomers and emerging second language learners.

Cognitive Academic Language Learning Approach (CALLA)

Similar to SDAIE, **CALLA** was developed in the 1990s and targets language minority students at the advanced beginner and intermediate levels of English language ability (Chamot & O'Malley, 1994). CALLA was designed to assist ELL students by providing transitional instruction from a standard ELL or bilingual program to the grade-level content classroom.

The CALLA model includes three components and instructional objectives in its curricular and instructional design: (1) topics from the major content areas,

(2) the development of **academic language** skills, and (3) explicit instruction in learning strategies and styles for both content and language acquisition.

The first component includes content area topics that are aligned with an all-English curriculum. Using this content, practice is provided with a selection of the actual topics students will encounter in the grade-level classroom.

The second component of CALLA, academic language development, includes all four language skills—listening, speaking, reading, and writing—in daily lessons in the content area. Language is used as a functional tool for learning subject matter. Students learn not just the vocabulary and grammar of the content area but also important concepts and skills using the academic language.

The third and central component of CALLA is instruction in learning strategies and styles (Chamot & O'Malley, 1994). This component emphasizes that students who are mentally active and who analyze and reflect on their learning activities will learn, retain, and apply new information more effectively. As both research and experience have shown, different students process information in different ways. Some are visual learners, some are auditory learners, and some are hands-on, tactile–kinesthetic learners. Keeping students engaged in content material requires teachers to present information through a variety of avenues. These avenues have changed dramatically since the 1990s, as new technology has been utilized in the classroom.

Along with this technological boom, the recent emphasis on standardized testing has had a tremendous impact on education. ELL students must pass a high-stakes test as a graduation requirement. They are a subgroup under the reauthorization of the **No Child Left Behind Act of 2001 (NCLB)**, and their scores on standardized tests count in determining the quality of schools and school districts.

While the components of CALLA transitional programs can be incorporated in newer programs, they are insufficient to meet all of ELL students' needs. Today, ELL students are immersed into mainstream content area classrooms from the day they enter school, regardless of their English language proficiency.

Stages of Second Language Development

To meet the needs of ELL students, content area teachers should know the developmental process of second language acquisition. Having this knowledge will make teachers aware of what to expect from ELLs at various stages and thereby help them better prepare lessons corresponding to the various stages.

Individuals go through four stages in learning and acquiring a second language: (1) preproduction, (2) early production, (3) speech emergence, and (4) intermediate fluency (see Table 1.1). More recently, these stages have been identified as stages of proficiency, with beginners identified as English language development (ELD) I, II, III, Sheltered/SDAIE in the areas of listening, speaking, reading, and writing (see Table 1.2). Although individuals may spend different amounts of time at these various stages, they generally pass through the stages in order. Table 1.2 provides some sample student behaviors, teacher behaviors, and questioning techniques for the five stages of language development (Rohac, 2001).

Table 1.1 Stages of Second Language Development

Stage	Sample Student Behaviors	Sample Teacher Behaviors	Questioning Techniques
Preproduction (May be in this stage 1–6 months)	Points or uses other nonverbal responses Actively listens Responds to commands Draws, circles, and matches pictures to words Engages in *role-playing* Creates illustrations	Uses gestures Uses language that conveys meanings and vocabulary development Uses repetition Does not force speaking Uses pictures, videos, and hands-on demonstrations	*Point to the . . .* *Find the . . .* *Put the . . . next to the . . .* *Do you have the . . . ?* *Is this a . . . ?* *Who wants the . . . ?* *Who has the . . . ?* *Show me the . . .* *Where is the . . . ?*
Early Production (May be in this stage 6–12 months)	Uses one-word and short utterances Names, labels, and categorizes Cuts and pastes Draws and describes Plays concentration-type games Does word puzzles	Asks questions that can be answered by *yes/no* and *either/or* responses Models correct responses Extends listening skills Plans activities that ask *who, what, when, where* questions	Yes/no responses: *Is this your homework?* One-word responses: *What utensil am I holding?* List-type responses: *What do you see on the board?* Two-word responses: *Where did he go?* and *What is . . . doing now?*
Speech Emergence (May be in this stage for 1–3 years; the longest stage)	Participates in small-group activities Demonstrates comprehension in a variety of ways Speaks in short phrases Recalls and retells Restates and summarizes Defines Predicts Identifies sequences and cause/effect relationships Compares and contrasts	Focuses on key concepts and expanded vocabulary Provides frequent comprehension checks Uses performance-based assessment Provides interaction activities and negotiates meaning Allows participation in mainstream classes	*How?* and *How is this like that?* *Tell me about . . .* and *Talk to me about . . .* *How would you change this part?* *Why is . . . so happy?* *Explain . . .* Short responses
Intermediate Fluency (May be in this stage for 3–5 years)	Participates in reading Produces connected narratives Expresses ideas orally and in writing Analyzes and examines Evaluates and justifies Creates	Fosters conceptual development and expanded literacy through content Incorporates reading and writing activities in the content areas	Create, predict, and describe: *What do you suggest?* and *How do you think the story ends?* Give an opinion: *What do you like? Why?* Analyze: *What is the story mainly about?*

Source: FLDOE, 2003.

Table 1.2 Stages of English Language Development

Old Descriptions				
Preproduction	Early Preproduction	Speech Emergence	Intermediate Fluency	
Beginning	Early Intermediate	Intermediate	Early Advanced	Advanced
New Descriptions				
ELD I	ELD II	ELD III	Sheltered/SDAIE	Sheltered/SDAIE
Listening	**Listening**	**Listening**	**Listening**	**Listening**
Emerges from silence into nonverbal communication Responds nonverbally when given simple directions and questions and dialogue with clearly spoken instructions Shows beginning signs of sound discrimination	Understands simple and social conversation Follows multi-step directions Recognizes basic information in simple stories	Understands • extended conversation and dialogue • simple stories with some details • simple idiomatic expressions	Demonstrates a higher level of understanding Listens critically to peer conversations Actively listens and responds to extended dialogue	Demonstrates an almost fluent understanding of English Approximates native English-speaking peers Understands complex and idiomatic presentations and conversations
Speaking	**Speaking**	**Speaking**	**Speaking**	**Speaking**
Silent phase Communicates nonverbally Uses one-word responses Participates in interactive and basic survival conversations Verbally identifies objects, people, places, etc. Repeats modeled language	Uses short phrases, gestures, and simple sentences Participates in guided discussion Expresses simplified idea, opinions, and feelings	Experiments with expanding vocabulary and grammar Answers questions in short sentences Participates in group discussions Takes more risks with language Solicits information for a variety of purposes	Interacts in a variety of speaking situations Uses language to express and defend opinions Paraphrases more complex ideas	Uses clear and comprehensible pronunciation Uses vocabulary appropriately Clarifies and uses idioms Rephrases ideas for comprehension purposes
Reading	**Reading**	**Reading**	**Reading**	**Reading**
Reads and understands words, phrases, and simple sentences with guided teaching	Understands main ideas when guided in the reading of simplified descriptive, narrative, and informational material	Understands main ideas and facts in simplified descriptive, narrative, and informational material when reading independently Draws conclusions and summarizes	Reads and understands main ideas and facts Draws conclusions Summarizes less simplified, longer texts	Reads a variety of literature and other printed material with an understanding of the underlying meaning

(continued)

Table 1.2 Stages of English Language Development (continued)

Old Descriptions				
Preproduction	Early Preproduction	Speech Emergence	Intermediate Fluency	
Beginning	Early Intermediate	Intermediate	Early Advanced	Advanced

New Descriptions				
ELD I	ELD II	ELD III	Sheltered/SDAIE	Sheltered/SDAIE
Writing	**Writing**	**Writing**	**Writing**	**Writing**
Recognizes all the letters of the alphabet	Engages in a variety of simple organization methods	Develops topic sentences and refines paragraphs	Develops thesis statements	Demonstrates writing skills that approximate native English-speaking peers
Uses patterns modeled by the teacher	Writes patterned poems and narratives	Writes using a variety of styles	Applies advanced editing and revising techniques to writing	Writes with a fluency for a wide variety of purposes and audiences
Practices writing complete sentences	Expands basic sentences	Uses varied word choice and expanded sentence structures	Writing multiparagraph essays	Independently uses advanced editing and revising techniques
Develops simple sentence structure	Develops paragraphs	Responds to writing prompts	Experiments with more sophisticated vocabulary and complex sentence structure	
Responds to writing prompts on familiar topics with short responses	Supports ideas	Applies editing and revising techniques		
Practices guided revision	Responds to prompts	Practices writing grade-appropriate multiparagraph essays		
Learns standard writing format	Uses graphic organizers			
Begins writing for fluency	Practices guided revision and editing			
Develops prewriting skills				

Source: Rohac, 2001.

$\int$heltered Instruction Observation Protocol (SIOP)

As part of a seven-year research project, Echevarria, Short, and Vogt (2004) have developed a model of **sheltered instruction.** Their **SIOP** model is grounded in two decades of classroom-based research, the experiences of skillful teachers, and findings from the professional literature. The researchers' work involved active collaboration with practicing middle school teachers in refining the model as they implemented it in their classrooms.

The SIOP model is a lesson-planning and delivery approach composed of thirty instructional strategies grouped into eight components:

1. Preparation
2. Building background

3. Comprehensible input

4. Strategies

5. Interaction

6. Practice/Application

7. Lesson delivery

8. Review/Assessment

SIOP teachers use the regular core curriculum. However, they modify their teaching to make the content understandable for ELLs and promote these students' academic English language growth. Many of the features embedded in the model have been drawn from effective English-as-a-second-language (ESL) methods developed during the last 20 years. In addition, the SIOP model offers a framework for organizing instruction, with key features that promote the academic success of ELLs, such as the inclusion of language objectives in every content lesson, the development of students' background knowledge, and the emphasis on academic literacy practice.

The research conducted by Echevarria et al. (2004) found that ELLs whose teachers were trained in implementing the SIOP model performed significantly better on an academic writing assessment than did a comparison group of ELLs whose teachers had no exposure to the model. The SIOP model may work best in ELL programs where all the students are ELL students and all the teachers have been specifically ELL trained in science, math, and social studies.

Sheltered Instruction

What is sheltered instruction? Unlike the traditional instructional practice of lecturing, sheltered instruction allows teachers to do the following:

- Pace the rate of speech and speak clearly, using gestures and facial expressions.

- Act out or illustrate meaning, using repetition and rephrasing.

- **Model** behaviors repeatedly, showing students what teachers want to see them do and produce.

- Maintain eye contact.

- Reduce the use of idiomatic expressions.

- Think aloud when solving problems, letting students hear the thought process they will be using, and relate lessons to students' prior learning.

- Use many visuals as tools of instruction, such as videos, photos, drawings, charts, and posters.

- Have special lessons on high-frequency vocabulary terms found in Bloom's taxonomy.

- Regularly use a variety of graphic organizers to chunk textual information, focusing on the lesson's important points and higher-order thinking skills.

- Teach key vocabulary by using word puzzles and games, and create a word wall of current vocabulary terms. Accompany the words with pictures.

- Allow students to interact with the content in cooperative learning groups. (Student-to-student learning in well-organized cooperative learning groups is an invaluable instructional tool.)

- Provide concrete examples to assist students in understanding complex concepts and skills.
- Ask questions in simple language that encourages students' reasoning abilities.

Given the NCLB emphasis on testing, schools have had to integrate ELL students into mainstreamed, inclusionary classrooms. In many cases, content area teachers have found it frustrating to deliver the same lesson at a variety of levels to avoid slowing down and discouraging their native English speakers or accelerating the pace and losing their ELL students' attention. These problems can be avoided by applying many of the features found in the SIOP method. Teachers must go further, however, in differentiating instruction to address the various proficiency levels found in classrooms today.

A documentary film called *Authentic Voices* was produced about a panel of 19 ELL students from eight different countries who attended two high schools in south central Florida (Keefe, 2008). Students responded to questions intended to elicit their feelings about what teachers do to help them be more successful in school and what makes learning difficult. The students also discussed what they want teachers to know about their culture and what gives them a sense of belonging at school. The purposes of the documentary were to provide a forum for English language learners to express their views in a nonthreatening environment, to help these students realize their important contributions to the world of education, and to allow teachers a glimpse of ELL students' reflections on their own learning.

The ELL students were quite forthcoming with their thoughts about the stresses they feel on a daily basis in the high school classroom. In their authentic voices, students revealed concerns about teachers' lack of appreciation for their culture and the challenges they face in trying to comprehend subject matter in their second language. They discussed being humiliated when arriving late to the classroom and working with native English speakers, who made fun of them when they tried to talk. The ELLs also remarked that teachers talk too quickly and that taking notes is very difficult. Only 1 ELL student out of 19 was involved in a sport or extracurricular activity. (That student was a member of the International Club, which met on campus after school.)

Based on the responses of the students in this video, teachers should adopt these practices for working with ELLs:

- Control and monitor group interactions for appropriate behaviors and verbal exchanges.
- Provide an accepting, comfortable classroom setting.
- Correct students in subtle ways.
- Speak at a slower pace.
- Advocate for and encourage ELLs to become more involved in campus activities.
- Demonstrate respect for the diverse ethnicities and cultures that ELL students represent.
- Attend refresher workshops on best practices for ELL instruction.

Many of the concepts in social studies, science, and math are abstract in nature. Teachers in these content areas can use the following additional sheltered instructional techniques to enhance learning for ELL students:

- Download radio programs about issues and current events from archived sources, such as National Public Radio and Voice of America.

- Contact the school media center or library to determine what information is available on the topic at an elementary level.

- Maintain a classroom library of supplementary books and workbooks that are written in simple English and have illustrations of problems.

- Provide biographies of significant men and women from different cultures.

- Collect comic books that portray historic and cultural events in simplified language.

- Limit the number of math problems that must be worked.

- Deemphasize the speed at which students work, and emphasize the accuracy of their work.

- Limit the number of variables in laboratory experiments.

- Have students prepare individual card files of specific vocabulary for the content area.

- Record difficult passages from textbooks for listening activities.

- Have students flag, underline, or highlight key words they do not understand so they can be explained in simpler English.

According to Ahmad and Szpara (2006), creating a socially supportive classroom for ELLs refers to developing a learning environment in which students feel comfortable learning both English and subject area content and making mistakes in learning both. By validating ELLs' home languages and cultures, teachers help provide an environment that assists students in overcoming the culture shock of entering a classroom setting that may be vastly different from what they experienced in their home country, if they attended school. Research also shows that allowing students to use multiple languages when making sense of new content allows them to strengthen their overall cognitive abilities, as well as their language knowledge and content-specific academic skills (Carrasquillo & Rodriquez, 1996; Crawford, 1999).

Displaying "Welcome" signs and hanging symbols of students' cultures makes the classroom setting socially supportive, thus promoting a sense of safety and encouraging risk taking.

The following list provides suggestions for creating a classroom environment that supports students' social learning needs in the ELL context:

- Be explicit in voicing high expectations of all students, and demonstrate willingness to help students overcome language, cultural, socioeconomic, and other barriers to high academic achievement.

- Specifically invite students to add comments based on their own cultural backgrounds.

- Establish cross-cultural subgroups for specific activities that require students to help each other see an issue from different cultural perspectives.

- Establish multilingual groups that have specific permission to talk in whatever language they prefer, even though their final work will be submitted in English.

- Learn basic greetings, polite phrases, and important classroom commands in students' native languages.

- Learn students' given ethnic names and how to pronounce them correctly.

- Learn as much as possible about students' cultures, family histories, home lives, and socioeconomic statuses.

- Ask for input from each student; track which students have responded to ensure that everyone has an opportunity to contribute.

Providing a classroom environment that is welcoming and accepting of ELL students' home languages and cultures will ease some of the affective tension they feel in learning new norms and vocabulary. This environment will also foster greater acceptance of diversity by all students and help reduce the stigma associated with being a newcomer in the school community.

Analyzing Textbooks

Trying to teach ELL students using textbooks written for native English speakers is frustrating not only for teachers but also for ELLs. These students find reading English language textbooks both difficult and intimidating.

Dwyer (2007) analyzed textbook vocabulary according to grade level. Based on his findings, he reports that the increased difficulty of social studies vocabulary by grade exceeds that in other content area textbooks, such as language arts texts. An excerpt from *The American Pageant*, a popular high school textbook, illustrates this quite well:

> The Non-Intercourse Act of 1809—a watered-down version of Jefferson's embargo aimed solely at Britian and France—was due to expire in 1810. To Madison's dismay, Congress dismantled the embargo completely with a bargaining measure known as Macon's Bill No. 2. While reopening American trade with all the world, Macon's Bill dangled what Congress hoped was an attractive lure. (Kennedy, Cohen, & Bailey, 2002)

Not only do ELL students need to know the meanings of discipline-specific words, such as *act* and *bill*, but they need to know the meanings of advanced vocabulary words, such as *embargo*, *dismantle*, and *dangle*. Clearly, students will not likely encounter the latter kinds of words in their everyday lives.

In addition, the structure of sentences in many textbooks is complex. For instance, cause-and-effect relationships may be embedded in ways that make them difficult for ELLs to recognize (Cho & Reich, 2008).

With these factors in mind, teachers must determine the language demands of their textbooks. Doing so is absolutely critical in promoting the success of ELL students and thus cannot be overstated. Teachers who teach the same content area can work together to review their district-adopted textbooks to determine the content vocabulary words that are essential to understanding. Then, from the perspective of an ELL student, teachers can design specific language focus lessons to introduce these new terms, use visual cues to accompany the text, and play word games that involve the new vocabulary.

One method for analyzing the language of textbooks is to determine the answers to these three questions (Ragan, 2005):

1. What should ELLs know after reading the textbook?
2. What language in the textbook may be difficult for ELLs to understand?
3. What specific language should be taught to ensure ELLs' understanding?

Textbooks are notoriously **text heavy** and contain content that is both linguistically and conceptually dense. After identifying the learning objectives of a given chapter or section, locate the main ideas you want students to know. Then identify the types of language that may cause difficulty for ELL students. These three types of language are most likely to cause reading problems for ELLs (Ragan, 2005):

ELLs have difficulty reading and understanding linguistically dense text without support, which can be provided in the form of a demonstration or a visual and/or graphic description of the text.

1. *Vocabulary:* Nonspecialized vocabulary words and idiomatic phrases that are known by most native speakers cause difficulty for ELLs due to the differences in the meanings of the individual words.
2. *Grammatical structures:* Problematic structures include conditional sentences, sentences with irregular verb tenses, and complex sentences with multiple imbedded clauses.
3. *Cohesive devices:* These devices include words, phrases, and punctuation marks that help show the relationship between one part of a sentence and another. Examples include ellipses (which indicate that text has been omitted within a quoted sentence), synonyms (words that have the same meanings), and conjunctions and transitions (linking words that connect related ideas).

Analyzing a textbook is a subjective process and requires a fair amount of judgment on the part of the teacher. To reiterate, conducting this analysis is critical in making content comprehensible to ELL students. Instructors must decide what academic language to teach by looking at the specific language that ELLs will need to understand main ideas, decipher key vocabulary words, and focus on essential skills. Realizing that ELL students can absorb only a certain number of new terms in a given time frame, teachers should limit the number of new terms presented at one time. New terms can be reinforced by having students play vocabulary games, such as Word Bingo, and completing crossword puzzles, word searches, and cryptograms. All these materials can be placed in student portfolios.

Table 1.3 contains criteria for selecting, adapting, and using content area materials for ELLs.

Table 1.3 Selecting and Adapting Content Area Materials

Criteria for Selecting Materials	Adapting Less-Than-Ideal Materials	Using Materials
Materials are clearly and simply written.	Select excerpts that contain key points.	Ask many questions to guide and check comprehension.
Length is manageable.	Find translations.	Teach students learning strategies for getting to essence of text.
Many pictures and graphs are provided that are closely related to written text.	Supplement with a more concrete and/or simple text.	Use text in combination with highly interactive activities.
Hands-on activities can be used with text.	Use concrete, specific examples of concepts.	Discuss **cultural bias** that is present.
Text is clearly organized with headings and subheadings, and important points are highlighted.	Provide many nonlinguistic aids, such as pictures, graphs, charts, artifacts, maps, and objects.	Encourage multiple perspectives on a topic.
Illustrations and background information reflect a **multicultural ideology.**	Focus on students' attention to the essentials.	
	Allow students to explore subject together, negotiating meaning through their native language.	

Source: Florida Reading Professional Development, http://forpd.ucf.edu

Sample Lesson Plan

The following is a lesson plan for an eighth-grade science unit on astronomy. The lesson contains many strategies for ELL students and examples of best practices in teaching in this content area and at this grade level. This lesson was designed specifically for a mainstream classroom containing both native and nonnative speakers of English.

Before reading the lesson, reflect on the things discussed so far about making lessons comprehensible, interactive, and cognitively challenging for ELL students. One way to build background and comprehensibility is to read aloud an elementary-level book on the topic. Lessons can be made more interactive by using cooperative learning activities that cultivate both positive interdependence and individual accountability.

As you review the lesson, critique it in terms of the three principles of designing lessons for ELL students in mainstream classes: (1) increase comprehensibility, (2) increase interaction, and (3) increase higher-order thinking skills (FLDOE, 2003). Keep these principles and activities in mind when critiquing the following lesson on astronomy:

- How well does the lesson address principle 1? (Comprehensibility)
- How well does the lesson address principle 2? (Interaction)
- How well does the lesson address principle 3? (Higher-order thinking skills)
- What is missing from the lesson? What specific suggestions can you offer for improvement?
- Overall, what grade (A, B, C) would you assign this lesson? Why?

Science/Astronomy

Created by Porolle V. Simm, Indiantown Middle School, reprinted with permission

Topic

Rockets in Space

Purpose

To explain how rockets travel in space.

Content Objectives

Students will be able to do the following:

a. Define key terms and terminology.

b. Explain the various purposes of rockets and satellites.

c. Explain how rockets and satellites travel in space.

d. Build a rocket.

Language Arts Objectives

Students will be able to do the following:

a. View a video on rockets and satellites, and take notes on the purposes of rockets and how they work.

b. Read a chapter selection that describes how rockets work.

c. Discuss the different elements that contribute to building a rocket.

Materials

Balloon for each student

Plastic or paper cups

Tape

Construction paper

Empty film canister

Water

Fizzing antacid tablets

Various books on rockets, satellites, and space exploration

Reference Materials

Science Explorer (Astronomy textbook)

Giant Science (Resource book, ESOL students)

Middle Grades Science Book (reproducibles)

U.S. Borne Science Encyclopedia (Internet linked)

Videos

Earth Science—Astronomy

Countdown to the Space Station

Discovery Channel

Websites

www.space.com

www.seasky.org/index.html

www.enchantedlearning.com

www.brainpop.com

Initiating Activity

Before students read the textbook, activate their prior knowledge by having them create Know, Want to Know, Learn (KWL) charts. Give students three minutes to brainstorm about rockets. Have them jot down in the "Know" column everything they know or think they know about rockets. Once students have completed this task, ask them to think about questions they may want answered about rockets in the "Want to Know" column. The students will write their answers and questions on their chart paper for future reference. After completing their charts, have students discuss what they know and what they want to know.

Introduction to Lesson

Have students watch a short video about rockets and satellites. They will be able to see inside a space station and how rockets and the space shuttle are launched.

Class Discussion

How Do Rockets Work? (Activity)

In this activity, students will use balloons to represent rockets. Ask each student to blow up a balloon and point it toward an area in the room or outdoors where there are no students. Have the student put his or her free hand behind the neck of the balloon, so the air will push against it, and then let go of the balloon. Ask students to repeat this activity twice.

Next, using the questions below, have the class discuss what this activity means in terms of rockets and how they work. Instruct students to add information to the "K," "W," or "L" column of their KWL charts.

Discussion questions

1. In which direction does the air push?
2. In which direction does the balloon go?
3. Does the balloon need to be pushed against something to move? Why or why not?
4. What does the balloon represent?

During the Lesson

Divide students into groups of four, and assign each group a section within the chapter. The group will be responsible for identifying at least two important points from the section and for selecting key words from it. Each group of students will become experts about their section.

Once the groups have completed this task, have students form new groups. Each new group will be comprised of one student from each original group. Students within the new group will be responsible for teaching one another what they learned in their original groups.

Based on the information from the video, reading, and discussions, have students answer the following questions. Again, they should add the information to their KWL charts.

Discussion questions

1. How does a rocket work?

2. What causes a rocket to move forward?

3. What is the difference between a multistage rocket and a single-stage rocket?

4. Name three uses of satellites and space stations. What are the differences between space shuttles and other rockets?

Hands-On Activity

Be a Rocket Scientist!

In this activity, students will work in pairs and build "rockets." Provide the directions as a handout with illustrations, and encourage students to follow the directions carefully.

Have students do the following:

1. Use a plastic or paper cup as the body of the rocket.

2. Cut out a paper nose cone, and tape it to the closed end of the cup.

3. Obtain an empty film canister with a snap-on lid.

4. Fill the canister about one-quarter full of water.

5. Put on goggles and go outside the room, preferably to a grassy area.

6. Add half of a fizzing antacid tablet to the film canister, and quickly snap on the lid.

7. Place the canister on the ground with the lid down. Place the rocket over the canister, and stand back.

Activity questions and observations

1. What happened inside the canister?

2. What form of energy was released?

3. How did the "rocket" react?

Culminating Activities

For students to really grasp the concepts in this lesson, they should take turns in researching various rockets, satellites, space stations, and space shuttles. Have students use the Internet to access information that was not available in their textbook. Many websites have interactive games, question/answer sessions, and quizzes about space exploration, rockets, and satellites.

Also take students on a field trip to the nearest planetarium. There, students will explore the exhibits, ask questions, participate in hands-on activities, learn where rockets and the space shuttle is launched, and have the opportunity to hear speakers talk about the future of space exploration.

Assessment

Performance-based assessment

1. Give students a quiz that includes questions about the various key terms and points outlined in the chapter. Each student should be able to answer the questions with 80% accuracy.

Hands-on activities

1. Were students able to build the "rocket" and answer the quiz questions with 80% accuracy?
2. Were students able to participate in the group activities and demonstrate teamwork?

Assessment modifications

Make modifications to the assessments for ELL students. Allow ELLs more time to complete the assessments, and let them use reference materials for assistance. Require ELL students to use a bilingual, picture dictionary during the lesson and the assessments.

By providing many of the features represented in the previous lesson plan and delivering understandable activities, teachers can integrate ELL students into both the classroom and the curriculum. Through conducting interactive activities, teachers can ensure that ELL students develop the academic language they need to participate in the content area classroom. When content teachers create a comprehensive and supporting learning environment, ELLs are more motivated in their own learning. Teachers can lighten these students' linguistic load without lowering the **cognitive demand** by using video streaming, demonstrations, and graphic depictions of content. By presenting important concepts and vocabulary in multiple and differentiated ways and by adjusting practices to avoid isolating and marginalizing ELL students, teachers become partners in their students' language learning and academic success.

Suggested Assignment

If this *ACEES* text is being used in a teacher-training course, the following is a suggested final activity/assignment that participants can complete for accountability. Here are the unit requirements:

A. The participant's final assignment will include a unit of lesson plans on a single topic; the lesson plans should cover one week of instruction in the participant's content area. The lessons will be due the last session of the course.

B. *Content Objectives:* Specify what students are expected to learn as a result of your lessons. *Language Objectives:* Specify the reading, writing, listening, and/or speaking activities students are expected to accomplish as a result of the lessons.

C. Provide several language focus lessons that cultivate new vocabulary. Introduce this vocabulary before students are asked to read it in context.

D. To cultivate genuine interaction, include cooperative learning activities that foster positive interdependence and individual accountability. Also provide graphic organizers, which lighten students' linguistic load.

E. Provide several graphic depictions of the content of each lesson. Activities should include pictures, videos, computer programs, and Internet sites and employ any of the ELL strategies presented in the course.

F. Create questions and activities that require higher-order thinking skills. Offer alternative assessments to assess learning; include a rubric (see Chapter 2) so students know ahead of time what constitutes the grade of an A, B, and so on.

G. For each lesson, provide all the information other teachers will need to conduct the lesson in their own classrooms. You do not need to include a detailed script of what to say at each stage of the lesson, but be sure to write the lesson in an organized, thoughtful, and detailed manner. Ensure that readers will be able to obtain a genuine sense of how the lesson might be implemented in a classroom setting.

H. Implement your unit of lessons with students. Then write a summary of the outcomes, such as how students reacted to the activities and how well they performed on the assessments.

I. Taking the perspective of an ELL student, write a one-page description of the strengths and weaknesses of the textbook your school district has provided for use in this content area. You might make a list of features in the textbook that are ELL student friendly, such as highlighted vocabulary and a bilingual glossary, and a list of features that an ELL student would have difficulty with, such as few illustrations.

References

Ahmad, I., & Szpara, M. (2006). Making social studies meaningful for ELL students: Content and pedagogy in mainstream secondary school classrooms. *Essays in Education, 16,* 1–14.

Branch, N., DeCrescentis, R., Chargualaf, S., & Reynolds, J. (2008). Extralinguistic Cues. *Educational Impact,* E. S. L., Retrieved on September 21, 2008, from http://secure.eionline.net/nsu/index.cfm

Carrasquillo, A., & Rodriquez, V. (1996). *Language Minority Students in the Mainstream Classroom.* Philadelphia: Multilingual Matters.

Chamot, A., & O'Malley, J. (1994). *The CALLA Handbook.* New York: Addison-Wesley.

Churches, A. (2008). *Bloom's Taxonomy Blooms Digitally.* Retrieved on September 21, 2009 from http://www.techlearning.com/article/8670

Cho, S., & Reich, G. (2008). New immigrant, new challenges: High school social studies teachers and English language learner instruction. *Social Studies, 99*(6), 235–242.

Crawford, J. (1999). *Bilingual Education: History, Politics, Theory and Practice.* Los Angeles: Bilingual Education Services.

Dwyer, E. (2007). *The power of social studies.* Paper presented at the annual meeting of TESOL, Seattle, WA.

Echevarria, J., Vogt, M. E., & Short, D. (2004). *Making content comprehensible to English learners: The SIOP model.* Boston: Allyn & Bacon.

Florida Department of Education (FLDOE), Center for Applied Linguistics, Sunbelt Office. (2003). *Enriching content classes for secondary ESOL students.* Tallahassee: Author.

Florida Reading Professional Development. University of Central Florida. Retrieved on May 3, 2008 from http://forpd.ucf.edu/courseinfo/syllabus

Keefe, M. R. (Producer/Researcher). (2008). *Voices of immigrant ELL high school students* [Video]. Martin County School District, Florida, TV Production Classes.

Kennedy, D., Cohen, L., & Bailey, T. (2002). *American Pageant* (12th ed.). Boston: Houghton Mifflin.

Krashen, S. (1989). *Language acquisition and language education.* New York: Prentice-Hall.

Martin County School District (MCSD). (2007). Professional development meeting, School Board Meeting Room, March 8, 2007.

Overbaugh, R., & Schultz, L. (2009). *Bloom's Taxonomy.* Retrieved on October 16, 2009, from www.odu.edu/educ/roverbau/Bloom/blooms_taxonomy.htm

Peregoy, S., & Boyle, O. (2005). *Reading, Writing and Learning in ESL.* Boston: Allyn & Bacon.

Rohac, R. (2000). S.D.A.I.E.—Specially Designed Academic Instruction in English. *ELT Newsletter.* Retrieved December 12, 2007, from www.eltnewsletter.com

Rohac, R. (2001). Educational Solutions (RES). Retrieved March 31, 2008 from www.rohac.com/images/sdaie_photos/Image1.jpg

Chapter 2

Equitable Assessment of ELL Students' Performance

What Teachers Make

Dinner guests were sitting around the table discussing life when one man, a CEO, decided to explain the "problem" with education. He argued, "What's a kid going to learn from someone who decided his best option in life was to become a teacher?"

The CEO reminded the other dinner guests that it's true what they say about teachers: Those who can't do, teach.

Then, to corroborate his gem of wisdom, the CEO said to another guest, "You're a teacher, Susan. Be honest. What do you make?"

Susan, who had a reputation for being honest and frank, gave this reply:

"You want to know what I make? I make kids work harder than they ever thought they could. I can make a C+ feel like the Congressional Medal of Honor and an A– feel like a slap in the face, if the student did not do his or her very best. I can make kids sit through 40 minutes of study hall in absolute silence. ! can make parents tremble in fear when I call home.

"You want to know what I make? I make kids wonder. I make them question. I make them criticize. I make them apologize and mean it. I make them write. I make them read, read, and vow to keep on reading. I make them spell *definitely* and *beautiful* over and over, until they will never misspell either one of those words again. I make them show all their work in math, and I make them hide it all for their final drafts in English.

"I elevate students to experience creativity through music and art and the joy of performance, so that their lives are made rich, filled with kindness and culture. All of that in order for them to learn to take pride in themselves and their accomplishments. I make them understand that if they have brains, then they must follow their hearts, for that is their natural destiny . . . and if someone ever tries to judge them by how much they make, to pay them no attention.

"You want to know what I make? I make a difference. What do you make?"

—Author Unknown

Studies show that it takes English language learners (ELLs) from three to five years to develop **oral proficiency** in their second language (L2) and from four to seven years to develop **academic language proficiency** in the L2 (Cummins, 1981; Hakuta, Butler, & Witt, 2000). Yet in this era of the **No Child Left Behind Act (NCLB)**, school districts cannot wait for ELLs to establish English proficiency before assessing them solely in English.

In response to a stronger national emphasis on the academic achievement of all students, schools are reevaluating the quality of instruction for English language learners. Studies suggest that ELLs who are starting high school hold high aspirations for education and are more likely than their native-English-speaking peers to spend more hours per week on additional reading not assigned by school and doing homework outside school (Keefe, 2008). The educational outcomes of ELLs vary, depending on the measures of achievement used and the specific population of students assessed. Individual characteristics—such as English language ability, immigrant status, and cultural and educational background—have been associated with students' level of educational attainment.

As teachers explore ways to assist and address ELLs' varying levels of language proficiency in testing situations, they must consider the language of the test. Many content assessments are rendered ineffective when ELL students cannot understand the test questions in English. Because most high-stakes tests are provided in English, it is often impossible to know if ELLs' low scores are due to their limited English or to their lack of knowledge of the subject tested (Maxwell-Jolly, Gandara, & Benavidez, 2007).

Much of the data on educational outcomes focuses not on English language learners specifically but on **language minority** and immigrant students, who may or may not be English language proficient. For example, data from the 2000 U.S. Census, which were analyzed by the Pew Hispanic Center, indicate that approximately one-fifth (21 percent) of Latino youth are high school dropouts. This compares with 8 percent of white youth and 12 percent of African American youth. Of the Latino youth who drop out, 40 percent speak English less than "well." The largest group of Latino youth who drop out are Mexican immigrants (39 percent), perhaps because students of Mexican ethnicity make up the largest number of Latinos. Overall, Latino youth have little more than a 50/50 chance of finishing high school with a diploma (Fry, 2003).

As discussed throughout this book, ELLs at the secondary level do not have enough time before they graduate to first become fluent in English and to then attend to both concrete and abstract concepts in science, math, and social studies classes. It is not fair to provide instruction to ELLs in **mainstream classes** without providing extra language support and otherwise being responsive to their learning skills and needs. It is noteworthy that research about overall adolescent literacy recommends changes to typical middle-level and high school content-focused classroom instruction that are similar to the recommendations made for effective content area instruction for ELLs (Hamann & Meltzer, 2006).

Training teachers in the best practices for meeting the needs of ELLs will promote content area literacy development and learning for all students. This is true because quality professional development in content area literacy includes explicit instruction and **modeling** of before, during, and after reading strategies (see Chapter 4). It also provides relevance and connections to students' lives and multiple opportunities for reading, writing, and speaking about content in all classes (Hamann & Meltzer, 2006).

Research on adolescent literacy has identified five sets of synergistic classroom practices that improve academic language development:

1. An emphasis on teacher modeling, giving explicit strategy instruction in context, and using formative assessment to improve reading comprehension

2. More time spent on reading and writing instruction

3. More time spent on speaking, listening, and viewing related to the discussion, creation, and understanding of texts

4. More attention to the development of critical-thinking and metacognitive skills as key parts of academic literacy tasks

5. Flexible grouping and responsiveness to learner needs

For ELLs, it is substantial work to learn how to break the code of how native English speakers read, write, talk, and think within a particular content area. If teachers truly want students to be able to think like scientists and write like historians, they must explicitly make students "apprentices" in the discourse of their particular disciplines.

Assessment Accommodations for ELLs: Implications for Policy-Based Empirical Research

Considered together, greater attention to large-scale assessments, the increase in the number of ELLs in schools, and recent inclusionary policies have made assessment **accommodations** a hotly debated issue. This is especially true regarding the validity of test results for ELL students (USDOE, 2005). In reviewing the research, Abedi, Hofstetter, and Lord (2004) found that the emphasis on inclusion introduces new, unintended consequences. Some of those consequences will be addressed in the following sections.

Policy Context for Using Test Accommodations

Under NCLB, the exclusion of certain groups from large-scale assessments may have been well intentioned in terms of fairness and validity. However, it has resulted in a lack of representation of these groups in debating broader educational policy and accountability and thus has diminished educational opportunities for ELL students (Abedi et al., 2004).

Not surprisingly, the recent focus on testing has yielded considerable controversy. Proponents highlight the importance of attaining and maintaining standards. They regard tests as the primary mechanism for rewarding high-performing schools and helping and/or sanctioning low-performing schools. Critics declare that standardized assessments measure socioeconomic status, innate ability, and noninstructionally related material, therefore yielding little valid information about student achievement. Yet if ELL students are not tested, they may be omitted from the accountability picture. They may not be considered in state or federal policy making, and their academic progress, skills, and needs may not be appropriately assessed.

In view of the many issues concerning the inclusion of ELL students in large-scale national and state assessments, it is clear that excluding them does more harm than good. Efforts must be made to modify assessment tools to make them more relevant to ELLs while not altering the constructs being measured.

Relationship between Language Proficiency and Test Performance

Research has amply documented the impact of students' language background on their test performance. Students who lack proficiency in the language of the test consistently perform at lower levels, and changes in the language of the test can result in changes in students' scores.

Recent experimental design studies conducted by the National Center for Research on Evaluation, Standards, and Student Testing further demonstrates that (1) test scores of ELLs are substantially lower than those of native English speakers in all subject areas and that (2) the linguistic complexity of test items may threaten the validity and reliability of tests of content area achievement, particularly for ELLs (Abedi, 2008). These studies indicate that as the language demands of individual test items decrease, the performance gap between ELL students and English-proficient students decreases. Studies suggest that reducing the impact of language factors on content-based assessments will improve the validity and reliability of such assessments for ELLs, resulting in fairer assessments (Abedi, 2008).

Tests in Students' Native Languages

Efforts to devise ways to make tests equitable and to develop international guidelines for test translation and adaptation have proven several things: that translated assessments are technically difficult, expensive to develop, time consuming, and not widely used (Abedi et al., 2004). Consider that a word or phrase in one language may not have an equivalent in another language. Some languages, such as Spanish, have multiple dialects, thus limiting the appropriateness of the translated version for certain student populations. Native language assessments are useful only when students can demonstrate their content knowledge more effectively in their native language, typically because they have received content area instruction in that language.

Extra Time

Giving ELL students extra time to complete test items is the most commonly permitted accommodation. Doing so is logistically feasible and does not require changes in the test itself. Some teachers feel that providing extra time is essential for ELLs to decode the language of the test until they become fully proficient in academic English.

To date, research on allowing extra time as a valid accommodation strategy is not conclusive. Abedi et al. (2004) found that ELLs benefited from this strategy. Raising student scores overall was a welcome result, even though the accommodation did not narrow the performance gap in this study.

Oral Administration

The strategy of oral administration includes several types of accommodation. For example, the test directions and/or test items may be administered orally. Rereading and paraphrasing of directions may be permitted if test security is not an issue. In addition, oral administration may be in the student's native language or in English. With any of these accommodations, there is a risk that the test administrator will provide unintentional cues—for example, through voice, rate of reading, or body language—thereby giving students more information than would be apparent from the printed words.

Preliminary studies suggest that ELLs prefer oral administration of the assessment in their native languages when they are new to the United States, are not literate in their home languages, and have little oral or reading proficiency in English (Abedi et al., 2004). In addition, studies suggest that oral administration of the test in English is preferred when students have been instructed in English in the United States for a long time and have attained a level of conversational oral proficiency in English but are not yet literate enough to read the test.

Implications for Education Policy and Practice

Evidence from a review of the empirical research strongly suggests caution in adopting a "one size fits all" approach to test accommodations for ELLs.

Students classified as ELL are not an homogeneous group. ELL students differ in many respects, including level of English proficiency.

The level of English proficiency of some students currently classified as ELL may be even higher than that of some low-performing native English speakers. Accommodations that are appropriate for ELL students at the higher end of the English proficiency distribution may not be relevant for ELL students at the lower end of the distribution. For example, ELL students with English proficiency sufficient to understand test questions may need additional time to process the information and therefore make good use of an extra-time accommodation. In contrast, students at the lower end of the English proficiency distribution may not understand the English vocabulary and structures in the test items and therefore not benefit from having extra time. For these students, providing a glossary of non–content area terms or a **customized dictionary** may be a more appropriate accommodation.

On the basis of previous research, these general conclusions can be drawn (Abedi et al., 2004):

1. Translating test items from English into another language does not appear to be an effective accommodation strategy when the student has studied the subject in a classroom where English is used. The language of assessment should match the student's primary language of instruction.

2. Some accommodations are more effective with certain student groups than others, depending on background factors such as English reading proficiency and length of time in the United States.

3. The performance gap between ELLs and other students can be narrowed by modifying test items to reduce the use of low-frequency vocabulary and complex language structures that are incidental to the content area knowledge being assessed. This accommodation strategy is effective and also valid because it does not appear to affect the performance of English-proficient students.

4. Customized dictionaries that translate words without providing definitions can offer an effective and valid alternative to commercial dictionaries. The use of customized dictionaries has been found to help ELL students while not affecting the scores of English-proficient students.

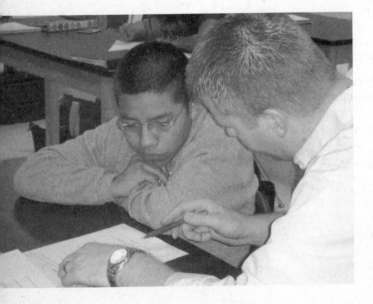

This teacher is reading aloud directions to the student in English.

All students should be provided with content area assessments that use clear language and provide sufficient time for demonstrating knowledge. In addition, customized dictionaries or glossaries can be provided for all students, regardless of their level of English language proficiency.

One of the most promising test accommodations—modifying the language but not the content of the test items—can reduce the performance gap between ELLs and non-ELLs but is rarely used. Native language translations are typically available only for Spanish-speaking students, because Spanish is the most common native language among ELLs in the United States. Since it is not cost effective to develop translated assessments in the many languages spoken by other ELLs, this accommodation strategy raises questions of fairness and equity for non-Hispanic students. Another consideration is that educators cannot assume that ELLs are sufficiently literate in their first language (L1) to read and write the translated version. Another question is whether reducing the language barrier through accommodations results in "dumbing down" tests and lowering expectations.

For all students to develop proficiency in English, teachers must provide them with the language experiences and tools needed to understand and use the academic language of classrooms, textbooks, materials, and tests. However, for assessments in the content areas—such as mathematics, science, and social studies—it is reasonable to minimize the use of language structures that are unnecessarily complicated and not relevant to the knowledge or skills being measured.

Considering ELL student accommodations and the limited research to date, the following recommendations can be made (Abedi et al., 2004):

1. In the future, the designs of large-scale content area assessments should take ELLs into account from the outset, rather than as an afterthought. Test developers should use straightforward, uncomplicated language when developing test forms. In addition, they should aim to create equitable assessments, rather than try to address language biases and other problems later by making adjustments in the testing process. The use of clear language, which is free of unnecessary complexity, and the provision of a customized dictionary can be elements of good assessment practice, not separate adaptations. The evidence from empirical research suggests that providing these elements for all students does not threaten test validity.

2. The specific language demands of academic materials and assessments should be identified and provided to teachers, so they can ensure that students have the language resources to demonstrate their content area knowledge and skills. Examining differential performance on original and modified English test items can help researchers identify those linguistic features that may affect the performance of some student groups.

3. Cost–benefit analyses should be conducted to compare the relative advantages and feasibilities of accommodation alternatives. Some accommodation strategies may be more expensive than others, and at present, the research data on the costs of accommodations are limited.

4. More research should examine how effective and valid particular accommodations are for various student groups. Student background variables are strong indicators of preparedness for participation in large-scale assessments. Accordingly, in planning who will be tested and how, states should collect and consider background information, including the language spoken in the home, English proficiency level, length of time in the United States, and years of schooling in both English and the native language.

5. The research base should be expanded to test and confirm the limited results reported here. Little empirical research exists on accommodations for K–12 ELL students in the content areas. Given this, educational practitioners are forced to base decisions about accommodations on anecdotal evidence and perceived notions of best practice, rather than on empirical evidence of validity. New and innovative assessment techniques should be developed and empirically tested to provide approaches that have proven effectiveness and validity for all of our students, including ELLs.

The "Right" English

In California, one in four students is an English language learner, for a total of 1.6 million ELL students in the state (Bielenberg & Fillmore, 2005). In comparing English-only students and ELL students, the average scores of ELLs on standardized math tests steadily decline over time, reaching their lowest points in the eighth and tenth grades. The reading and language standardized test scores of ELLs in California have shown similar declines as students matriculate to the tenth grade.

The significant test score gap in all academic areas between ELLs and other students is a serious concern, because performance on these tests matters. Perhaps most critically, high-stakes tests have the potential to undermine ELLs' opportunities for high school graduation and education beyond high school. Considering the trends in the performance of ELL high school students on standardized tests in reading, language, and math, it can be predicted that most ELLs will find high school exit exams difficult, if not impossible, to pass because these exams cover not just English literacy and mathematics but also concepts in science and social studies. Twenty-six states currently implement or plan to implement state high school exit exams (Zabala et al., 2007). These tests involve the highest possible stakes in public education because they have the power to limit subsequent economic opportunities for the students who fail them. This cannot be overstated.

As long as tests stay close to the skills and materials covered in basic skills instruction, students perform reasonably well, even when their proficiency in English is limited. By middle to high school, however, when tests require a higher level of English proficiency and a greater understanding of the content areas, ELL students' performance begins to decline (Bielenberg & Fillmore, 2005).

What ELLs need and teachers should provide is training in the academic English skills that are foundational to literacy, mastery of subject matter, and superior test performance. The term *academic English* is based on a distinction that Jim Cummins (1979) made when he argued that proficiency in language involves layers of skills and knowledge. Once students reach the middle and high school grades, the linguistic demands of school quickly change. The language of textbooks and instruction evolves to a markedly different form to allow communicating more advanced and complex subject matter. The language becomes more precise in reference and more complex in structure.

Here is an example of a typical statement in science:

> If we had provided the soil with essential nutrients, the plant would have grown larger.

To understand this statement, students have to linguistically unpack the conditional, hypothetical mood (*If*), the past-perfect verb structure (*had grown*), the comparative (*larger*), and background knowledge of *nutrients* and *soil*.

Here is a statement conveying the same information but in a more linguistically simplified form:

> The plant did not grow larger because we did not give the dirt, or *soil*, enough food, or *nutrients*.

These examples offer evidence that content area teachers must bridge linguistic gaps for ELLs (Bailey, 2006).

Problems with language also present themselves in math tests, and these problems are perhaps more worrisome because they can go unnoticed. Even the simplest word problem calls for the test taker to interpret the text and recognize that ordinary words may have quite specialized meanings in the math. This issue is evident in the following sixth-grade math test item from the Massachusetts Comprehensive Assessment System (Bailey, 2006):

> Students in Mr. Jacob's English class were giving speeches. Each student's speech was 7 to 10 minutes long. Which of the following is the best estimate for the total number of student speeches that could be given in a 2-hour class?
>
> A. 4 speeches　　B. 8 speeches　　C. 13 speeches　　D. 19 speeches

The only technical math term used in this problem is the expression *best estimate,* which tells the test taker that the correct answer will be more believable than the other answers. At first glance, this problem is simply stated, and both the vocabulary and the calculations called for are fairly straightforward: The estimate will fall between the number of 7-minute speeches that can be given in 120 minutes (17) and the number of 10-minute speeches that can be given in the same time period (12). Therefore, C (13 speeches) is the correct answer.

For ELL students, however, the problem is not that simple. They must understand that the time given for each speech is a *range,* a word with several different meanings. In this case, it means that each speech is between 7 and 10 minutes long. Test takers must also successfully interpret the question posed. To do this, they will need to unpack several grammatical features typical of academic English structures. The first is a complex noun phrase structure: *the best estimate for the total number of student speeches that could be given.* This contains a complex prepositional phrase: *for the total number of student speeches.* In addition, the complex noun phrase contains a passive construction—*could be given*—which is frequently encountered in academic English but difficult for ELLs to decipher.

The following problem, taken from preparation materials for the California High School Exit Examination (www.cde.ca.gov/ta/tg/hs/resources.asp), provides another illustration:

> A submarine is 285 feet under the surface of the ocean. A helicopter is flying at 4,500 feet above sea level. Given that the helicopter is directly above the submarine, how far apart are they?
>
> A. 285 feet　　B. 4,215 feet　　C. 4,785 feet　　D. 4,500 feet

Mathematically, this is a simple arithmetic problem: 285 + 4,500 = 4,785. However, students find it difficult. First, test takers must be able to envision the scene described in the problem. It calls for considerable background knowledge, triggered by specific vocabulary and expressions, such as *helicopter, submarine, surface of the ocean,* and *sea level.* The test taker must know that the words *sea* and *ocean* are used as synonyms here, and that *sea level* and *surface of the ocean* refer to the same baseline. It would help to know that the term *sea level* is an abstraction, and that it can apply to places miles away from an ocean. For example, Denver is a mile above sea level, and Death Valley is 282 feet below sea level but not literally under the surface of the ocean.

There are other difficulties with the problem, as well. It asks how far apart the helicopter and the submarine are. It does not specify whether the distance is to be thought of as horizontal or vertical. The student must interpret this information from the positions given for the submarine and the helicopter: The first position is 285 feet under the surface of the ocean, and the second is 4,500 feet above sea level. Important information in the problem is contained in a conditional construction, *given that,* which ELLs may never before have encountered. Test takers most likely will have difficulty realizing that the information introduced by this expression is crucial to interpreting the problem. Prepositional phrases are notoriously difficult for native English speakers, as well as ELL students, and this short math problem contains five. English language learners may also have difficulty interpreting pronoun references. The word *they* tends to be especially problematic, because it can refer to people or objects. Students may not understand that the pronoun in the test item refers to the helicopter and the submarine. This example highlights the vocabulary reinforcement crucial for ELLs to understand what is being asked (Bailey, 2007; Bielenberg & Fillmore, 2005).

In Project Challenge, Boston University researchers and teachers studied 100 fourth-graders, two-thirds of whom were ELLs (McNeil, 2007). Each day, students received an hour of **scaffolded** instruction from their teachers that emphasized integrating their knowledge of various topics and taking responsibility for their own learning. Teachers encouraged students to talk about their reasoning processes in understanding the problems they were working on.

Using a technique called **revoicing,** a teacher repeated some or all of what the student had just said, modeling a more fully realized version of the student's statement. The teacher also asked students to restate the contributions of classmates: "Can you repeat what he or she just said in your own words?" Students in the program came to realize that they not only had to listen to one another, but they also had to try to understand what had been said so they could paraphrase it for the class. This involved higher-level thinking skills.

Project Challenge teachers also asked students to comment on their classmates' understanding of a problem and the reasoning behind it: "Do you agree or disagree with him or her, and why?" Doing so allowed students to practice at the evaluative higher-order thinking level, as students became more aware of their own and their classmates' thinking processes and various techniques used in problem solving.

Although Project Challenge was conducted at the elementary level, the strategies used in it are also appropriate at the secondary level. These strategies keep ELLs involved and engaged at a comprehensible level of input. They also avoid the **unconscious marginalization** of ELLs and the watering down of content. English language learners can make the grade, even on the toughest tests, when they get the instructional support they need.

Siegel, Wissehr, and Halverson (2008) have discussed concerns of secondary science teachers in Missouri schools, who teach ELLs mainstreamed into regular science classes. These researchers have configured five principles of equitable assessment, entitled *The McCes: Sounds Like Success: A Framework for Equitable Assessment,* to assist teachers in evaluating ELL students' written classroom assignments. The acronym McCes stands for these elements:

M   Match the learning goals and the language of instruction.

c   [Be] comprehensible for English learners, both linguistically and culturally.

C   Challenge students to think about difficult ideas.

E   Elicit student understanding.

S   Scaffold the use of language and support student learning.

The sample test questions on the high-stakes tests from California and Massachusetts and the research conducted in Missouri provide fractional evidence of the larger issues involved in the equitable assessment of ELLs. By considering these concepts and ideas and adopting better assessment techniques, teachers can meet the learning needs of their students through providing equitable assessment opportunities.

Assessment Strategies, Tools, and Techniques

Adequate Yearly Progress (AYP)

Under NCLB, the success of ELL students is connected to meeting **adequate yearly progress (AYP)** by individual schools. Considered a tool, AYP is used to guide schools in assisting all students to attain certain goals and standards. The emphasis on testing that has occurred since this legislation was enacted in 2001 has left teachers and administrators scrambling to find the optimal ELL instructional program. Many ELLs manage to reach the goal of earning a passing score in math, but they continue to struggle with earning a passing score on the verbal components of tests.

One effective strategy for improving students' scores is to reproduce the answering formats of high-stakes tests in daily and weekly formative testing situations throughout the year. When teachers design and simulate the response formats on these tests, students become familiar with the question/answer formats and will likely perform better when it comes time to take the actual test.

Questioning Strategies

Involving ELL students in content discussions can be frustrating if teachers do not develop strategies for asking questions. To do so, teachers should consider the language of the question: Is it testing the language skills of the student, or is it testing his or her understanding of the content?

Teachers can structure the form of the question to the ELL student's current language ability and accept single words or phrases as correct answers. Teachers should not insist that students speak in full sentences. Rather, they should let ELL students know in advance which questions they will be responsible for answering. Teachers should allow students think time to prepare an answer.

Here is an example of hierarchy of questioning:

■ Ask newcomers to point to a picture or word to demonstrate basic knowledge—for example, "Point to the porpoise."

■ Using visual cues, ask simple *yes/no* questions: "Is a porpoise a fish?"

- Ask *either/or* questions, for which the answer is embedded: "Is a penguin a mammal or a bird?"

- Break complex questions into several steps: "Look at the mammals. Find the tiger, the goat, and the bat. Why are these animals all mammals? How are they the same?"

- Ask simple *how* and *where* questions that can be answered with a short phrase or sentence: "Where do porpoises live? How do bats hear?"

- Do not expect ELLs to answer broad, open-ended questions, such as "How do fish breathe underwater?" Rather, ask "What do fish have that helps them breathe?" This question requires just a one-word answer.

Modifying Multiple-Choice Tests

The use of multiple-choice format recognizes the emerging linguistic skills of intermediate and advanced ELL students. It also encourages the development of ELLs' test-taking skills, which will be necessary for them to perform well on required standardized tests. However, since students at these levels of development still have specific linguistic needs, careful and deliberate test construction is required. Consider the following guidelines for making **modifications:**

- Provide only three answer options.

- Make all answer options about the same length.

- Be sure the answers are not ambiguous and relate to the question.

- Be sure answer options are grammatically correct.

- Keep the vocabulary and syntax simple, and use simple sentences.

- Provide answer options that require careful reading, not outside knowledge.

- Focus on the essential concepts of the lesson.

- Do not use double-negatives, as in this example:

    The way not to get hit by the bat is:
    - A. to not stand away from the batter
    - B. to not stand behind the batter
    - C. to stand farther from the batter

- Finally, do not use the answer options "All of the above," "None of the above," or "A and B but not C."

Modifying Fill-in-the-Blank Questions

When utilizing the fill-in-the-blank form of questioning, teachers should use clear, brief, and simple statements. They should also provide a box containing a list of word or term options, rather than ask ELL students to produce the vocabulary on their own.

It is good to use a variety of formats in any one test. Teachers should use a few multiple-choice, a few true/false, and some fill-in-the-blank items. In addition, teachers should reproduce the answer formats ELLs will encounter on their standardized tests. Doing so familiarizes students with these kinds of test items and prepares them for sitting down to take high-stakes tests.

Guidelines for Modifying Assessments

To help ELL students avoid dreading every testing situation, teachers must make modifications for them to be successful. Here are some modifications teachers can make in providing **alternative assessments:**

- Reduce response materials for content area testing.

- Provide a version of the test with simplified language.

- Simplify directions.

- Read test questions aloud.

- Supply word banks for tests.

- Provide matching activities.

- Allow extra time to complete tests.

- Use peer interpreters.

- Allow students to respond orally, rather than in written form.

- Double-grade students, providing one grade for content and one for structure, particularly for narratives and essays in all content areas.

- Use **portfolios** to assess student progress authentically and allow them to view their progress.

Culturally Biased Tests

It is important for curriculum developers and test writers to make sure ELLs can figure out the cultural content of test questions through context. Depending on an ELL's cultural heritage, he or she may be completely unfamiliar with what is considered common to most U.S. students (Brown University, n.d.). **Cultural bias** takes place when items on a test require the student to have certain background knowledge and experience to answer correctly.

For instance, consider the following sentence:

Josef had some humus and baklava before noon.

A Portuguese-speaking ELL who just arrived in the United States would find it nearly impossible to figure out the meanings of the words *humus* and *baklava*. However, when two minor changes are made to the sentence, it becomes clear that *humus* and *baklava* refer to food:

Josef ate some humus and baklava for lunch.

Including the words *ate* and *lunch* makes it possible for the reader to infer that the words *humus* and *baklava* refer to food items.

Other more subtle aspects of **culture,** such as the concept of credit, can further confuse ELLs. Many students come from countries and cultures that operate on a cash economy, where credit is never used for financial transactions. In such countries and cultures, the majority of people have no credit cards or checking accounts but instead line up to receive a salary or pay rent in cash. The notion of paying for something with "plastic" might be foreign to students from such countries and cultures. Although these ELLs may know what a credit card looks like, they will be less likely to understand the concept of credit as well as their peers. Compared to ELL counterparts who have been raised in the United States, these ELLs will have difficulty understanding that interest is like rent paid to use money.

The following example is a word problem that would challenge even a student born and raised in the United States. Consider how much harder it would be for an ELL who has grown up in Belarus, a small country in Eastern Europe, where cash is the only negotiable currency:

Alex bought a new sweater that cost $200. He paid for the sweater with a credit card with a simple interest rate of 1.7 percent per month and late charges of $10 per month. If Alex's first payment of $50 is late, what will be the balance on his next monthly statement?

This word problem can be made more comprehensible for ELLs by adding explanations of *simple interest rate* and *late charges*. The curriculum could also be modified to ensure that ELLs have a thorough understanding of not only the language but also the underlying concepts and cultural content involved. This type of question assumes the student already understands the cultural content of the question, which is *interest on credit.*

The following is an example of a text question that could be construed as culturally biased:

One of the most important speeches was given by Kennedy.

If the purpose of this sentence is to assess whether students remember from their course of study that Kennedy was a famous U.S. president, then the sentence is fine as written. However, if the purpose of the sentence is to determine something else, it could be considered culturally biased against ELLs, who could easily lack background knowledge about U.S. presidents. To correct the problem, the sentence should be rewritten:

One of the most important speeches in U.S. history was given by President Kennedy.

Here is another example of a biased item:

Kate won at archery because she could _____ straighter than Rosie.

1. show   2. run   3. draw   4. aim

This item is biased because it takes more than an ability to read and comprehend the question to answer it correctly. It takes culturally specific knowledge not contained within the question. Specifically, the reader must know about the sport of archery, as well as the vocabulary words within the question and answer choices. A picture of a bull's eye target might help students understand the reference to the game. The question would be better if revised:

Kate had more points than Rosie, so she won the game of archery. Kate's score was _____ than Rosie's score.

1. lower   2. taller   3. higher   4. shorter

To help determine if a test is culturally biased or culturally responsive, teachers should ask these questions about it:

- Are enough supporting details provided so that students can comprehend the cultural content?

- Do the test items show bias in terms of race/ethnicity, gender, culture, religion, socioeconomic status, or processes?

- Are different cultural and socioeconomic groups represented and portrayed positively?

- Will the cultural content be comprehensible to all test takers?

- Are the cultural content and language accurate and up to date?

Alternative Assessments

Standardized tests remain the most reliable and practical way to measure the overall abilities of large groups of students. Thus, developing the academic skills needed to perform well on a conventional test is still looked at as important. However, educators today realize that assessing academic intelligence is only one way to measure the overall abilities of a student. Because people are considered to have multiple areas of intelligence, the use of alternative assessments to measure these intelligences has become more widely accepted (Lederman & Burnstein, 2006). The twenty-first century workplace demands that employees have problem-solving and computer skills and can work well on a team with a variety of people.

Given this, today's classroom must develop both interdependent and independent, problem-solving abilities. Students should work in **cooperative learning** environments, expressing divergent thinking and discussing concepts and ideas from **multiple perspectives.** It is unrealistic and unfair, as well incomprehensive, to test students through traditional paper-and-pencil, multiple-choice tests. For example, suppose students have been asked to form two groups and debate whether the atom bomb should have been dropped on Japan at the end of World War II. Assessing the rationale for students' opinions using a fill-in-the-blank or multiple-choice test seems illogical. An alternative format will be more appropriate—for instance, one that will ask students to explain their opinions, how they arrived at those opinions, and what influenced their decision making (Brookhart, Moss, & Long, 2008).

Alternative assessments are called *alternative* because they are more global than traditional assessments. They ask more from students than a conventional test. Related terms are *performance assessment* and *authentic assessment.* As instruction becomes more thematic and geared to higher-order thinking skills, assessment should move in the same direction. One problem with traditional tests is that they tend to assess lower-order thinking skills, even when teachers claim to value and teach complex thinking.

Using alternative assessments has a number of advantages:

- It helps students integrate and use their learning.

- It shows students what they can do, not what they can't.

- It better accommodates varying student interests, learning styles, backgrounds, and language levels.
- It encourages student responsibility.

In an alternative assessment situation, the time is more flexible and the setting is relaxed and cooperative. These factors set the tone for assessment so that all students can experience a measure of success. Alternative kinds of activities mirror real workplace scenarios in many jobs and businesses.

Forms of Alternative Assessments

The list that follows identifies forms of alternative assessments that elicit higher levels of thinking and engage students. These alternative forms ask students questions, such as *why* and *how,* and have them redefine, prioritize, and organize:

Personal interview	Exhibit team	Group testing
Content retelling	Diagrams	Word associations
Group project/Presentation	Tables or graphs	Lists
Graphic representation	Organizers	Portfolios
Student self-rating/Evaluation	Short answers	Word problems
Teacher rating checklist	Summary of findings	Writing samples
Peer interviewing	Oral responses	Computer or online tests

Self-Evaluation

One way to determine how ELLs feel about their own learning is to have them complete self-evaluation forms (see Figures 2.1 and 2.2). Having students evaluate themselves not only increases teachers' understanding of their learning channels and styles, but it also offers teachers insights into the kinds of activities ELLs feel comfortable doing. Based on students' responses, teachers can provide more individualized academic achievement plans. Self-evaluation forms can be made bilingual using online free translation resources, such as www.google.com/ig.

Figure 2.1 Self-Evaluation Form

Name _____ Date _____

Title of Assignment _____

For each of the following statements, put an X in the box that shows how often you do the behavior mentioned. Add comments.

When I have problems talking or writing in English, I:

Behavior	Never	Sometimes	Often	Comments
Use my native language.				
Ask for help from other students.				
Look for answers in the textbook.				
Use nonverbal communication, such as facial expressions and hand gestures, to communicate.				
Use a word that I think has the same meaning.				
Make up new words.				
Simplify what I want to say.				
Do not say anything.				
Use my bilingual dictionary.				

Figure 2.2 Self-Evaluation Form

Name _____ Date _____

Title of Assignment _____

Put a checkmark in the box that best describes how well you use English. Add comments.

Ponga una marca en la caja que describe mejor cuán bien usted puede utilizar inglés.

Task	Not Very Well No Muy Bien	Okay Bueno	Very Well Muy Bueno	Comments Comentarios
I can describe objects and people. *Puedo describir objetos y a personas.*				
I can summarize a story. *Puedo resumir un cuento.*				
I can give an oral report. *Puedo dar un informe oral.*				
I understood the main idea/concept of the lesson. *Entendí el idea/concepto principal de la lección.*				
I can describe past events. *Puedo describir los acontecimientos pasados.*				
I can listen to and understand video and television. *Puedo escuchar y entender video y televisión.*				
I can state an opinion. *Puedo indicar una opinión.*				
I can agree and disagree. *Puedo concordar y no puedo convenir.*				
I can listen to and understand radio programs. *Puedo escuchar y entender programas de radio.*				
I like and learn working in groups of students. *Quiero y aprendo trabajar en grupos de estudiantes.*				

Rubrics

Teachers can also use **rubrics** to evaluate students' understanding of social studies, science, math, or language arts topics. A rubric can be applied to numerous tasks in the classroom. It can evaluate the depth, breadth, creativity, detail, completeness, and conceptual framework of an essay, presentation, skit, poster, project, report, portfolio, and so on.

Rubrics are assessment tools that provide feedback along these scoring criteria:

Summative: Provide information about a student's knowledge

Formative: Provide information about a student's strengths and weaknesses

Evaluative: Provide ways to create instruction that fits a student's needs

Educative: Provide the student with an understanding of how he or she can learn and perform in a particular content area

In the classroom, the use of rubrics can make assessment more meaningful, clarify expectations, and yield better feedback. Specifically, a *rubric* is a matrix that defines in advance what is expected in a learning situation. For students, having a rubric prevents them from receiving a mysterious grade at the end of a unit, project, paper, or presentation. The rubric gives them insight and direction about what is important about the activity and what levels of effort and ability are needed for certain scores.

There are two predominant types of rubrics: holistic and analytical (see Figures 2.3 and 2.4). A **holistic rubric** is a description of requirements that are assigned terms such as *proficient* for the higher score and *limited* for the lowest score. An **analytical rubric** is a description of requirements that are assigned numbers or points, according to the aspects of the project.

The most beneficial aspect of incorporating rubrics into assignments is that doing so lets students know before they begin work what they need to do to achieve an A in a project or report, a B, and so on. That way, students

Figure 2.3   Holistic Rubric for Science Experiment

Proficient – 3 points	The project has a hypothesis, a procedure, collected data, and analyzed results. The work is thorough, and the findings are in agreement with the data collected. There are minor inaccuracies that do not affect the quality of the project.
Adequate – 2 points	The project has a missing component, and the work is not as thorough as it could be. A few areas have been overlooked. There are a couple of inaccuracies that affect the quality of the project.
Limited – 1 point	The project has more than one missing component, and the work is not thorough. There are many inaccuracies that affect the quality of the project.

Source: Mueller, 2009.

Figure 2.4 Analytical Rubric for Science Experiment

Criteria	4 points	3 points	2 points	1 point
Plan for investigation	The plan is thorough	The plan lacks a few details	The plan is missing several details	The plan is incomplete and limited
Use of materials	Uses all materials responsibly	Uses materials responsibly most of the time	Mishandles some of the materials	Does not use materials properly
Data collection	Has collected all the data	Has collected some of the data	Major pieces of data are missing	Minimal data have been collected

Source: Mueller, 2009.

can decide how much effort and ability to put into a project or report, thus assuming responsibility for the outcome. This eliminates comments from students such as "The teacher gave me a C"; rather, students will remark "The grade that I earned is a C."

Guidelines for Constructing Rubrics

To construct effective rubrics, teachers should follow these guidelines:

■ Know the goals for instruction. What are the learning outcomes?

■ Decide on the type of rubric: holistic or analytical. Which best fits the task?

■ Determine the levels of performance. Are there levels specific to all the criteria?

■ Share the rubric with students. They should have an opportunity to see, discuss, and even design the rubric *before* beginning the project or activity to be evaluated.

■ Have the class brainstorm ideas about what should be included in the rubric. Students should identify three to five important criteria and assign values to them.

■ Consider what grade level and ability level are appropriate when choosing areas to grade.

Figures 2.5 and 2.6 provide additional examples of rubrics. Note that in using the social studies discussion rubric (Figure 2.5), scores of 4 and 2 could be used to rate in-between behaviors. This would be useful, in particular, if a student disagreed with the teacher's evaluation and could demonstrate that his or her project falls between the descriptions of scores indicated in the rubric. Taking this approach would allow for discussion of students' awareness of the degree of effort and knowledge necessary to earn a certain score. It provides an opportunity to foster individual student ownership of the grade/score and reinforces the value of contributing positively to student cooperative learning activities.

Figure 2.5 Rubric for Group Discussion in Social Studies

Criteria	5	3	1
Participation	Actively participates; para-phrases; encourages others; is patient; is enthusiastic	Shares some ideas; requires encouragement; needs reminders to stay on task	Is off task; is distracted; makes inappropriate responses or contributions
Critical Thinking	Clearly identifies the problem; considers others' viewpoints; helps formulate conclusions; applies extended learning	Identifies the problem by restating the main points; shows a general understanding; shows some limited application of ideas	Demonstrates little comprehension of the problem; makes little contribution to conclusions; shows little consideration for others' viewpoints
Communication of Ideas	Has a well-defined position; uses questioning; para-phrases and clarifies ideas; displays appropriate body language; supports others; is convincing	Demonstrates ideas in a general way; demonstrates limited paraphrasing and questioning; displays passive interaction	Has vague, indecisive positions; is confrontational; shares views in a negative fashion or is withdrawn
Use of Knowledge	Shares knowledge respect-fully; applies and relates knowledge to or of past experiences, issues, and discussions	Shares a general knowledge of the issue; engages in limited sharing, engagement, and discussion of the issue	Refrains from contributing any knowledge; criticizes others' expressions of knowledge

Source: www.teachnology.com/web_tools/rubrics/socialstudies

The beauty of rubrics is that they provide both the criteria that students need to consider in doing the work and the specifics teachers need to evaluate that work. Rubrics provide a very equitable tool for assessment.

Bloom's Taxonomy

Teachers should continually challenge ELL students by asking higher-order thinking questions. On many high-stakes tests, 60 percent of the items fall into the upper levels of **Bloom's taxonomy:** evaluation, synthesis, and analysis (PBCSD, 2000). The following sections describe these three levels of thinking, identifying the skills demonstrated at that level, question cues to use at that level, sample tasks for that level, and question prompts for that level (Churches, 2008; Overbaugh & Schultz, 2009).

Figure 2.6 Rubric for Mathematics Problem Solving

Areas of Activity to Be Evaluated	Novice (Lowest)	Apprentice	Practitioner	Expert (Highest)
Understanding	Misses fundamental steps and concepts underlying the problem.	Understands some of the major steps and concepts in solving the problem but misses others.	Has a solid understanding of the major steps and concepts in solving the problem.	Has a solid understanding of the major steps and concepts in solving the problem. Indicates alternative approaches, and provides details to support understanding.
Strategies, Reasoning, and Procedures	Does not demonstrate knowledge of common strategies and procedures for solving the problem. Reasoning is unsure or incorrect. Work cannot lead to a correct solution.	With assistance, can manage common strategies and procedures for solving the problem. Reasoning shows a possible approach to the problem. Work could lead to a correct solution but does not include all steps.	Cleary understands the plan for solving the problem, and applies the main procedures and strategies. Reasoning is essentially correct, except for minor errors.	Shows clear evidence of a plan for solving the problem, and clearly understands all strategies and procedures. Reasoning is clear, errors are minimal, and details are correct.
Communication	Does not provide a clear explanation. Is confused about or missing specific steps.	In the explanation, shows some of the steps have been taken. Needs help to give a full explanation.	Provides an explanation that is clear and includes all the major steps. Is missing some details, and uses some imprecise language.	Provides a clear and complete explanation. Indicates more than one solution, and shows understanding through details of the solution.

Source: www.teachnology.com/web_tools/math

Evaluation Level

The skills demonstrated at the evaluation level, which is the highest level, are as follow:

- Compare and discriminate between ideas.
- Verify the value of evidence.
- Recognize subjectivity.
- Assess the value of theories.
- Make choices based on reasoned arguments.

Question Cues

Assess	Recommend	Rank	Decide
Convince	Grade	Support	Judge
Measure	Conclude	Test	Select

Sample Tasks

- Prepare a list of criteria to judge a . . . show.
- Form a group to discuss a topic. State guidelines for discussion.
- Prioritize and rate a set of items or ideas.
- Make a booklet about five rules you value.
- Write a letter to . . . advising changes needed.
- Prepare points of view for a debate panel.

Question Prompts

- Do you believe . . . ?
- How would you feel if . . . ?
- Is there a better solution to . . . ?
- Do you think . . . is good or bad? Why?
- Judge the value of . . .

Synthesis Level

These skills are demonstrated at the synthesis level:

- Predict and draw conclusions.
- Use old ideas to create new ones.
- Generalize from given facts.

Question Cues

Rearrange	Rewrite	Plan	Prepare
Formulate	Compose	Substitute	Modify

Sample Tasks

- Create a poster that advertises a story with the goal of persuading others to read it.
- Write a story from just a title.
- Revise the roles of fiction or nonfiction characters to create a different outcome.
- Create an original character, and work him or her into an existing work of fiction or nonfiction.
- Design a book, record, or magazine cover.
- Write or rewrite a screenplay about a real or fictitious situation.

Question Prompts

- What might be a new way to . . . ?
- How many ways can you . . . ?
- What might be a new use for . . . ?
- What would happen if . . . ?
- How would you compose a new . . . about . . . ?

Analysis Level

The skills demonstrated at the analysis level include these:

- Recognize hidden meanings.
- See patterns.
- Identify components.

Question Cues

Arrange	Classify	Connect	Infer
Explain	Analyze	Order	Separate

Sample Tasks

- Distinguish what can happen from what cannot.
- Differentiate fact from fiction.
- Compare and/or contrast characters/issues.
- Construct a graph to illustrate information.
- Write a biography.
- Design a questionnaire or survey to gather information.
- Review a work of art for form, texture, dimension, and color.

Question Prompts

- What is the turning point in the story or event?
- What must have happened when . . . ?
- How is . . . similar to . . . ?
- What is the underlying message or theme of . . . ?
- Distinguish between . . . and . . .

See also Table 2.1, which contains all this information. This table can be printed on colored paper, laminated, and placed in a lesson plan book for easy reference.

Experiential Activities

Experiential activities provide opportunities for language acquisition for ELLs at all stages of language development. These activities can encompass experiences in science, social studies, art, and music. They include games, problemsolving activities, cooking, crafts, models, field trips, and **role-playing**.

Activities to Assess Students at the Early Production Stage

- Pair an ELL student with another student who can help translate.
- Label objects in the room.
- Before discussing the lesson, identify illustrations and graphs, conduct *Text Quests*, and examine maps in the content area textbooks.
- Make word cards, with a picture on one side and a word on the other.

Table 2.1 Bloom's Taxonomy

	Evaluation		Synthesis		Analysis	
Skills Demonstrated	■ Compare and discriminate between ideas. ■ Verify the value of evidence. ■ Recognize subjectivity. ■ Assess the value of theories. ■ Make choices based on reasoned arguments.		■ Predict and draw conclusions. ■ Use old ideas to create new ones. ■ Generalize from given facts.		■ Recognize hidden meanings. ■ See patterns. ■ Identify components.	
Question Cues	Assess Recommend Rank Decide Convince Measure	Grade Conclude Support Judge Test Select	Rearrange Rewrite Plan Prepare	Formulate Compose Substitute Modify	Arrange Classify Connect Infer	Explain Analyze Order Separate
Sample Tasks	■ Prepare a list of criteria to judge a . . . show. ■ Form a group to discuss a topic. State guidelines for discussion. ■ Prioritize and rate a set of items or ideas. ■ Make a booklet about five rules you value. ■ Write a letter to . . . advising changes needed. ■ Prepare points of view for a debate panel.		■ Create a poster that advertises a story with the goal of persuading others to read it. ■ Write a story from just a title. ■ Revise the roles of fiction or nonfiction characters to create a different outcome. ■ Create an original character, and work him or her into an existing work of fiction or nonfiction. ■ Design a book, record, or magazine cover. ■ Write or rewrite a screenplay about a real or fictitious situation.		■ Distinguish what can happen from what cannot. ■ Differentiate fact from fiction. ■ Compare and/or contrast characters/issues. ■ Construct a graph to illustrate information. ■ Write a biography. ■ Design a questionnaire or survey to gather information. ■ Review a work of art for form, texture, dimension, and color.	
Question Prompts	■ Do you believe . . . ? ■ How would you feel if . . . ? ■ Is there a better solution to . . . ? ■ Do you think . . . is good or bad? Why? ■ Judge the value of		■ What might be a new way to . . . ? ■ How many ways can you . . . ? ■ What might be a new use for . . . ? ■ What would happen if . . . ? ■ How would you compose a new . . . about . . . ?		■ What is the turning point in the story or event? ■ What must have happened when . . . ? ■ How is . . . similar to . . . ? ■ What is the underlying message or theme of . . . ? ■ Distinguish between . . . and . . .	

Source: Churches, 2008; Overbaugh & Schultz, 2009.

- Make a collage with known objects.
- Assign the *ABCs of a Topic* activity.

Activities to Assess Students at the Speech Emergence Stage

- Conduct role-playing to illustrate and reinforce new information.
- Keep a **dialogue journal** with the ELL student.
- Brainstorm about what students know about a topic.
- Create a **graphic organizer** to identify the main idea/concept and significant supporting details.
- Identify the information that is essential for students to know, and give it to ELLs in advance of the lesson.
- Modify activity sheets.
- Use the *Give One, Get One* student-generated vocabulary activity.
- Check comprehension through drawing, free writing, peer discussion, and other illustrations.

Activities to Assess Students at the Intermediate Fluency Stage

- Play games that enhance language development, including board games and vocabulary Tic-Tac-Toe, Bingo, and Concentration using pictured content cards.
- Play games such as Guess the Object, in which a variety of realia or pictures are placed on a table. Students are asked questions about objects that they have to identify.
- Create a crossword puzzle or cryptogram with salient vocabulary.
- Play Jeopardy with vocabulary terms.
- Have student groups design test questions.

Portfolios

A *portfolio* is a collection of student work representing a selection of performances over a certain amount of time. The student selects the materials to include and is responsible for keeping them organized. The content in portfolios is built from class assignments and as such corresponds to the classroom curriculum. The teacher should provide students with specific directions, along with clear guidelines and examples, to get started on creating a portfolio.

By building a portfolio and explaining the basis for selecting materials, students generate criteria for good work with teacher and peer input. Portfolios capitalize on students' natural tendency to save work and are an effective way to get students to take a second look at their work and think about how they might improve it in the future. All students benefit from maintaining a portfolio.

Portfolios are useful in supporting new instructional approaches that emphasize the student's role in constructing understanding and the teacher's role in promoting understanding. Portfolios are valued as an assessment tool because as representations of classroom-based performance, they can be fully integrated into the curriculum.

Using the template shown in Figure 2.7, teachers can help students create a Table of Contents page that identifies the contents of their portfolios. This page could be stapled to the inside-left flap of a manila folder, providing one folder per student. Each student could print his or her name on the tab of the folder. The teacher can make a transparency of this form and keep adding assignments as they are done. Students can record each new assignment on their Table of Contents form as the teacher writes it on the transparency.

Figure 2.7 Template for Table of Contents Page for a Portfolio

Table of Contents		
Assignment #	**Title of Assignment**	**Date**
1.		
2.		
3.		
4.		
5.		
6.		
7.		
8.		
9.		
10.		
11.		
12.		
13.		
14.		
15.		
16.		
17.		
18.		
19.		
20.		

When students have been absent, they will see that they have a blank line. They can find the missing assignment in the teacher's "Make-Up Work Box." Doing so helps promote the metacognitive skills of organizing and knowing where to find information.

Teachers should use different colors of folders to differentiate between blocks of classes. Teachers should also provide a file box in which students can place their folders as they leave the classroom. New folders should be created at the middle or end of the grading period.

It is very important for ELLs to see their progress from week to week, month to month. This encourages students and fosters greater motivation in tackling content in their second language. All portfolios—across diverse curricular settings, student populations, and administrative contexts—involve students in their own education. They take charge of their personal collection of work, reflect on what makes some work better than other work, and use this information to make improvements in future work.

References

Abedi, J. (2008). Measuring students' level of English proficiency: Educational significance and assessment requirements [Part of a special issue entitled *Assessment of English Language Learners*]. *Educational Assessment, 13*(2/3), 193–214.

Abedi, J., Hofstetter, C., & Lord, C. (2004). Assessment accommodations for English language learners: Implications for policy-based empirical research. *Review of Educational Research, 74*(1), 1–28.

Bailey, A. (Ed.). (2006). *The language demands of school: Putting academic English to the test.* New Haven, CT: Yale University Press.

Bielenberg, B., & Fillmore, L. W. (2005). The English they need for the test. *Educational Leadership, 62*(4), 45–49.

Brookhart, S., Moss, C., & Long, B. (2008). Formative assessment that empowers. *Educational Leadership, 66*(3), 52–57.

Brown University. (n.d.). Education Alliance. Retrieved November 1, 2006, from www.alliance.brown.edu

Churches, A. (2008). *Bloom's Taxonomy Blooms Digitally.* Retrieved on September 21, 2009 from www.techlearning.com/article/8670

Cummins, J. (1979). Linguistic interdependence and the educational development of bilingual children. *Review of Educational Research, 49,* 221–251.

Cummins, J. (1981). Age on arrival and immigrant second language learning in Canada: A reassessment. *Applied Linguistics, 2,* 132–149.

Fry, R. (2003). *Hispanic youth dropping out of U.S. schools: Measuring the challenge.* Report published by Pew Hispanic Center, Washington, DC.

Hakuta, K., Butler, G., & Witt, D. (2000). *How long does it take English learners to attain proficiency?* Report published by University of California, Linguistic Minority Research Institute.

Hamann, E., & Meltzer, J. (2006). Literacy for English learners and regular students, too. *Education Digest, 71*(8), 32–40.

Keefe, M. R. (Producer/Researcher). (2008). *Voices of immigrant ELL high school students.* [Video]. TV Production Classes, Martin County School District, Florida, TV Production Classes.

Lederman, L., & Burnstein, R. (2006). Alternative approaches to high stakes testing. *Phi Delta Kappan, 87*(6), 429–432.

Maxwell-Jolly, J., Gandara, P., & Benavidez, L. M. (2007). *Promoting academic literacy among adolescent English language learners.* Report published by University of California, Linguistic Minority Research Institute.

McNeil, T. (2007). Exponential promise. *Bostonia: Boston University Alumni Magazine.*

Mueller, J. (2009). Authentic Assessment Toolbox. Retrieved on March 31, 2009, from http://jonathan.mueller.faculty.noctrl.edu/toolbox/rubrics.htm

National Center for Secondary Education and Transition (NCSET). (2004). *Topical report: A national study of graduation requirements and diploma options for youth with disabilities.* Retrieved on November 13, 2008, from www.ncset.org/publications/related/NCSETgradreport.pdf

Overbaugh, R., & Schultz, L. (2009). *Bloom's Taxonomy.* Retrieved on October 16, 2009, from www.odu.edu/educ/roverbau/Bloom/blooms_taxonomy.htm

Palm Beach County School District (PBCSD), Department of Elementary and Secondary Education. (2000). JETS workshop.

Siegel, M., Wissehr, C., & Halverson, K. (2008). Sounds like success: A framework for equitable assessment. *Science Teacher, 75*(3), 43–46.

U.S. Department of Education. (2005). Office of English Language Acquisition. Retrieved February 24, 2006, from www.ed.gov/about/offices/list/oela/index.html

Zabala, D., Minnici, A., McMurrer, J., Hill, D., Bartley, A., & Jennings, J. (2007). *State High School Exit Exams: Working to Raise Test Scores.* Report published by the Center on Education Policy, Washington, DC.

Second Language Acquisition

Reasons Why English Is Hard to Learn

The bandage is wound around the wound.

The farm was used to produce produce.

The dump was so full that it had to refuse more refuse.

He could lead if he could get the lead out.

The soldier decided to desert his dessert in the desert.

Since there is no time like the present, he decided to present the present.

I did not object to the object.

The insurance was invalid for the invalid.

They were too close to the door to close it.

The wind was too strong to wind the sail.

After a number of injections, my jaw got number.

Upon seeing the tear in the painting, I shed a tear.

I had to subject the subject to a series of tests.

There is no egg in eggplant, nor ham in hamburger, neither apple nor pine in pineapple.

We take English for granted as we explore its paradoxes, we find that quicksand can work slowly and boxing rings are square.

If the plural of tooth is teeth, why isn't the plural of booth beeth?

If teachers taught, why don't preachers praught?

If a vegetarian eats vegetables, what does a humanitarian eat?

In what language do people ship by truck and send by cargo?

Have noses that run and feet that smell?

How can a slim chance be a fat chance, while a wise man and a wise guy are opposites?

You have to marvel at the unique lunacy of a language in which your house can burn up as it burns down, in which you fill in a form by filling it out, and in which an alarm goes off by going on.

These are just a few of the reasons why English is so hard to learn.

—*Author Unknown*

Native-speaking children enter school with a working knowledge of their language. Moreover, they learned to speak and understand this language at a very early age and with little or no formal teaching. Children learn their spoken language by making hypotheses based on the language spoken by adults and others in their environment. During this process, children test a series of language strategies and learn through feedback whether their speech makes sense to people. Once they go to school, children use these same cognitive skills in learning to read and write.

It appears that children acquiring a second language follow the same developmental sequence of linguistic patterns as children acquiring their native language. Differences do exist, however, between first and second language acquisition (Krashen, 1981).

If English language learners (ELLs) are literate and can read and write in their first language (L1), this can facilitate learning their second language (L2). However, many ELL students can speak and understand their L1 as it is spoken but cannot read or write this language and have had no formal education in this language. Moreover, in U.S. classrooms and beyond, ELLs will most likely be assessed in English. Therefore, instruction must stress English language learning.

Test Your Knowledge

The following list identifies common notions about effective ELL instruction. Some of these ideas have been proven true by research, and others have been proven false (Grognet et al., 2000). Consider each statement and read the analysis to see if your original thought on the matter agreed or disagreed with the research:

1. *Children acquire a second language primarily through imitation and repetition.* FALSE. Krashen's (1989) **input hypothesis** suggests that learners acquire a second language by understanding language input that is just slightly beyond their current level of competence. If the input is either too easy or too difficult, language acquisition will not be facilitated.

2. *Maintaining the student's first language in the home will facilitate and enhance his or her acquisition of English.* TRUE. Concepts learned in the first language will transfer to the second. If the student's parents are limited in their English skills, however, they will not be good language models, and what they teach their child will be based on their limited English.

3. *Oral fluency is a sufficient indication that an ELL student has mastered the new language.* FALSE. English language learners who are socially proficient in English will struggle in the content area classroom if they have not yet acquired **academic language proficiency**. **Academic language** is more complex, whereas **social language** is less complex.

4. *It may take some ELLs five to seven years to develop academic language proficiency.* TRUE. Cummins (1979) explains that it takes five to seven years for students to develop academic proficiency in the second language. Doing so is necessary to achieve a passing score on a high-stakes standardized test.

5. *The only real difference between academic language and social language is the academic or technical vocabulary.* FALSE. There are several differences between social and academic language. While academic or technical vocabulary distinguishes academic language from social language, there are several additional differences. For example, social language focuses on the present and has a more simple sentence structure, while academic language focuses on more abstract topics and has a more complex sentence structure. Social language is developed in a natural way by all speakers of any language, while the development of academic language occurs through education in that language.

6. *An initial silent period can benefit a second language student, because it allows him or her an opportunity to process and decode the new language.* TRUE. Language develops in stages. A student in the preproduction stage of language development may experience a **silent period,** in which his or her language skills develop at the receptive level. This phase of language development applies to students who have limited experience in English. Students at this level are

listening to the new language and trying to make sense of it. Many students at this stage are not yet ready to produce or speak the target language, however. Asking appropriate questions will allow them to respond with a one-word or physical response, rather than an extended verbal response.

7. *Placing a student who has limited English proficiency in a mainstream English-speaking classroom will ensure that he or she will acquire English quickly.* FALSE. If the instruction and language in the **mainstream classroom** are not made **comprehensible**, an ELL student will not comprehend the lesson or the language. Students must receive comprehensible instruction via classroom strategies and approaches if they are going to acquire English.

8. *Bilingual aides can be very helpful to beginning ELL students by providing concurrent translations for them.* DEBATABLE. Establishing a pattern of concurrent translations tends to promote dependence on those translations and may delay a student's acquisition of English. The student may not try harder to understand English. However, when an ELL understands the concept in his or her thinking (or native) language, then the student can transfer that understanding and continue to absorb the terms and vocabulary of the content areas in the second language. In many classrooms, several different native languages are spoken by students. Clearly, a Spanish-speaking aide would not have the capacity to facilitate a Vietnamese or Haitian **Creole** speaker.

9. *Correcting students' language errors is an effective way to enhance their acquisition of correct structure.* FALSE. Krashen's (1989) **acquisition versus learning hypothesis** suggests that the most effective way to develop students' second language proficiency is by helping them acquire that language much like they acquired their first language. This approach is more effective than having students learn the language by focusing on error correction. Just as parents do not correct the language errors of their toddlers, teachers should not correct the errors of ELL students who are in the early stages of second language development. Doing so can be counterproductive. Modeling correct language structures is a more effective approach.

This native-Spanish-speaking student is allowed to write in Spanish when participating in small-group activities.

Among secondary ELL students, issues of identity development and adolescent transitions complicate educational motivation and focus. Adolescent ELLs are more likely to be embarrassed over their lack of competence in English. Teachers' inability to communicate the academic content of the class and address these students' social and personal issues poses difficulties in encouraging and motivating them (Maxwell-Jolly, Gandara, & Ben, 2007).

Research indicates that teachers' perceptions of how a second language is learned often run contrary to research findings in second language acquisition (Reeves, 2006). Two misconceptions were evident: (1) that ELLs should be able to acquire English within two years and (2) that ELLs should avoid using their native languages as they acquire English. These misconceptions about language acquisition may color teachers' attitudes toward ELLs and ELL inclusion, leading them to misdiagnose learning difficulties or misattribute student failure to lack of intelligence, ability, or effort (Reeves, 2006). These research findings suggest the importance of all ELL teachers having a basic understanding of L2 acquisition processes.

Language Principles

Language principles are examples of manifestations of language in the process of development. These language principles have been discussed in the literature as important variables in second language acquisition (Carrasquillo & Rodriquez, 1996):

- Language learners go through a silent period before they begin to produce language orally. Speech emerges in natural stages.

- Motivation influences the ease and speed of acquiring a second language. The desire to be a valued member of the community by learning a second language is positively related to L2 acquisition.

- Language learning represents a collaborative, meaning-making process. Successful L2 learners effectively use interpretation, expression, and negotiation of meaning. Making errors is a natural part of language learning. Language acquisition is not based on learning grammatical structures but rather meaning.

- Language learners' goals and empowerment skills are essential in the process of second language acquisition. Successful learners share a sense of confidence building and ego enhancing, and they have a quest for competence in some domain of knowledge or skill.

- Language helps to perpetuate **culture** and, as a tool for that purpose, is vitally connected to a person's cognitive and affective development. A teacher can validate a student's home language and culture by referring to it during class.

Integrating language and content is a current method that uses many of Stephen Krashen's concepts and focuses on learning language through content. In language classes, this means that the topics of the class are the content, not grammar. In school, math, science, and social studies classes are used as the mediums for students to learn both language and content. Thus, content area teachers should pay attention to students' language development, as well as content knowledge.

Krashen's Hypotheses

In the past 15 to 20 years, perhaps the strongest influence on second language teaching and learning has been Krashen's (1981) theory of second language acquisition. Krashen's theory was developed on the assumption that first and second language acquisition are similar in important ways. Prior to Krashen's theory, people often learned a second language through grammar study or memorization of dialogue.

Krashen's (1989) theory contains five hypotheses, each of which will be explored in the following section:

1. The natural order hypothesis
2. The acquisition versus learning hypothesis
3. The monitor hypothesis
4. The input hypothesis
5. The affective filter hypothesis

Natural Order Hypothesis

The **natural order hypothesis** states that a person *acquires,* not *learns,* the grammatical structures of a language in a predictable order. This idea reflects Noam Chomsky's (1987) revolutionary notion that everyone has a built-in **language acquisition device (LAD),** which within the first year of life begins to enable the understanding and acquisition of language. This means that certain grammatical structures tend to be acquired early and others are acquired late. For example, in English, the *–ing* ending and plural *–s* marker are among the earliest acquired grammatical structures. The third-person singular ending *–s* is acquired much later.

One of the implications of the natural order hypothesis is to discourage error correction, because errors tend to fall away when the learner reaches a certain stage of development. Krashen (1989) would encourage placing learners in a rich language acquisition environment, where they would hear and be exposed to a lot of rich, natural, complex language. In that environment, learners unconsciously begin to internalize patterns. When the input is controlled or adjusted to contain only certain grammatical structures, learners' natural acquisition process is undermined.

When error correction is used, it should focus on errors of meaning. Teachers should use modeling and encouragement directed at students' self-correction whenever possible.

Acquisition versus Learning Hypothesis

Krashen (1989) believes that there are two distinct ways of developing ability in a second language: acquisition and learning. *Language acquisition* is a natural, subconscious process of absorbing a language, similar to how children develop their first language. *Language learning* is a formal, conscious process that often involves learning grammar, vocabulary, and rules. Acquisition requires meaningful **interaction** in the target language. This should involve natural communication, in which speakers concentrate not on the forms of their utterances but on the act of communicating.

From Krashen's view, acquisition is the most important process in developing second language ability. As such, the classroom should provide rich, natural, hands-on language acquisition experiences.

Monitor Hypothesis

Krashen's (1989) **monitor hypothesis** suggests that conscious learning—that is, the outcome of grammar instruction and other traditional practices—serves only as a monitor or editor for language students. For example, individuals make corrections *as* they speak or write or *after* they speak or write. To use conscious learning to make corrections, individuals must have time, be consciously thinking about correctness, and know the rule for correctness.

One place the monitor can be used appropriately is in the editing phase of **process writing.** When students are speaking or writing to get their ideas down by brainstorming, they cannot be worrying about grammatical correctness.

Input Hypothesis

The input hypothesis suggests that people acquire language in only one way: by understanding messages, or by receiving *comprehensible input* (Krashen, 1989). If the input is either too easy or too difficult, it will not promote

Manipulatives, such as algebra tiles, can be used to provide comprehensible input of concepts to students.

improvement as effectively. The language learner must understand the message of the input for it to help him or her acquire the related language. Several learners at different levels can benefit individually from a rich, interesting, and comprehensible lesson. It is helpful for teachers to use gestures and visual aids when speaking to children, even if they cannot respond, as this helps provide comprehensible input.

Affective Filter Hypothesis

Finally, Krashen's (1989) **affective filter hypothesis** proposes that a mental block, caused by affective or emotional factors, can prevent input from reaching the student's language acquisition device (LAD). Anxiety and other negative feelings, such as low motivation or self-confidence, will raise the filter, providing a barrier to effective language acquisition. Optimal language acquisition occurs in a state of low anxiety and high motivation and self-confidence. For example, consider a mother and child in a relaxed setting, reading a picture book.

Some researchers contend that there is not a clear distinction between language acquisition and language learning. They contend that intake is more significant than input and that intake is influenced by factors such as motivation, interest, and the social and cultural environment in which the learning takes place. Producing comprehensible output significantly aids language acquisition, some contend, and the interaction involved in group work is essential for language acquisition.

Taken together, Krashen's (1989) hypotheses offer a practical, elegant, and appealing theory of language acquisition and learning. Consider applying the hypotheses to ELL students. If they are presented with comprehensible input and if the affective filter is low, they can absorb and use the input to aid in acquiring new language. Some parts of the language will naturally be acquired before others. When students produce language, it may contain errors, because it is in a state of development. In a few circumstances, when ELLs focus on correctness, they can monitor themselves to make some self-corrections. However, this focus can conflict with a focus on fluency and the content of the message. Excessive error correction is not effective in classrooms where the focus is on acquiring a second language.

Table 3.1 provides an overview of the stages of second language development.

Table 3.1 Another Look at Stages of Second Language Development

	Preproduction Stage	Early Production Stage	Speech Emergence Stage	Intermediate Fluency Stage
Learner Behaviors	Points to items Follows commands Listens primarily Has limited receptive vocabulary	Gives one- and two-word responses Labels and matches items Lists items Shows improvement in productive vocabulary	Utters phrases and simple sentences Compares and contrasts using graphic organizers Describes items in simple terms Shows increase in productive vocabulary	Shows beginning CALP Engages in dialogue and discourse with errors Begins reading and writing more decontextualized passages with support
Modified Teaching Strategies	Total physical response (TPR) Matching words and pictures Matching sentence strips and pictures Video presentations	Simple role-playing with little verbal expression Cooperative learning in pairs Graphic organizers using pictures and words Hands-on activities Video presentations	Simple poems and songs Word banks Cooperative learning Fill-in-the-blank phrases Graphic organizers and diagrams Demonstrations Video presentations	Directed reading thinking activities (DRTA) Level-appropriate tests Process writing *Into, Through, and Beyond* reading strategy
Modified Input and Interaction	Use gestures Use repetition Provide pictures and props Ask simple *yes/no* questions Provide illustrations	Model tasks and language Ask *either/or* questions Ask simple *who* and *where* questions Refer to picture dictionaries Use think-alouds Rephrase content	Focus content on key concepts Highlight key words/terms Use bulleted lists, not extended text Make frequent comprehension checks Expand vocabulary through paraphrasing and teaching synonyms Ask simple *how* and *why* questions	Provide alternative assessments Check for language and cultural bias Provide additional contextual support and interaction through cooperative learning Check for idioms and complex structures

Source: FLDOE, 2003.

Social Language (BICS) versus Academic Language (CALP)

It is easier to acquire social language than it is to acquire academic language. Social language takes two to three years to acquire. It is acquired on the playground, in the neighborhood, and in the classroom, and it is usually spoken face to face in an informal setting. Precise understanding is seldom required.

Academic language takes five to seven years to acquire (Cummins, 1979), and it is generally acquired in the classroom. It contains technical vocabulary and is often spoken in lecture-style communication or in reading a textbook. Fewer situational clues to meaning are provided in academic language, and precise description or explanation is required.

Mastering an academic second language is much more difficult and takes longer than mastering a second social language. To conceptualize the differences between academic language skills and skills in everyday conversation, Cummins (1979) uses the terms **cognitive academic language proficiency (CALP)** and **basic interpersonal communication skills (BICS)**. Academic language has a cognitive component, in that it must be used for thought as well as for speech, and academic language proficiency is facilitated by background knowledge of the topic under consideration. CALP is the level of language proficiency a student must have to achieve a passing score on a norm- or criterion-referenced and/or standardized test.

All instructional planning and programming for ELL students should consider the two dimensions described by Cummins (1979):

- Level of **contextual support** refers to the number and nature of clues, such as pictures and video, available to a speaker or listener that can assist in conveying the meaning of the language. A high degree of contextual support can make the content comprehensible. The more contextual support, the easier it is to understand the language and communicate.

- Level of **cognitive demand** refers to how easy or difficult the topic or content is for the language learner. For example, the task of understanding the Emancipation Proclamation would be very difficult for someone who does not know about the American Civil War. Someone who has already studied slavery and the Civil War would experience less cognitive demand. The degree of cognitive demand for any given activity depends on the individual's prior knowledge of the topic.

Cummins' Quadrants

These two levels can be further detailed into **Cummins' quadrants** (1979) (see Figure 3.1). Quadrant I represents the language that is easiest to master. It is characterized by a high degree of contextual support—that is, a lot of visual clues and realia to aid understanding—and a low degree of cognitive demand. Quadrant IV represents language with a high degree of difficulty. Not only are the contextual clues greatly reduced, as in lectures and textbooks, but the topics addressed by the language are unfamiliar and pose a greater cognitive challenge. Quadrants II and III are intermediary areas between Quadrant I and Quadrant IV.

A language program that progresses from Quadrant I to II promotes language learning that is not overwhelming. Gradual progression to Quadrant III reinforces language learning and promotes comprehension of academic content. Unfortunately, in many cases, second language learners are frequently moved from ELL classes and activities, as represented by Quadrant I, to classes and activities represented by Quadrant IV with little opportunity for transitional language experiences, as characterized by Quadrants II and III (Jameson, 1998).

Teachers who do not recognize ELLs' difficulty in making these kinds of movements may well set the stage for their academic failure. However,

Figure 3.1 Cummins' Quadrants

Quadrant I (easiest) High context, low cognitive demand	Quadrant III High context, high cognitive demand
Music class Art class Face-to-face conversation	AV-assisted content lessons Social studies lesson with maps & photos Science demonstration
Quadrant II Low context, low cognitive demand	Quadrant IV (most difficult) Low context, high cognitive demand
Grocery list Social telephone conversation Spelling list	Written directions Math word problems Academic lectures without props Essay writing End-of-chapter review questions

Source: Based on Cummins, 1979; Jameson, 1998. Adapted with permission.

by addressing both language dimensions and organizing appropriate techniques of lesson presentation, schools and teachers can provide more effective instruction and better assistance to ELL students.

So, how can content in Cummins' Quadrant IV be presented with a high level of context? How can information that falls into this quadrant—such as math word problems, academic lectures, and textbook chapter reviews in history—be adapted to fit into Quadrant III? Strategies for contextualizing content and providing comprehensible input in content areas for ELLs include the use of **graphic organizers,** pictures (and more pictures), hands-on activities, demonstrations, **cooperative learning** projects, video streaming, role-playing, software programs, website links, PowerPoint presentations, realia, puzzles, Word Bingo, drawings, and vocabulary games.

Quadrant Identification Activity

For each of the following tasks, indicate the quadrant in which it belongs: I, II, III, or IV.

____ 1. Art class

____ 2. Music class, with tambourines, whistles, drums

____ 3. Reading a grocery list on the fridge

____ 4. Telephone conversation with a good friend

____ 5. Written directions for a new task

____ 6. Science demonstration

____ 7. Math word problems

____ 8. Audiovisual-assisted content classes

____ 9. Learning a spelling list

____ 10. Face-to-face conversation

____ 11. Social studies lesson with maps and photos

____ 12. Writing a short essay on alternative energy

____ 13. Academic lectures without props

____ 14. Answering end-of-chapter review questions in American History

Source: Based on Jameson, 1998. Adapted with permission.

Instructional Scaffolding

Working in the early 1900s, Russian psychologist Lev Vygotsky introduced a useful concept about learning and development when he pointed out that what learners can do with assistance today, they can do alone tomorrow (Daniels, 2001). Teaching, he urged, must aim not at today's but at tomorrow's development, or the **zone of proximal development.**

Thus, students need to be challenged but also supported and encouraged. With assistance, they can move to the next level of development and therefore progress in learning (Peregoy & Boyle, 2005). The assistance that permits this performance is referred to as **scaffolding.** Scaffolding comprises the encouragement, support, and assistance from teachers that ELLs need to reach higher levels of comprehension.

Scaffolding is a metaphor based on the temporary structures that are put up around buildings to hold equipment and workers while repairs and construction take place. In learning and development, students are constructing the ability to carry out complex processes, and scaffolds are temporary supports that permit full participation and learning at a level that would not be possible without assistance. Some examples of scaffolding are teacher think-alouds, wait times for students' responses, graphic organizers, buddy journals, story mapping, and **directed reading thinking activity** (**DRTA**). In summary, scaffolding helps students perform at a level somewhat beyond their unassisted capability (Peregoy & Boyle, 2005).

Instructional scaffolding should be used as an intentional strategy in the form of supportive activities that engage learners in interactions that help them perform beyond their current level of competence (Walqui, 2004). Some types of scaffolding include the following:

- **Modeling** by teachers who provide clear examples of what students are to do, independently or in groups

- **Contextualization** by providing manipulatives, videos, pictures, and other types of sensory experiences to make the language more accessible and content more engaging

- **Schema building**, which involves weaving information into structures of meaning by previewing information, searching for information through Text Quests, or chunking information on a graphic organizer, chart or diagram

- **Bridging**, or laying a foundation for understanding the concept by tapping into students' prior knowledge and making the concept relevant

- **Text re-presentation** by having students write a poem, draw a picture, role-play, or demonstrate the concept by transforming content from one genre to another, or from a text to another form of presentation

- **Reciprocal teaching**, which involves pairs or groups of students questioning each other, discussing questions that go beyond recall, and being guided through their practice of problem solving

The *Students as Teachers* strategy is very effective in getting students to engage in and understand the material and should be used in classrooms more than traditional teacher lecturing. Good ELL practice ensures that "student talk" occurs at a higher rate than "teacher talk."

Corpus Linguistics

A *corpus* (plural *corpora*) is a collection of linguistic data, either compiled as written texts or as a transcription of recorded speech. The main purpose of a corpus is to verify a hypothesis about language (Crystal, 1992), such as to determine how the usage of a particular sound, word, or syntactic construction varies. *Corpus linguistics* deals with the principles and practice of using corpora in language study. A *computer corpus* is a large body of machine-readable texts. The main focus of corpus linguistics is to discover patterns of authentic language use through analysis of actual usage. The only concern of corpus linguistics is the usage patterns of the empirical data and what they reveal about language behavior, or the *pragmatics* of the language (Krieger, 2003).

To understand how corpus linguistics can be used in classroom practice, consider the example of contextual analysis done using *modal verbs,* which are auxiliary verbs that can be used to change the grammatical mood of a sentence (Al Saeed & Waly, 2009). Students are given a number of sentences obtained from any of the two corpora, *have to* and *must,* used in this analysis. Students should try to analyze the context of each to see why one modal verb is used rather than the other.

In the following sentence, why is *have to* used instead of *must?*

In Colorado, for example, you have to renew your license every year after age 75.

Students will be expected to explain that *have to* is used because the obligation to renew comes from outside. The context indicates that this is the law in Colorado.

Other examples to explore include the following:

You must be happy with your new car.
You should be getting the field trip registration information soon.
I have to go to Boston, where the award ceremony will be.

Express Yourself (Al Saeed & Waly, 2009) is a fun activity that exposes students to a large number of sentences using modal verbs. The sentences all express suggestion and/or obligation. The teacher writes the sentences on small pieces of paper, folds them in half, and collects them in a box or hat. The teacher then writes a situation on the board. Students randomly draw pieces of paper and read the sentences on them. Some sentences will be relevant to the situation on the board, and some will not. Students negotiate the meanings of the sentences and decide which can be used and which cannot.

Here is an example situation written on the board:

Give your sick friend advice.

Here are some examples of sample sentences:

You have to attend the meeting at 7:00 p.m. (Irrelevant)
You should take a break. (Relevant—advice)
You must see a doctor. (Relevant—strong advice)
You should go ask the superintendent of the cemetery. (Irrelevant but funny)

A *Situation Analysis* can be done after students are introduced to the different uses and meanings of apologies. For this activity, students are divided into groups. Each group receives flashcards containing corpus-based dialogues about apologizing. Students decide the meaning and level of sincerity of each apology (Al Saeed & Waly, 2009).

Determine the meaning and sincerity of the apology in each of the following statements or short dialogues:

1. We apologize for the delay, which has been caused by a traffic jam.

2. I am sorry, but I will have to leave.

3. I am sorry, but this table is reserved.

4. *Mr. Ahmed:* Go and get me the papers, Angel.
   Angel: I'm sorry. Are you talking to me?

5. *Manager:* We regret the delay in service.
   Martha: Is that all you have to say?

6. *Jeramiah:* Sorry you didn't do well on your exam.
   Anne: You *should* be, too.

7. *Terrance:* Excuse me, but I think that is my seat.
   Sandra: I'm sorry, but I don't see a "Reserved" sign.

8. I am sorry to hear about your accident.

Students can also be provided with situations and work in groups to determine whether the speaker in each situation should *apologize* or say he or she is *sorry*. The differences between these two expressions can be subtle, and knowing when to use them appropriately aids in clarity of communication.

Consider these examples of situations:

1. You accidentally spill some water on your friends.

2. You have to tell your friend that his team has lost the game.

3. The doctor's office called to tell you that your appointment has been cancelled because the doctor is not in today.

Idiomatic expressions are notably confusing to English language learners. After training students on how to use online corpora, such as http://corpus.byu.edu, teachers can ask them to search for idiomatic expressions. Doing a concordance analysis of expressions allows students to see how idioms are **contextualized** and used by native speakers (Al Saeed & Waly, 2009).

The following are some idiomatic expressions using the verb *break:*

1. To *break bread* means to eat together.
   Joshua Morris had invited her to break bread in Broomfield Saturday evening.

2. To *break the mould* means to do something in a different way.
   This seemed a refreshing attempt to break the mould of British politics.

3. To *break a heart* means to emotionally abandon somebody.
   She broke his heart when she went to the prom with someone else.

4. To *break the bank* means the monetary cost of something is high.
   When we were on vacation, we went to a restaurant that nearly broke the bank for the rest of the trip.

5. To *break the ice* means to try to get through awkwardness when talking to someone for the first time.
   To break the ice at the party, we played a word game.

6. To *break free* means to get rid of tensions, fears, and difficulties.
   Panic gave her the strength to break free of the thorns.

7. To *break new ground* means to do or make something new.
   It is difficult to break new ground in the oil drilling business.

Doing these kinds of activities helps ELLs understand how a word or phrase can be used in multiple ways. Visualizing idioms can also assist students in comprehending phrases. Using corpus will help ELLs determine what word or phrase is appropriate for the statement. Students will be able to develop a more authentic vernacular of English use.

Influences from Native Languages

Most of the errors that second language acquirers make as they work to become more proficient in their new language (L2) are due to natural language development. In other words, the errors ELLs make are normal and the same across language groups (Kenfield, 2004). Thus, a Japanese speaker acquiring English will make many of the same kinds of errors that a Russian speaker will make. However, some of the errors can be traced to influence from the native language (L1).

Phonology

Phonology is the sound system of a language. People from Asia often have difficulty pronouncing the English /r/. Mandarin does have this phoneme, but Cantonese, Japanese, and Korean do not. Japanese and Korean do not have /r/ or /l/; rather, they have a sound that falls between these two phonemes. Tagalog (a language of the Philippines) and Spanish also do not have the English /r/, but they have other *r*-like sounds. For example, the /-r-/ between vowels in Spanish and Tagalog is pronounced almost identically to the English /-d-/ sound that is heard as the medial consonant sound in *ladder, butter, little,* and *middle.*

Consonant clusters are very difficult for many speakers whose second language is English. English uses many final and double consonants. Spanish and Vietnamese use only a limited number, and speakers of other languages may omit the final consonant when speaking English. The sound "th" in English does not exist in many other languages. For this reason, common pronunciations include "I'm going tru da door," "Dey are my friends," and "I sink you are right." The "sh" sound in English does not exist in Spanish or Hmong, a language of Laos. A Spanish speaker having a problem with the "j" sound may likely say "The car is in the garotch." Phonological influence from the L1 is evident when a Spanish speaker says "I espeak Espanish in eschool." No words in Spanish begin with the *s–* plus a consonant. In English, the /p-/, /t-/, and /k-/ are aspirated. The speaker who places a hand in front of his or her mouth and says "paper" will feel a puff of air from the initial sound. But a Spanish speaker will not aspirate the /p/ in saying "papel." Most other languages do not aspirate these sounds.

Certain vowel sounds in English often provide difficulty for Spanish and Haitian Creole speakers, because the English phonological system has twice as many vowel sounds as these languages' sound systems. Typically, problems occur with the short vowel sounds, which do not exist at all in these two languages. The ELL student must be able to hear these sounds before producing them will be possible.

Syntax

Syntax refers to the structure and organization of a language. English uses the auxiliary verb *do* or *does* to form a question or a negative statement, as in "Do you want to go? He doesn't want to." This is unique to English. A Spanish speaker might say or write "What eats Juan for lunch?" A Tagalog speaker might say or write "Not have he book," while a Chinese speaker might say "He not have book."

There are no articles (*the, a, an*) in many languages—for example, Chinese and Korean—so speakers of these languages often say "This is book." Sometimes, they have difficulty with correct use of the indefinite article. "I want one cookie," instead of "I want a cookie," is a typical utterance for a speaker of Spanish, Korean, Japanese, or Chinese.

Prepositions are also hard for many ELLs. The difference between "In the store" and "at the store" is tricky for Spanish speakers and speakers of Asian languages, since these languages have only one preposition for both functions. Spanish speakers also often translate directly from a Spanish expression: "He lives near of me" or "I am angry when they laugh of me." Both of these constructions in Spanish use the preposition *de,* as the speaker is simply translating it to *of.*

Most languages do not have an equivalent to the pronoun *it.* A Spanish speaker is used to saying "*Es azul,*" meaning "It's blue"; the *it* is already in the verb. In Asian languages, pronouns do not have gender, so it is common to hear an Asian student say "John is my friend. She is nice."

In Spanish, Vietnamese, Laotian, and Cambodian, the adjective follows the noun, whereas in English, the opposite is the case. A native Spanish speaker, for instance, may follow Spanish syntax and say "milk cold," rather than "cold milk."

Morphology

A **morpheme is** the smallest units of meaning in a language. Nonnative speakers may make morphological errors in their speech when they overgeneralize a morpheme, such as plural –s. There is no plural morpheme in most Asian languages, as nothing is added to a noun to make it plural. A Vietnamese speaker might say in English "many book" because in his L1, no suffix is added for plurality. A Tagalog speaker would use "onga" in the L1 to make the noun following it plural; for example, "onga bata" means "children." In English, the Tagalog speaker might say or write "many child."

Verbs are not conjugated in most Asian languages. For example, nothing is added to a verb to make it past tense. A Vietnamese speaker might say "Yesterday, we go to the store." Another difficulty with plurals comes with the English nouns that are never made plural. Once speakers of Asian languages learn the rule about adding –s, they may overgeneralize it, as in "I eat many butters" and "She has lots of waters."

Each language has its own rhythm and movement that is punctuated by bits of silence and emphases on certain words and syllables. Learning how to deal with intonation and pauses will help the second language learner speak more naturally and fluidly. An example of the use of stress can be found in compound words. For instance, a "hotdog" is not the same as a "hot dog." In writing, the difference is easy to see, but in conversation, the distinction may be lost. The meanings of the sentences "The hot dog is big" and "The hotdog is big" can only be determined by the stress given or not given to the word *dog*.

Grammatical Interference

As noted earlier, some language devices learned in the first language are different from those of the second language and thus interfere with the correctness of speech in the L2. This phenomenon is called **grammatical interference.**

Grammatical Interference for Spanish Speakers

- Use of the subject: Because verb conjugations in Spanish carry person, as well as tense, the use of the subject in spoken language is sometimes optional. There is no mandatory use of the subject. *Example:* "Is big" instead of "It's big."

- Use of the verb *be* to express age, state of being, and temperature: In Spanish, the verb *have* is used to express these concepts. *Example:* "I have eight years" instead of "I am eight years old."

- Use of *not* as a negative form: Spanish uses the same word to express *no* and *not*. *Example:* "He no eat" instead of "He does not eat."

- Use of *–er* and *–est* to form comparative and superlative forms: In Spanish, comparatives and superlatives are formed with *more* and *the most*. *Example:* "Ana is more pretty" instead of "Ana is prettier."

- Use of possessive pronouns in reference to body parts: The definite article *the* is used to refer to parts of the body. *Example:* "I'm going to wash the hands" instead of "I'm going to wash my hands."

- Use of a person's title alone preceding the name: In Spanish, the definite article is used before a person's title. *Example:* "The Mrs. Smith is here" instead of "Mrs. Smith is here."

Grammatical Interference for Haitian Creole Speakers

Haitian Creole has only recently undergone the standardization process needed to become a written language. What is interesting about Haitian Creole is that its structure is based on African languages, while its vocabulary stems primarily from French and other European languages. Thus, the grammar interferences for Haitian children will be somewhat different from those for Hispanic children.

- Distinction between the pronouns *this/that* and *these/those:* Haitian Creole does not make these distinctions; instead, context determines meaning. Pronouns in Haitian Creole are invariant. The same form is used for *I/me/my* and *they/them/their*, for example. Meaning in these cases is determined by word order: If the pronoun occurs before the verb, it is the subject. If it occurs after the verb, it is an object.

- Pronouns: As discussed previously, pronouns in Haitian Creole do not denote gender. One form is used for *he/she/it* and the corresponding forms. For this reason, Haitian children may tend to use the pronoun *he* when referring to a female or inanimate object.

- Verbs: In sentences that describe a state of being or location, no verb is used in Haitian Creole, whereas the verb *be* would be used in English. With verb conjugations in Haitian Creole, verb forms remain invariant. Tense is indicated by the particle placed before the verb. Haitian students may thus be confused when they have to add an *–s* for the third person or change the verb form for irregular past tense.

Although grammatical interference will never completely disappear from the language of ELLs, teachers will find it easier to work with these students if they know what problems may arise from the L1. Students will also feel more comfortable knowing that their teacher has taken the time to tailor instruction to their particular needs. Together, teachers and students can work to achieve maximum results in the L2 acquisition process.

References

Al Saeed, N., & Waly, S. (2009). *Corpus for classrooms: Ideas for material design.* Paper presented at the Southeastern TESOL Conference in Atlanta, Georgia, on September 18, 2009.

Carrasquillo, A., & Rodriquez, V. (1996) *Language minority students in the mainstream classroom.* Philadelphia: Multilingual Matters.

Chomsky, N. (1987). *The Chomsky reader.* New York: Pantheon Books.

Crystal, D. (1992). *An encyclopedic dictionary of language and languages.* Oxford, England: Blackwell.

Cummins, J. (1979). Linguistic interdependence and the educational development of bilingual children. *Review of Educational Research, 49,* 221–251.

Daniels, H. (2001). *Literature circles: Voice and choice in the student-centered classroom.* York, ME: Stenhouse.

Florida Department of Education (FLDOE), Center for Applied Linguistics, Sunbelt Office. (2003). *Enriching content classes for secondary ESOL students.* Tallahassee: Author.

Grognet, A., Jameson, J., Franco, L., & Derrick-Mescua, M. (2000). *Enhancing English language learning in elementary classrooms: Study guide* (pp. 38–42). Washington, DC, & McHenry, IL: Center for Applied Linguistics and Delta Systems, Inc.

Jameson, J. H. (1998). *Enriching content classes for secondary ESOL students: Trainer's manual* (Appendix, p. 8). Washington, DC, & McHenry, IL: Center for Applied Linguistics and Delta Systems, Inc.

Kenfield, K. (2004). The basics of sheltered instruction. Materials distributed at a workshop in Orlando, FL.

Krashen, S. (1981). *Second language acquisition.* Oxford, England: Pergamon.

Krashen, S. (1989). *Language acquisition and language education.* New York: Prentice-Hall.

Krieger, D. (2003). Corpus linguistics: What it is and how it can be applied to teaching. *Internet TESL Journal, 10*(3). Retrieved on September 21, 2009, from http://iteslj.org/Articles/Krieger-Corpus.html

Maxwell-Jolly, J., Gandara, P., & Benavidez, L. M. (2007). *Promoting Academic Literacy Among Adolescent English Language Learners.* Report published by University of California, Davis, School of Education, Linguistic Minority Research Institute.

Peregoy, S., & Boyle, O. (2005). *Reading, writing, and learning in ESL.* Boston: Allyn & Bacon.

Reeves, J. (2006). Secondary teacher attitudes toward including English-language learners in mainstream classrooms. *Journal of Educational Research, 99*(3), 131–142.

Walqui, A. (2004). Teacher quality initiative. *WestEd Communications.* Retrieved July 28, 2006, from www.wested.org/cs/we/view/feat/36

Chapter 4

ELL Students' Reading and Literacy Development

*A*cquire knowledge.
It enables its possessor to distinguish right from wrong.
It lights the way to heaven.
It is our friend in the desert, our society in solitude,
our compassion when friendless.
It guides us to happiness, and sustains us in misery.
It is an ornament amongst friends, and armor against enemies.

—*Prophet Mohammad Hadith*

Math, science, and social studies teachers do not have the time or capacity to assess individual students' reading abilities using running records, phonetic assessments, reading inventories, or reading matrixes. However, reading skills are required to succeed in all content areas. Reading is a multifaceted and complex process. Secondary content area teachers, who often lack expertise in teaching basic literacy skills such as reading, must understand the process to work effectively with English language learners (ELLs) (Maxwell-Jolly, Gandara, & Benavidez, 2007). Let us begin this discussion by describing that process.

The Reading Process

Reading is a language process, which means that it enables people to communicate. Oral language is the cornerstone on which reading is built. Students have been using oral language to communicate with parents, siblings, peers, and teachers. Given this, their oral language should not be viewed as an obstacle to their reading development. Instead, oral language provides the foundation for reading and writing before students enter school, and it reveals what students understand when they read.

Reading is a cognitive process, and therefore, teachers should provide many opportunities for students to interact with both the text and **print-rich environment** of the classroom. Reading is also an affective and social process. Positive experiences with reading help develop a student's positive self-concept. If reading is valued at home and at school, the student will also likely value it. By providing reading material of interest to students and allowing them to interact about reading selections, teachers foster the love of reading.

Reading is also a physiological and developmental process. Visual acuity and neurological functioning, as well as socioeconomic status, affect the reading process. Since literacy development begins at birth, students' ability to read and write is related to developmental milestones by having appropriate sensory, cognitive, perceptual, and social skills as they progress through school years.

Reading Challenges for ELLs

English language learners face many obstacles when reading literature in English. Most literature is **culture** bound (Ladson-Billings, 1995). Students are expected to have prior knowledge of literary genres, such as fairy tales, myths, legends, and tall tales. If the teacher has not activated students' prior knowledge or built background information, reading comprehension will suffer. Knowing the vocabulary is only part of comprehending the text. English language learners may be able to read the individual words, but they may not understand the meanings of the whole sentences they read (Keefe, 2008). These students are not aware of information that author has left unsaid—the information that "everyone knows."

Some specific challenges that ELLs face when learning to read material in English include the following (Haynes & O'Loughlin, 2003):

- Use of homonyms and synonyms
- Density of unfamiliar vocabulary
- Word order, sentence structure, and syntax
- Abundance of idioms and figurative language
- Grammar usage, especially the exceptions to the rules
- Difficult text structure, with a topic sentence, supporting details, and conclusion
- Unfamiliarity with the connotative and denotative meanings of words
- Imagery and symbolism
- Use of regional U.S. dialects
- Fear of participation and **interaction** with students in **mainstream classes**
- Confusing story themes and endings
- Lack of knowledge of literary terms for story development
- Unfamiliarity with drawing conclusions, analyzing characters, and predicting outcomes

Adaptations in Content Area Reading

The Executive Summary on the National Literacy Panel on Language Minority and Youth (August & Shanahan, 2000) makes four potentially important general recommendations for teaching ELLs:

1. Being literate in the native language is an advantage.
2. It is helpful to provide substantial coverage of the five essential elements of reading: phonemic awareness, phonics, fluency, vocabulary, and comprehension.
3. Reading programs for ELLs should include intensive language development, as well as instruction in literacy strategies and skills.
4. Instruction needs to be adjusted to meet the needs of ELL students.

Research discusses effective reading instruction for ELLs by centering on the five essential elements just mentioned (Irujo, 2007):

1. *Phonemic awareness* is difficult for ELLs, because they may not have had enough experience with English to be able to distinguish how its sounds differ

from those of their native language. Therefore, extensive practice speaking English is recommended.

2. *Phonics* is problematic because many sounds are similar, and there is no regular system of correspondence between sounds and letters. To address these problems, reading instruction should be combined with intensive development of oral language. In addition, a print-rich environment should be created, providing appealing reading materials in varied genres. Most ELLs will need additional time to master phonics.

3. *Fluency,* or automatic recognition of frequent words, is important because it helps mitigate the lack of proficiency that slows down ELLs. These students cannot achieve fluency in oral reading before they have achieved fluency in speaking. Repeated readings of texts that contain unfamiliar vocabulary and sentence structures will not increase fluency. To develop fluency, students should read aloud texts they are familiar with and understand.

4. The *vocabulary* of ELLs is a fraction of the size of that of native English speakers. English language learners must learn not just content vocabulary but also words that are crucial for understanding the text, words that are encountered in a wide variety of contexts, words with multiple meanings, words used in figurative language, and words from academics that indicate relationships among other words, such as *because, therefore,* and *since.* Handing out a list of words and definitions is not a meaningful exercise for teaching ELLs vocabulary. Explanations of unknown words should include **contextual support**, as discussed previously. That support can be provided through real objects, pictures, word games, photographs and drawings, gestures, examples, demonstrations, and experiments that accompany the verbal explanations.

5. *Reading comprehension* instruction needs to be modified for ELLs so they can understand content area concepts. One approach proven effective in reading literature is called *Into-Through-Beyond* (Corrigan & Davies, 2008). Content area teachers should engage in **schema building** before the reading process by setting goals for reading, building background knowledge, and recognizing discipline-specific terms. Here are examples of activities for the *Into, Through,* and *Beyond* stages:

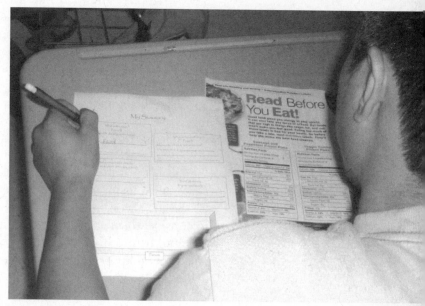

This student is using a graphic organizer to summarize an article.

Into Activities

- Brainstorming has been proven an effective strategy in that it pools students' existing knowledge. That knowledge can be recorded in a mind map or a graphic organizer, such as a Know, Want to Know, Learn (KWL) chart or semantic web.

- Previewing the glossary, scanning, formulating questions, and using semantic mapping are excellent before reading activities.

- Discussing discourse competence and determining whose point of view is represented in the material are also valuable activities.

Through Activities

- Build schemata during the reading process by understanding cultural terms and practices and explaining beliefs and behaviors as they occur in the reading.

- Gradually complete a Venn diagram or compare and contrast chart to identify differences and similarities or to explicate content. Use group discussion to identify possible main ideas and supporting details; then gradually complete a graphic organizer, such as *Parts of a Paragraph* or *My Summary*.

- Discuss what is implied but not stated outright, making inferences and visual images of the setting, character, and problem. Use one of these graphic organizers: *Story Web*, *Problem Solution*, or *Character Attribute Web*.

- Work with students to obtain information from pictures, charts, and graphs and to guess meaning from context.

- Have groups of students complete the *Group Member Assignment* activity (see Chapter 7).

- Have groups of students produce a *Pass the Poster* activity.

- Continue building vocabulary by having students identify words they do not know, and create glossaries using the graphic organizer *Student Glossary*.

Beyond Activities

- Build schemata after the reading process by rewriting the story. For instance, set the story in another culture, or have students put themselves in the places of characters from other cultures.

- Ask students to retell a fictional story or nonfictional event (such as in social studies) from an outline, recalling key ideas and completing a graphic organizer, such as *Story Web*, *Character Attribute Web*, and/or *My Summary*.

- Create a student-generated list of vocabulary words found in the reading. Then, in less than thirty words, have students write a description of the plot.

- Have **cooperative learning** groups rewrite and then act out favorite parts of a reading selection.

Since textbooks and their materials are the resources most secondary teachers use in their classrooms, conducting these kinds of activities provides a way for ELLs to read in the content areas (Balderrama & Diaz-Rico, 2006). Conducting these kinds of activities also provides comprehensible input for both ELL students and native speakers of English who struggle with reading comprehension.

Second language learners often know most of the vocabulary in a reading, if the vocabulary has been given in a word list. Students will know one meaning of the word but may not understand the meaning when the word is used in an unfamiliar context. For example, an ELL student may understand the meaning of the word *cold* as it refers to temperature but not as it refers to personality, as in "She is a cold person."

Because word meanings are context sensitive, misunderstandings can lead to considerable confusion in text interpretation and overall reading comprehension. Before ELLs can effectively interpret text, they need to build their background knowledge, or schemata, through interactions in the classroom and outside school.

Teachers need to analyze the language demands of the different content areas, which include the language of curriculum and classroom participation, and then teach students subject-specific vocabulary. These language demands are different from those of the beginning-level ELL class or the type of **social language.** Because of this, they need to be taught specifically and practiced in the context of actual subject-matter learning.

Six Key Elements of Research-Based Vocabulary Instruction

A language-rich environment is one in which students encounter, work with, and become curious about words. In such an environment, students hear words used in natural contexts, such as engaging read-alouds and rich discussions, and manipulate words through word play, graphic organizers, and writing activities (Beck, McKeown, & Kucan, 2002).

Following these guidelines will help teachers provide the language-rich environment needed for vocabulary growth in the English language classroom:

1. *Introduce words through natural contexts.* Read-alouds and discussions give ELLs exposure to engaging materials that they would find quite difficult to read independently.

2. *Explain words in language students can understand.* Explain the meanings of words in simplified language. For example, state that "The dictionary definition of *incredulous* is 'disinclined or indisposed to believe; skeptical.' A student-friendly definition is 'something is very hard to believe.'"

3. *Provide multiple contexts for each word.* Help ELLs build depth of understanding by using each word often and in different contexts. For example, the word *instrument* describes a musical device, but it can also mean a tool used in medical surgery.

4. *Build a strong and flexible knowledge of words through lively discussions and word manipulations.* Encourage students to think about situations in their lives that relate to the new words. Use games, discussions, word play, and semantic word maps to build confidence in English learning.

5. *Provide opportunities for students to encounter words in and out of the classroom.* Use the words as much as possible, both verbally and in writing during class time. If possible, provide lists of the words and their meanings in the ELLs' first languages.

6. *Assess vocabulary continually.* During the course of the lessons, check for understanding and adapt instruction accordingly. When playing Word Bingo, incorporate words learned in previous lessons with newer words.

Research suggests that vocabulary instruction must be direct and systematic for both native English speakers and English language learners. Students must learn sophisticated vocabulary through repeated encounters and varied contexts. This type of robust instruction helps ELL students bridge the language gap (Carlo et al., 2004).

In a video documentary of interviews with ELL high school students, entitled *Authentic Voices* (Keefe, 2008), students commented that vocabulary flashcards were very helpful. Students enjoy playing in pairs a gamelike activity using student-made flashcards that have a word on one side and its definition on the other. One student holds up each card with the word facing the other student and the definition facing him or her. That student then reads the definition and guesses the correct word. Then the partners switch roles. Each student can be timed, and the student who took the shortest time to identify all the words correctly can earn extra credit or some other reward. Individuals can win, and pairs can compete against other pairs.

Directed Reading Thinking Activities (DRTAs)

Some students, including many ELLs, need explicit guidance from the teacher to comprehend their texts. **Directed reading thinking activities (DRTAs)** provide this kind of explicit guidance.

DRTAs are not typically conducted with an entire class of students. Rather, they are usually conducted with a small group of students who need more explicit instruction from the teacher to comprehend their reading. This small group of students may include only ELL students, or it may include ELLs and some native speakers of English, who also need explicit instruction.

Here are the steps involved in conducting a DRTA (FLDOE, 2003):

1. *Preview* the reading: Have students look at the title, headings, summary, and pictures; discuss prior knowledge and experiences; and identify key vocabulary.

2. *Predict* the content: Have students form questions from the headings to help identify what they want to learn from reading. Also ask them to identify what they already know. Ask these questions: What is this chapter about? What seems important in this chapter? What seems interesting?

3. *Read* in sections: Instead of assigning students the entire chapter, assign them a section or chunk to be read silently.

4. *Check* the predictions: Lead a discussion to review the reading. Focus on answers and evidence students have found related to their initial questions and predictions. Ask students to show the part of the reading that answered each question. Use higher-order thinking questions and strategies. After students check their predictions, the cycle begins again with students forming new predictions/questions before reading the next predetermined section of text.

5. *Summarize* the main points: Ask students to summarize and state the main points of what they learned in their own words, either orally or in a short written form.

Graphic Organizers for Reading

Graphic organizers are effective tools that help lighten the linguistic load of text in district-adopted textbooks. Using organizers, students can chunk the important pieces of information contained in discussions and text in a way that provides comprehensible input. In addition, these teaching and learning tools can be referred to when students are doing tasks independently.

Figures 4.1 through 4.12 provide examples of graphic organizers for reading. These student samples were completed in a high school language class.

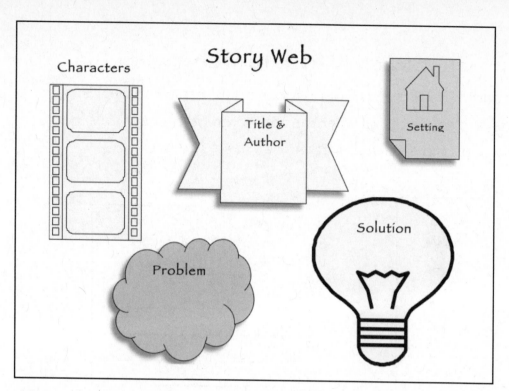

Figure 4.1   Sample Story Web Template

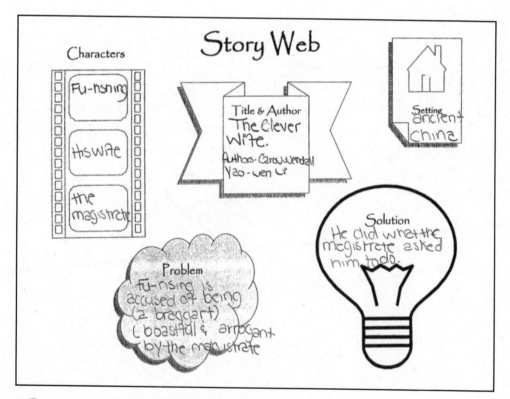

Figure 4.2   Sample Story Web

Character Attribute Web

This helps you gather clues the author provides about what a character is like. Write words or phrases about what the character looks like, how s/he feels, what s/he does and says in the story.

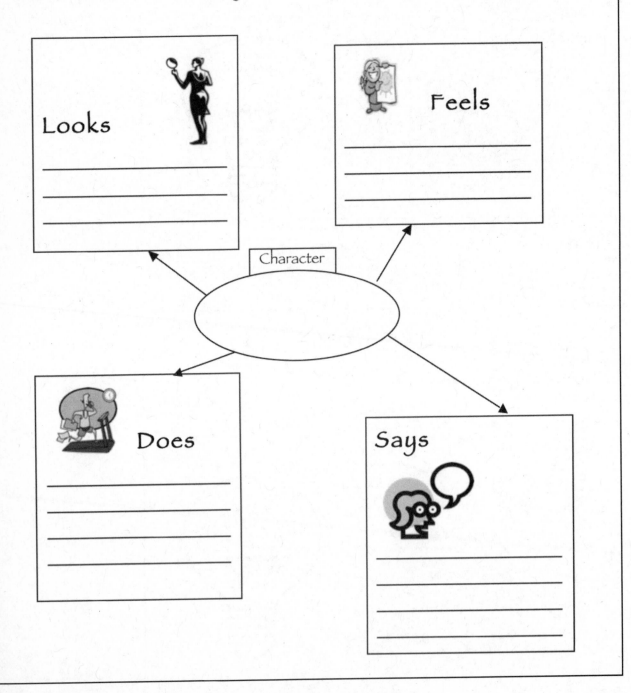

Figure 4.3 Sample Character Attribute Web Template

76

Chapter 4

Character Attribute Web

This helps you gather clues the author provides about what a character is like. Write words or phrases about what the character looks like, how s/he feels, what s/he does and says in the story.

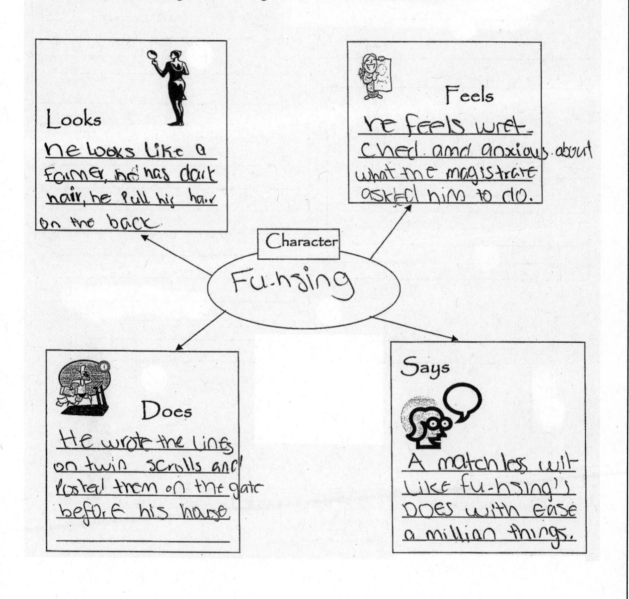

Looks

He looks like a farmer, he has dark hair, he pull his hair on the back

Feels

he feels wret-ched and anxious about what the magistrate asked him to do.

Character

Fu-hsing

Does

He wrote the lines on twin scrolls and posted them on the gate before his house.

Says

A matchless wit like fu-hsing's does with ease a million things.

Figure 4.4   Sample Character Attribute Web

My Summary

What is the topic? Prove It
(words identifying the topic)

The topic is _____

_____

_____

What is the main idea? Prove It
(key words in first & last sentences)

The main idea is _____

_____

_____

_____

What are 3 important details?
(who, what, where, when, why & how)

It tells that _____

_____

Also, _____

_____

and it discusses_____

_____

_____

Your Summary...In your own words

_____

_____

_____

_____

_____

_____

_____

Picture

Figure 4.5   Sample My Summary Template

My Summary

What is the topic?
Prove It
(words identifying the topic)

The topic is Flight to Freedom brings Custodia to SFHS from Cuba

What is the main idea?
Prove It
(key words in first & last sentences)
The main idea is People had to scape Cuba to find a better life.

What are important details?
(who, what, where, when, why & how)

It tells that 2 people in Cuba had a different life before 1965
Also,
After Fidel Castro took over life changed

Your Summary
In your own words
Fidel Castro took over Cuba but this couple didn't mind and they wanted to have a better life so the escape.

United States

Cuba

Picture

Figure 4.6 Sample My Summary

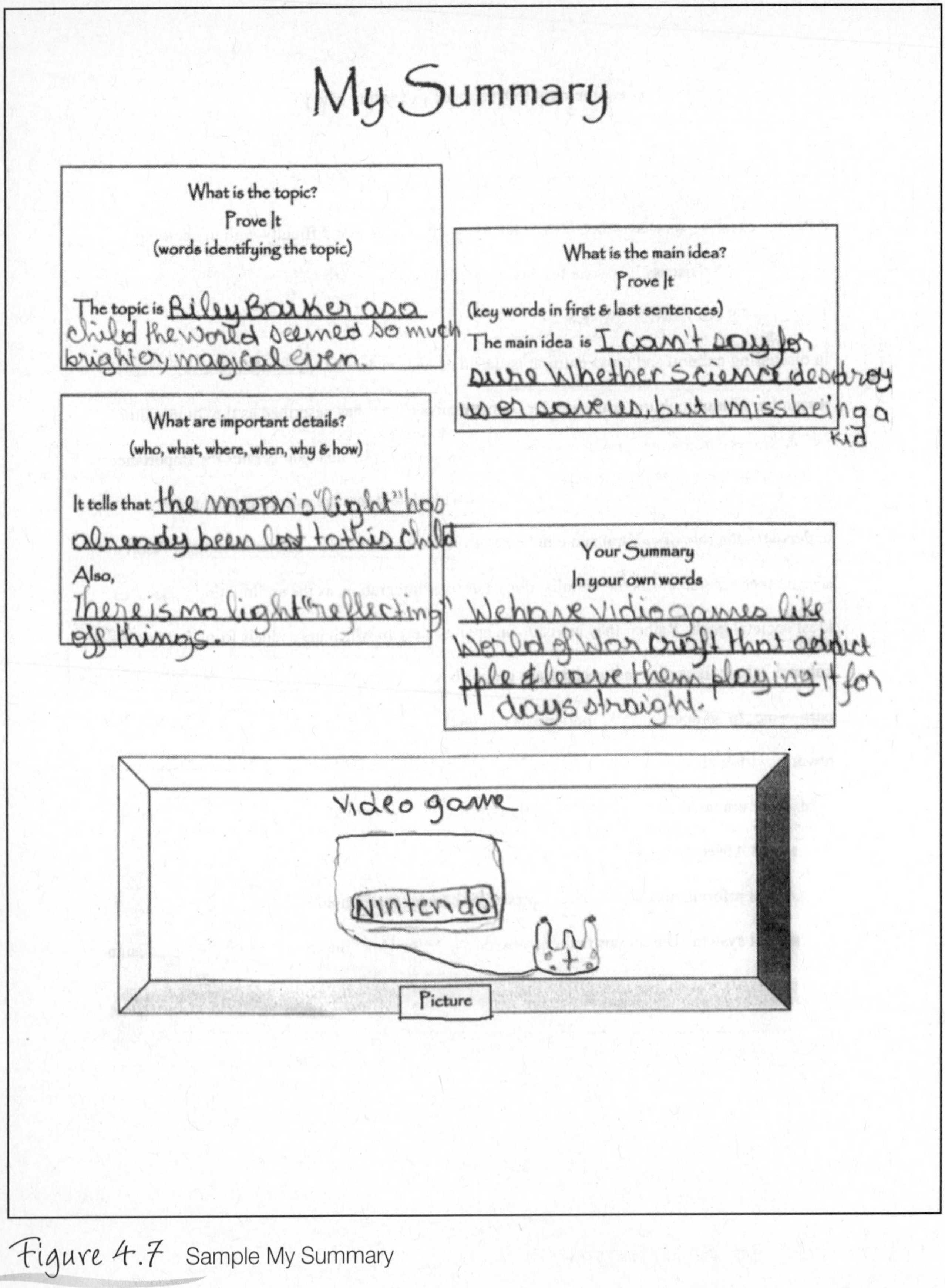

My Summary

What is the topic?
Prove It
(words identifying the topic)

The topic is _Riley Barker as a child the world seemed so much brighter, magical even._

What is the main idea?
Prove It
(key words in first & last sentences)

The main idea is _I can't say for sure whether science destroy us or save us, but I miss being a kid_

What are important details?
(who, what, where, when, why & how)

It tells that _the moon's "light" has already been lost to this child_
Also,
There is no light "reflecting" off things.

Your Summary
In your own words

We have video games like World of War craft that addict pple & leave them playing it for days straight.

Video game

Nintendo

Picture

Figure 4.7   Sample My Summary

My Summary

What is the topic?
Prove It
(words identifying the topic)

The topic is <u>dolphins trains</u>

What is the main idea?
Prove It
(key words in first & last sentences)

The main idea is <u>Working with any</u>
<u>animals requeres lots of</u>
<u>hur work and Patience.</u>

What are important details?
(who, what, where, when, why & how)

It tells that <u>Gina trains dolphins</u>
<u>in Orlando, Fl. now and she hae to be</u>
<u>wet all day and swim perfect.</u>
Also,
<u>She loves animals</u>

Your Summary
In your own words

<u>She workin with them every</u>
<u>day, she start at 5:00 am</u>
<u>and she also teach them</u>

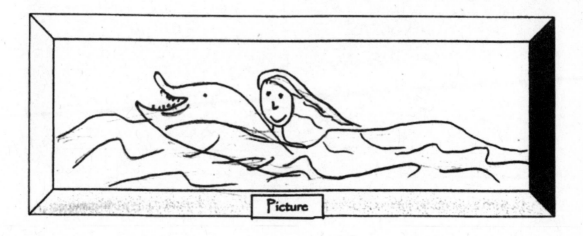

Picture

Figure 4.8 Sample My Summary

My Summary

What is the topic?
Prove It
(words identifying the topic)

The topic is ___Michael phelps___

What is the main idea?
Prove It
(key words in first & last sentences)
The main idea is _if he does, he_
will have won more medals
than any olympic athlete.

What are important details?
(who, what, where, when, why & how)

It tells that _Michael was the first American_
olympic
to win eight medals
Also,
michael is smooth in the water

Your Summary
In your own words

He is a strang man because
he never lose the hope to
keep going and make his dream
real.

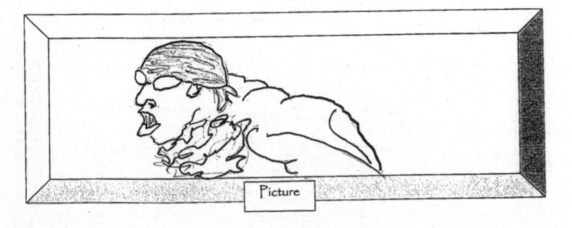

Picture

Figure 4.9   Sample My Summary

Figure 4.10   Sample Semantic Map Template

NEW Word

Write the new word in the star, find the definition, write a synonym, draw a picture of the word and then create a sentence with the new word.

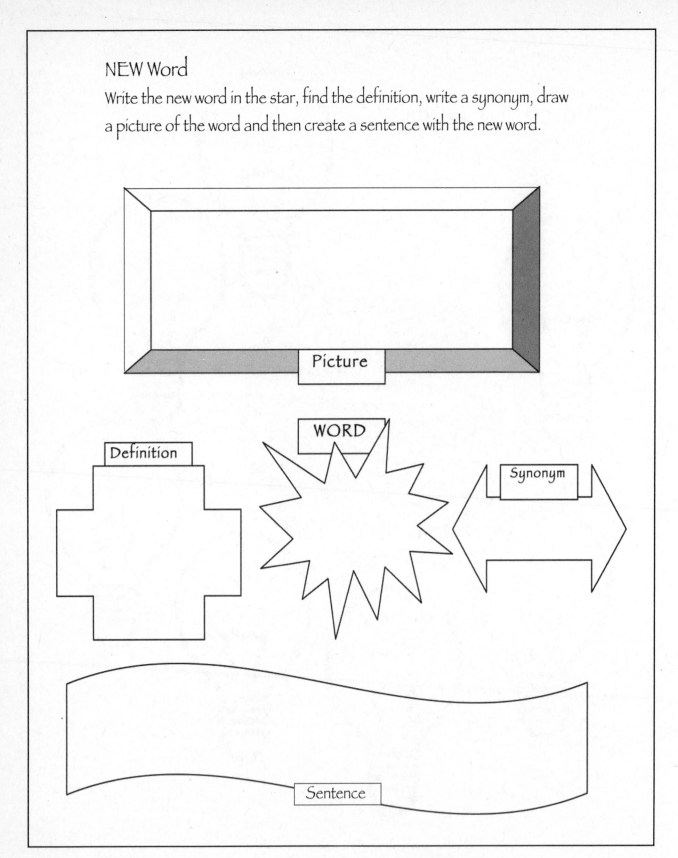

Picture

Definition

WORD

Synonym

Sentence

Figure 4.11   Sample New Word Template

Word Construction Site

Student Name: _____ Date: _____

Assignment: _____ Period: _____

The WORD is:	
Part of Speech (noun, verb, adjective)	Synonym (same) & Antonym (opposite)
Symbol or picture	Definition
Sentence with WORD	

The WORD is:	
Part of Speech (noun, verb, adjective)	Synonym (same) & Antonym (opposite)
Symbol or picture	Definition
Sentence with WORD	

Figure 4.12 Sample Word Construction Site Template

Adolescent Literacy and ELLs

The consequences of being underprepared in literacy are dire for all **language minority** students, but for Hispanic ELLs—who comprise the largest group of ELLs in the United States—the consequences are particularly grim. This group has the lowest graduation rate of all students (Ruiz de Velasco, 2005). Of every 100 Hispanic students, only 61 will graduate from high school. Thirty-one of those who graduate will complete some postsecondary education, and only 10 will graduate with a bachelor's degree (Koelsch, 2006). For too many ELLs, graduation from high school, let alone college, remains but a dream.

Adolescent literacy at the high school level entails the development of disciplinary knowledge and the use of that knowledge in oral interactions, reading, and writing. Consequently, states and districts need to redesign literacy work for ELLs in high school, moving away from remediation and toward academic acceleration and enrichment.

Effective literacy instruction includes teaching students to read critically in the content areas in multiple modalities, including the Internet. In grades 6 to 12, content area teachers are also literacy teachers who teach students to discuss ideas and read and write in their disciplines. To help these teachers retool their teaching, new strategies are required. The overrepresentation of ELLs in special education classes (see Chapter 10) points to the importance of teachers being knowledgeable about the development of literacy for adolescent ELLs.

An important component of change is developing the skills and dispositions of accomplished teachers of English language learners (Walqui, 2004). The need for sustained, rigorous professional development that strengthens teachers' capacity to promote rich literacy practices among adolescent ELLs is central to improving literacy achievement for all students. Part of improved literacy instruction also involves having high expectations for student performance and offering strong support so students achieve.

One of the most effective activities, used initially to introduce new concepts, is to identify the language demands of the content area course. Content area teachers should examine their curriculums from a language perspective:

- What features of English do students need to know and apply to succeed in the class?

- What is the readability of the textbook, and are students required to take notes from the text?

- Does the course require students to write comparison/contrast or cause/effect essays?

- Are students going to make oral presentations? If so, how will the technical vocabulary be taught?

By reflecting on the language demands of their courses, teachers can provide comprehensible input. Specifically, they can focus on activities that promote learning about various aspects of the English language in the content areas.

Teachers may also consider these guidelines in approaching ELL instruction (Walqui, 2004):

1. *Plan language objectives for all lessons, and make them explicit to students.* Teachers can help students learn to read and write in specific content areas

by conducting prereading activities, such as previewing the textbook chapter by examining the section, headings, illustrations, and chapter summaries and using graphic organizers to chunk information within the chapter.

2. *Activate and strengthen background knowledge.* Many ELLs struggle with curriculum content, because they lack background knowledge of the topic or have gaps in what they have learned. For example, immigrant students may not have studied the Vietnam War in their native countries, but they may have studied another war or even experienced a military conflict firsthand. By tapping into what students know about such conflicts, the teacher can set the context for a lesson on the Vietnam War. Graphic organizers, such as semantic maps, and brainstorming activities can also be used to establish the context for topics to be studied.

3. *Emphasize academic vocabulary development.* English language learners' academic vocabulary can be expanded by moving beyond the highlighted or italicized words in a textbook. Teachers should discuss and communicate meanings of terms for higher-order thinking skills used throughout content, such as *infer, convince, decide, compose,* and so on. Applying strategies such as word walls, semantic webs, and relational vocabulary cards can help students organize new words in meaningful ways. Other ways to cultivate content vocabulary include conducting demonstrations, discussing illustrations, completing art projects, utilizing *New Word* and *ABCs of a Topic* graphic organizers, and letting students select specific vocabulary words to study.

4. *Promote oral interaction and extended academic talk.* Developing ELLs oral language skills can help them acquire literacy skills and access new information. Teachers should talk less and engage students in extended discussions, encouraging ELLs to give more than one-word responses. After a student responds, the teacher might say "Tell me more about that" or "Why do you think so?" This is a more effective approach than saying "Good" and moving on to the next question.

By establishing discussion routines, teachers provide structures for this kind of discourse and teach students to be active listeners. By encouraging ELLs to share their thoughts with a partner before reporting to the whole class, teachers promote risk-taking in oral expression.

Five Key Learning Habits

Developing the five key learning habits described in this section will help ELLs acquire the language of school. The learning habits draw on research from language acquisition theory, **academic language** development, and constructivist learning methods (Zwiers, 2004/2005):

1. *Teach students to use context to interpret meaning.* Teachers can do this by "scoping out the neighborhood where the word lives," which shows how this "neighborhood" provides clues to the word's meaning. When students encounter an unknown word, they can first guess at its meaning by using the context. Then they can refine their guesses with a partner or check the dictionary to make concrete–abstract connections.

2. *A principal role of academic language is to recognize words that describe thinking skills*—particularly, higher-order thinking processes, such as comparing, analyzing, and evaluating. After teachers ask students to *compare* or *analyze*, they should pause to discuss the meaning of the term. Teachers

should also work with students to pick out key terms and expressions from text, such as *rather, therefore, justify, support,* and so on. Regularly encountered terms should be posted on the wall, providing an ever-evolving reference tool to help students understand, value, and use academic language.

3. *English language learners should have the opportunity to read challenging but understandable materials.* Teachers should read aloud to students as they follow along, stopping at times to **model** thinking out loud, to go over new words, or to talk about what is happening in a passage. The use of visuals and gestures can help ELLs conceptualize the reading selection.

4. *Allow students to take risks in the new language by providing nonthreatening opportunities for them to orally express themselves.* English language learners might hesitate to give an opinion, waiting to speak until they can formulate a grammatically perfect sentence. Teachers should encourage students to speak up, even if it means stating an imperfectly constructed message. Students learn actively from genuine conversation and connect directly to what is said. Teachers should also use these opportunities to model the correct grammar, thus validating students' responses, as well as the correct way to say something, and keeping the focus on the meaning of the conversation.

5. *It is vital for ELLs to converse with native speakers about academic topics.* Every conversation offers a chance to learn something new. English language learners should be encouraged to practice conversing in English with other students, recording on a note card how the talk went. When the dialogue focuses on the topic of class discussion, it can be used as an evaluative tool, for which the ELL can earn a grade.

To cultivate these habits in students, teachers must first reflect on their own academic language proficiency. Doing so takes considerable thought and honesty, as it is hard to notice the habits we automatically engage in to comprehend language.

One way to provide comprehensible input is to teach specific *language focus lessons,* which concentrate on English vocabulary and usage, not curricular content. Teachers should devote a class session to the language being used in a particular lesson, rather than the content itself. The lesson should include an activity that allows teachers to observe students' mastery of the English language.

A good resource for observing best practices in teaching ELLs is the ESOL TAPESTRY website, developed by the University of South Florida (http://tapestry.usf.edu). This site provides video streaming of actual classroom situations, as well as printable pages of resources used in the video.

Activites for ELLs

ABCs of a Topic

This activity can be done on any topic by students working in groups, in pairs, or independently. Given a particular topic, students are asked to think of words representing a person, place, thing, or action related to that topic. One word must begin with A, another with B, another with C, and so on throughout the alphabet. To create an ABCs poster, students can illustrate each word by drawing or coloring pictures or cutting out images from magazines (see Figure 4.13).

Abigail Adams 	Bunker Hill 	Colonies 	Death 	End of the War 1783
F	G	H	I	J
K	L	M	N	O
P	Q	R	S	T
U	V	W	X	Y/Z

Figure 4.13 ABCs Poster

One of the benefits of this activity is that students generate the vocabulary. This factor makes the activity appealing to high school students. The topic in the example poster in Figure 4.13 is the American Revolution.

Word Bingo

As mentioned earlier, playing *Word Bingo* is another fun way of learning and reinforcing new vocabulary. This game can be used for learning vocabulary in any content area, such as science and social studies, as well as language arts and reading.

To prepare for the game, the teacher should create Bingo cards for 9 or 16 words, depending on the number of words he or she wants students to work with. (To conserve paper, the teacher can print out two Bingo cards per page or on the front and back to make four cards per page.) If the teacher wants to include more words in the game, he or she should mix in words students already know with the new words. It is important to keep in mind that ELLs can absorb only a limited number of new words at a time.

Here are the steps for playing Word Bingo:

1. Write the words on the board or overhead, and distribute the Bingo cards to students (one per student). Have students copy the words at random on their cards, one word per space. This means that students' Bingo cards will not look alike.

2. Read a definition out loud. Ask students to find the word on their cards and place a checkmark in that space.

3. Tell students that when they have checked all the spaces across, down, or diagonally, they should yell out "Bingo!" To verify the winner, ask the students to read his or her words. The student might also provide the definitions, stated in their own words, for extra points. Other students might also be asked to provide definitions for extra points.

References

August, D., & Shanahan, T. (Eds.). (2006). Executive summary. *Developing literacy in second-language learners: Report of the National Literacy Panel on Language-Minority Children and Youth*. Mahwah, NJ: Lawrence Erlbaum. Available online at www.cal.org/projects/archive/natlitpanel.html

Balderrama, M., & Diaz-Rico, L. (2006). *Teaching performance expectations for educating English learners*. Boston: Allyn & Bacon.

Beck, I. L., McKeown, M. G., & Kucan, L. (2002). *Bringing words to life: Robust vocabulary instruction*. New York: Guilford Press.

Brown, C. (2007). Supporting English language learners in content reading. *Reading Improvement, 44*(1), 32–39.

Carlo, M. S., August, D., McLaughlin, B., Snow, C. E., Dressler, C., Lippman, D. N., Lively, T. J., & White, C. E. (2004). Closing the gap: Addressing the vocabulary needs of English language learners in bilingual and mainstream classrooms. *Reading Research Quarterly, 39,* 188–215.

Corrigan, K., & Davies, B. (2008). Into-Through-Beyond: A lesson-planning framework for using YES! In the classroom. Retrieved July 28, 2008, from www.yesmagazine.org/article.asp?ID=1006

Florida Department of Education (FLDOE), Center for Applied Linguistics, Sunbelt Office (FLDOE). (2003). *Enriching content classes for secondary ESOL students*. Tallahassee: Author.

Haynes, J., & O'Loughlin, J. (2003). *Challenges for ELLs in content area learning*. Paper presented at the 2003 TESOL Annual Convention, March 25–29, Baltimore, MD. Available online at www.everythingesl.net/inservices/challenges_ells_content_area_l_65322.php

Irujo, S. (2007). What does research tell us about teaching reading to English language learners? *ELL Outlook*. Retrieved February 2, 2007, from www.coursecrafters.com/ELL-Outlook/

Keefe, M. R. (Producer/Researcher). (2008). *Voices of immigrant ELL high school students* [Video]. Martin County School District, Florida, TV Production Classes.

Koelsch, N. (2006). *Improving literacy outcomes for English language learners in high school: Considerations for states and districts in developing a coherent policy framework*. National High School Center at the American Institute for Research. Retrieved January 25, 2007, from www.betterhighschools.org

Ladson-Billings, G. (1995). Toward a theory of culturally relevant pedagogy. *American Educational Research Journal, 32,* 465–491.

Maxwell-Jolly, J., Gandara, P., & Benavidez, L. M. (2007). *Promoting academic literacy among adolescent English language learners*. Report published by University of California, Linguistic Minority Research Institute.

Ruiz de Velasco, J. (2005). Performance-based school reforms and the federal role in helping schools that serve language-minority students. In A. Valenzuela (Ed.), *Leaving children behind: How "Texas-style" accountability fails Latino youth*. Albany: State University of New York Press.

Walqui, A. (2004). Teacher quality initiative. *WestEd Communications*. Retrieved July 28, 2006, from www.wested.org/cs/we/view/feat/36

Zwiers, J. (2004/05). The third language of academic language. *Educational Leadership, 62*(4), 60–63.

Chapter 5

ELL Students' Writing, Listening, and Speaking English

*One of the obligations of the writer is to say or sing all that he or she can,
to deal with as much of the world as becomes possible to him or her in language.*

—Denise Levertov

Reading and writing go hand in hand, and writing is not only a key to academic success but also a means for self-expression. While the process of writing in English is essentially similar for both first and second language writers, there are some important differences in what the two groups bring to the task. First, students new to English will likely experience some limitations in their expressive abilities, in terms of vocabulary, **syntax,** and idiomatic language. In addition, English language learners (ELLs) may not have had the exposure to written English that comes from being read to and reading. As a result, they may not have a feeling for how English conventionally translates to the written form. The more ELLs read or are read to in English, the easier their writing will become.

To introduce a writing topic, teachers should use brainstorming or flash writing, in which students write about the topic quickly and abundantly, without using a dictionary or worrying about structure and grammar (Lange & Park, 2009). In doing this activity, students generate words and phrases about the topic, without stopping to organize their thoughts or waste time erasing. They later can select those words or phrases they determine are best suited for addressing the writing prompt. In assisting ELLs to become competent writers, teachers must find a balance between writing for fluency, such as flash writing, and academic writing for the purpose of improving accuracy.

Research has shown a number of benefits from using **process writing** with ELLs and indeed with all students (Hoch, 2008). These benefits include the built-in aspect of process writing that allows students to make a variety of mistakes, recognize these mistakes either on their own or with a peer, correct these mistakes, and continue to write. Upon considering the variations in systems of logic across **cultures,** it becomes evident that the process writing approach has even more advantages for ELLs and teachers.

Process writing demands that students write more than single words and sentences. It encourages the creation of lengthy, original writing samples, which can provide a window to how students think. Teachers who use process writing are enhancing and increasing their knowledge of each ELL student as an individual member of a particular ethnic and cultural group. And once teachers and students are better able to understand each other, it seems logical that they will be able to increase learning opportunities on a daily basis. A teacher who has ample evidence of how a student thinks, based on an examination of his or her writing, can more easily prepare lessons and develop strategies that will help that student become more proficient in English (Hoch, 2008).

In addition, teachers may be able to use process writing to point out to ELLs the cultural differences in logic that are present between their native languages and English. By helping ELLs make connections, teachers help increase the likelihood that they will transfer what skills they can and recognize those skills they still need to work on in their language acquisition process (Yoon, 2007). In this way, teachers of ELLs, as well as the students themselves, build a partnership in learning, in which both play active roles in the quest for academic success and effective communication.

Writing Activities

Writing Workshop

Writing workshop can be used successfully with ELLs because of the collaborative setting of the activity and because it is based on the writing process of prewriting, drafting, and editing. During prewriting, students talk and listen about shared experiences, do brainstorming, and have peer conferences. Doing so helps them generate, explore, test, and integrate ideas. Students benefit from the questions they ask each other as they shape ideas.

The drafting stage of the writing process allows ELLs to be more concerned with fluency, rather than accuracy. Writers capture ideas quickly, getting their ideas down on paper without worrying about syntactical and grammatical accuracy. Graphic organizers, such as the *Parts of a Paragraph,* can be helpful for students in organizing their thoughts. Peers are allowed to review one another's writing in an informal setting. Their responses offer feedback to the writer about the content, point of view, and tone of the work and help the writer focus on the message he or she intends to communicate.

The editing stage is vital to making writing interesting to read. Editing cleans up the writing, in effect, making the assignment a more acceptable product while keeping the message intact. Self-correction is most desirable and a skill that will help students improve their own writing. An excellent tool for guiding students is the *SOS* graphic organizer.

Figure 5.1 is a sample *Writing Partners' Rubric*. This **rubric** can be modified to fit more specific writing purposes and prompts. Figure 5.2 is a type of graphic organizer for relational vocabulary, which will help cultivate any content area vocabulary. Figure 5.3, an editing checklist, can be used by students to edit writing independently or with a partner.

Discussion of Sample Student Writings

On the following pages are several samples of students' writing, which students created in response to given prompts. The writings that appear in Figures 5.4 through 5.8 were done by tenth and eleventh graders considered "newcomers"—that is, new to the school and having limited English language experience. These ELLs have the same bilingual English/Spanish teacher and take an

Figure 5.1 Writing Partners' Rubric

4	Plan writing together. Share ideas respectfully. Talk together in quiet, library voices. Listen to each other.
3	Let your partner do most of the work. Talk a little about other things. Get some words down on paper. Be somewhat distracted.
2	Whisper to other friends. Talk a lot about other things. Just get a few words on the paper. Be distracted.
1	Ignore each other. Be disagreeable. Show inappropriate behavior. Be off task.

Figure 5.2 Graphic Organizer for Relational Vocabulary

Relational Vocabulary	
Word	Something I can use to help me remember the definition
A picture of what the word reminds me of	What the word means in my own words

Figure 5.3 Editing Checklist

We Edit: Partners' Editing Checklist

Names (1) _____ and (2) _____

Title _____

Writer _____ Date _____

Spelling

I/we . . .

☐ Found words that don't look right.

☐ Checked for tricky words.

☐ Used the dictionary, thesaurus, or another resource.

Comments: _____

Content

I/we . . .

☐ Checked to see if words or parts of words are missing.

☐ Checked sentences: Too long? Too short? Confusing?

☐ Read and retold to the writer to make sure of understanding.

Comments: _____

Grammar

I/we . . .

☐ Checked for periods, commas, question marks, and exclamation marks.

☐ Checked for capital letters, proper nouns, and breaks in paragraphs.

☐ Discussed what was needed to create the final copy.

Comments: _____

Source: www.kent.k12.wa.us/curriculum/tech/unit_plan_2community.doc

elective course entitled Developing Language Arts through ESOL two periods of a four-period day for at least two grading periods. The first semester begins in the fall and consisted of two grading periods. The second semester begins in January and also consisted of two grading periods. Most likely, these students will be with this teacher for an entire academic year. Then, the next school year, they will be with the same teacher for at least one class per day the first semester and possibly the second semester. These students are tested twice a year for English language proficiency. They will continue to receive this academic support until testing shows they have developed a high enough level of English language proficiency to be successful in **mainstream classes** in the content areas.

English language learners enjoy writing in journals, since the purpose is to write informally, without worrying about syntactical or spelling correctness (Keefe, 2008). The samples of journal writing in Figures 5.4 and 5.5 are typical of the early production stage of second language development. Journal writing provides an equitable way of evaluating ELLs' understanding and writing skills, from which their progress can be assessed.

The sample in Figure 5.4 was written in response to this prompt: "Write about foods you like." The student wrote the following:

Foods That I Like

1. General Mills cereal—I eat cereal in da morning.
2. Caramels—I eat caramels in middy [midday].
3. Apples—I like apples in da day.
4. Coca-cola—I dat [don't] like coca-cola in da morning.
5. Apple strudel—I like apple strudel in da naight [night].
6. Cupcake—I like cupcake in da naight [night].
7. Cheese—I like cheese.

The instructional purpose and focus of this assignment was for ELLs to express themselves by demonstrating they understood the topic and could respond with sensible, meaningful information. Students did not have to be concerned with grammatical correctness but rather expression.

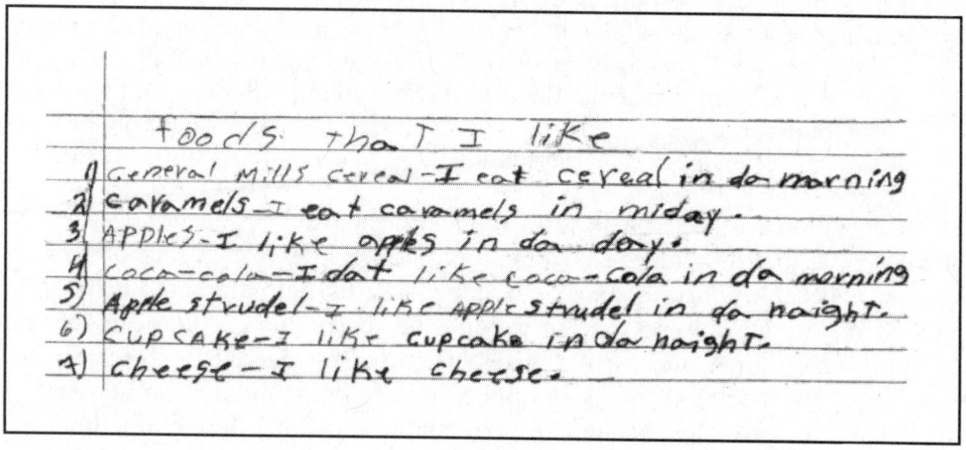
foods that I like
1) General Mills cereal-I eat cereal in da morning
2) caramels-I eat caramels in miday.
3) Apples-I like apples in da day.
4) coca-cola-I dat like coca-cola in da morning
5) Apple strudel-I like apple strudel in da naight.
6) cupcake-I like cupcake in da naight.
7) cheese-I like cheese.

Figure 5.4 Sample Journal Entry

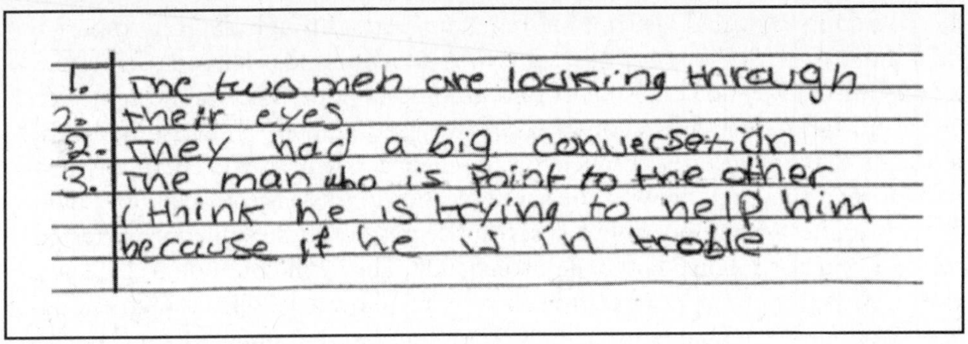

1. The two men are looking through
2. their eyes
2. They had a big converseti'on
3. The man who is point to the other
I think he is trying to help him
because if he is in troble

Figure 5.5 Sample Journal Entry

The sample in Figure 5.5 was written in response to viewing a black-and-white photograph (found in the book entitled *Looking at a Picture—Look, Think and Write,* by Leavitt and Sohn). In describing and interpreting the photo, the student wrote the following:

1. The two men are looking through their eyes
2. They had a big conversetion [conversation].
3. The man who is point to the other I think he is trying to help him because if he is in troble [trouble].

The teacher of the student who wrote this journal entry often does this assignment with this level of ELLs: having them look at a picture and then write a description of what they see. Again, this is an assignment that demonstrates students understand the directions and can respond in a meaningful way without being concerned with spelling or grammar accuracy. This type of assignment also prepares students for writing a descriptive narrative.

The sample shown in Figure 5.6 was written in response to the prompt "What makes you sad?" Here is what the student wrote in her journal:

> The thing that make me sad is that my brothers got mad with and my dad too, he does not talk to me and everyone in my family is mad with my sister because yesterday she talked with a psychologist about when my dad hit us and that became a big problem an my family and I am upset about my little sister because she told me tha she thought she did the righ thing and now she is so sad, because she hurt my mom and dad feelings and my dad told her that the love that they have to her is going to change is not going to be the same.

The response of this female student caused the teacher concern, as the student describes difficult issues going on at home. Here is evidence of how culture plays an important role in students' lives, in that values and behaviors in students' native cultures may or may not be acceptable in American culture.

In this case, the teacher can address the student's concerns with confidentiality. The teacher also has an opportunity to lend guidance and possibly some ideas for how the student can better communicate at home. Reading about a student's home life might give the teacher insight into the reasons the student is not performing well academically that day or week. The teacher may recommend that the student speak with a counselor, depending on the

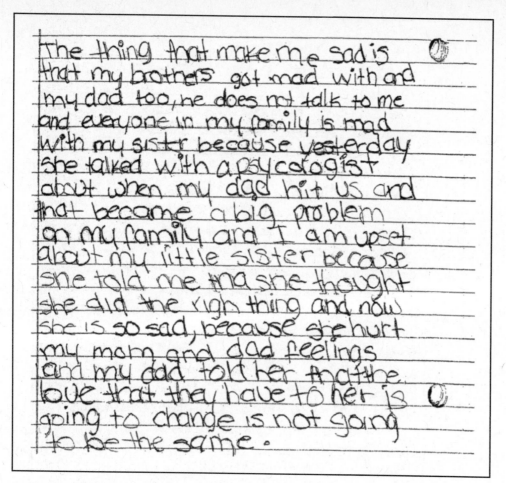

The thing that make me sad is
that my brothers got mad with and
my dad too, he does not talk to me
and everyone in my family is mad
with my sister because yesterday
she talked with a psycologist
about when my dad hit us and
that became a big problem
on my family and I am upset
about my little sister because
she told me tha she thought
she did the righ thing and now
she is so sad, because she hurt
my mom and dad feelings
and my dad told her that the
love that they have to her is
going to change is not going
to be the same.

Figure 5.6   Sample Journal Entry

seriousness of the issue and the length of time the student continues discussing it. Students must have some way of sharing their feelings, and writing in a **dialogue journal** with the teacher is a safe avenue through which they can express their concerns.

The journal entry in Figure 5.7 was written in response to this prompt: "Write about a topic of your choice." The student wrote the following:

Journal

Write about a topic of your choice.

The topic I would like to talk about is "Bad day." First of all is all about me, I'm gonna talk now because I know I hat about me I really know don't know about others. During 2 months of school I started for this year I had so many bad days some-time foreal I felt uncomtable uncomfortable at those time but when I thought about that I mean when I question myself I said It's doesn't matter because I wanna reach my goal. Its all about my "language". Sometime when I talked in people made funny at me, and they also asking me if am I speaking Creole? and people start laughing at me you know but they don't even if English is not my first language at all. I'm like they're "stupid" because I'm not born in America. All I know that won't keep on going like that. I think it gonna change one day I hope I'm gonna speak well one day

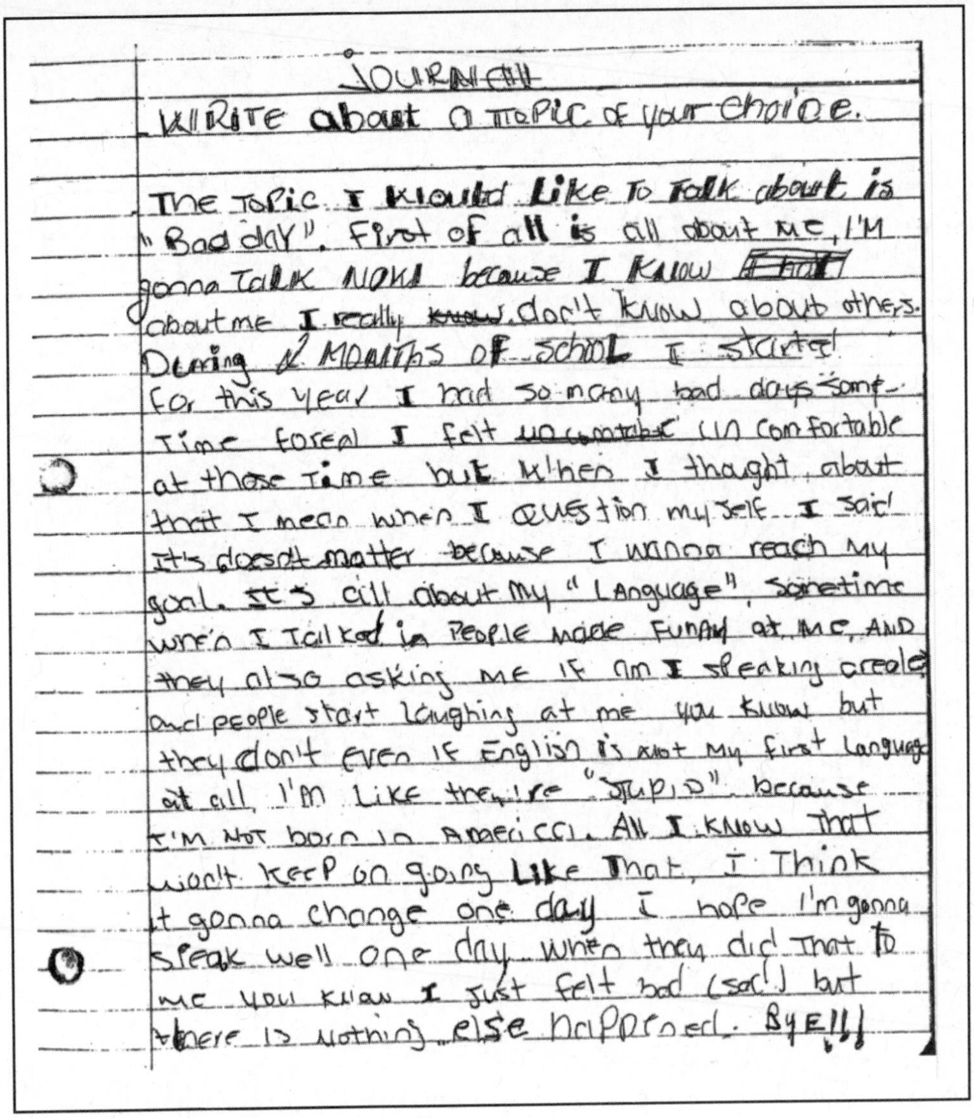

Figure 5.7 Sample Journal Entry

when they did that to me you know I just felt bad (sad) but there is nothing else happened. Bye!!!

This passage was written by a male student and describes how students laugh at him because he does not speak English correctly and how students make him feel stupid because he was not born in the United States. Dialogue journals can elicit these kinds of writings. As such, they give teachers the opportunity to address some of ELL students' concerns by discussing ways to alleviate the disappointments they experience and giving them encouragement as they struggle with learning the English language.

The strikethrough words in this writing sample can be considered evidence of Stephen Krashen's (1979) monitor hypothesis and Noam Chomsky's (1987) language acquisition **device** (see Chapter 3). Again, journal writing is one way students can express their feelings through a nonthreatening medium.

In Figure 5.8, the sample was written in response to the prompt "Why are your friends important?" The student wrote the following journal entry:

> Friends are important to me because sometimes when I have problems they can help me or they can teach me when I don't know some things always I have friends in everywhere sometimes they are fany [funny] and some of them are angry but if you have a friend you need to talk something what they make happy always I am a good friend with every body, in my house in school in everywhere in this world.

Note that in writing a response, the teacher took the opportunity to reinforce the student's comments, noting "You are likable" and thus building self-esteem (see bottom of Figure 5.8). This sample journal entry, as well as the others, reveals the depth of ELL students' thought processes and demonstrates

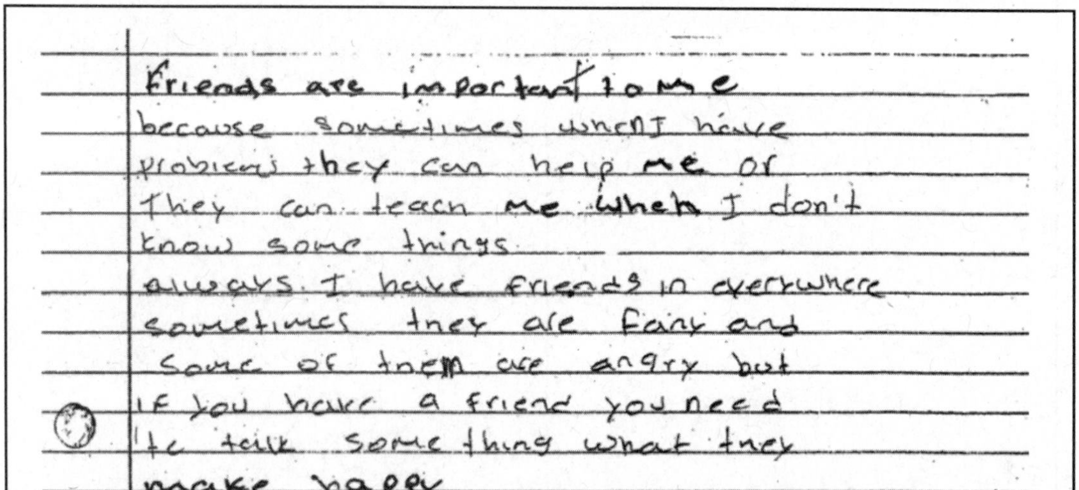

Friends are important to me
because sometimes when I have
problems they can help me or
They can teach me when I don't
know some things.
always I have friends in everywhere
sometimes they are fany and
Some of them are angry but
if you have a friend you need
to talk some thing what they
make happy
always I am a good friend
with every body, in my house
in school in everywhere in this
world.

Yes - I think you have
the qualities of a
good friend and
you are also the
type of person
many people like!
You are likable...

Figure 5.8 Sample Journal Entry

their commitment to completing assignments by considering responses and answers thoughtfully.

Graphic Organizers for Writing

Figures 5.9 through 5.13 are examples of graphic organizers designed specifically for assisting ELLs with improving writing skills. With guided practice

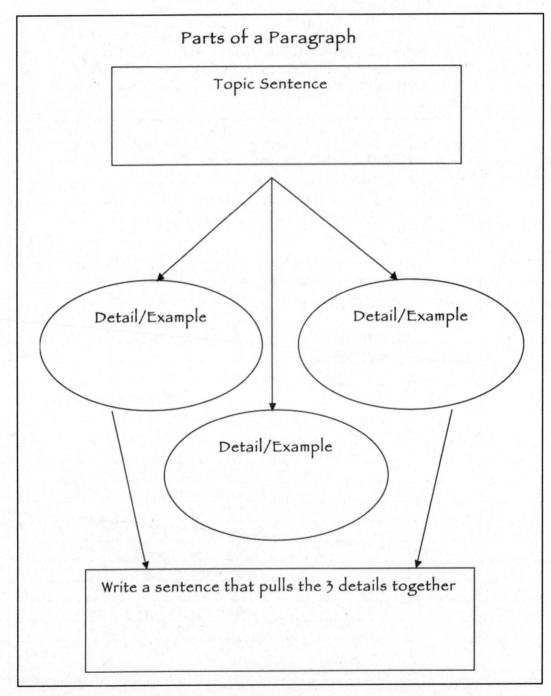

Figure 5.9 Sample Parts of a Paragraph Graphic Organizer Template

and frequent use, these graphic organizers can assist students in becoming better writers and in fostering their independent work.

Parts of a Paragraph, shown in Figures 5.9 and 5.10, helps students organize the elements of a good paragraph, including a topic sentence and supporting details or examples. Students can use this graphic organizer to record these elements before actually writing the paragraph.

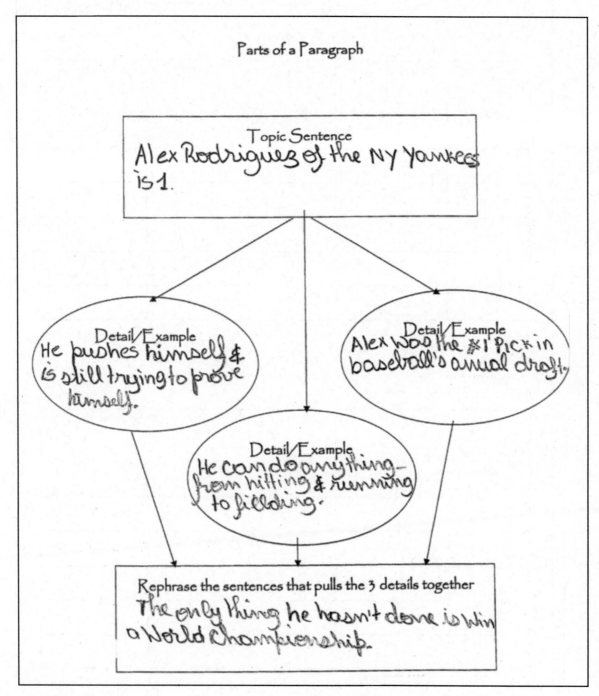

Parts of a Paragraph

Topic Sentence
Alex Rodriguez of the NY Yankees is 1.

Detail/Example
He pushes himself & is still trying to prove himself.

Detail/Example
Alex was the #1 pick in baseball's annual draft.

Detail/Example
He can do anything— from hitting & running to fielding.

Rephrase the sentences that pulls the 3 details together
The only thing he hasn't done is win a World Championship.

Figure 5.10   Sample Parts of a Paragraph Graphic Organizer

The *SOS* organizer helps students analyze and edit what they have written and guides them to edit their work more effectively, producing a better final draft (see Figures 5.11 and 5.12). This form of organizer also alerts students to parts of speech, helping to reinforce grammar and syntax.

S. O. S. – Sentence Opening Sheet

Sentence Number	First 4 words in the sentence	Subject (noun)	Verb (action word)	Special Features (adjective/adverb)

Edited/Changed Version

Sentence Number	First 4 words in the sentence	Subject (noun)	Verb (action word)	Special Features (adjective/adverb)

Figure 5.11 Sample SOS Graphic Organizer Template

S.O.S. – Sentence Opening Sheet

Sentence Number	First 4 words in the sentence	Subject (noun)	Verb (action word)	Special Features (adjective/adverb)
1	Fu-hsing was remarkably proud	Fu-hsing	was	Remarkably proud
2	His wife laid a calming hand	his wife	Laid	calming
3	She alway thought of a solution.	she	thought	solution
4	Fu-hsing continue to wring his hand	Fu-hsing	continue	Wring

Figure 5.12   Sample SOS Graphic Organizer

The *Persuasive Paragraph* organizer helps students form an opinion about a given topic by considering another student's opinion on the same topic (see Figure 5.13). This graphic organizer also asks students to identify supporting reasons for their opinions—a necessary step in any kind of persuasive writing.

Figure 5.14 is a typical writing example of a student who is in the speech emergence stage of second language acquisition. This student would benefit from using the *SOS* graphic organizer in editing a writing assignment. In the third paragraph, notice the number of times the word *and* is used to link thoughts and the lack of subject/verb agreement. Despite these problems, the student correctly identifies the topic of the text and conveys understanding of the main ideas, which were the objectives in this writing exercise. Therefore, the student should be graded accordingly.

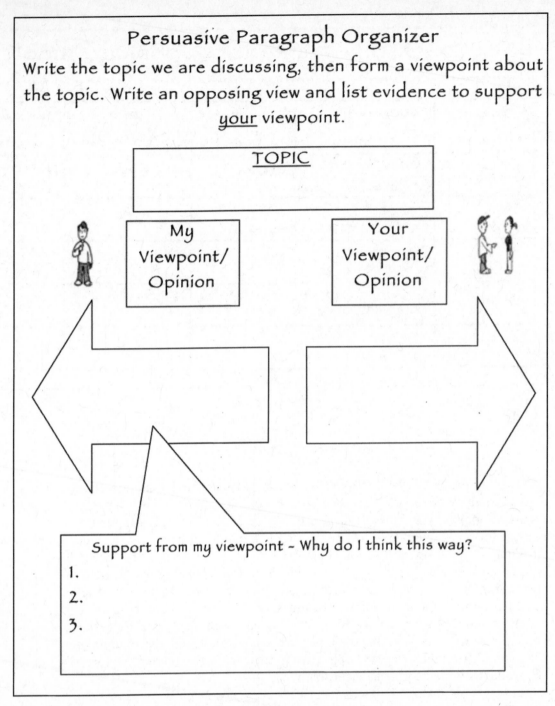

Persuasive Paragraph Organizer
Write the topic we are discussing, then form a viewpoint about the topic. Write an opposing view and list evidence to support _your_ viewpoint.

TOPIC

My Viewpoint/ Opinion

Your Viewpoint/ Opinion

Support from my viewpoint - Why do I think this way?

1.

2.

3.

Figure 5.13 Sample Persuasive Paragraph Graphic Organizer Template

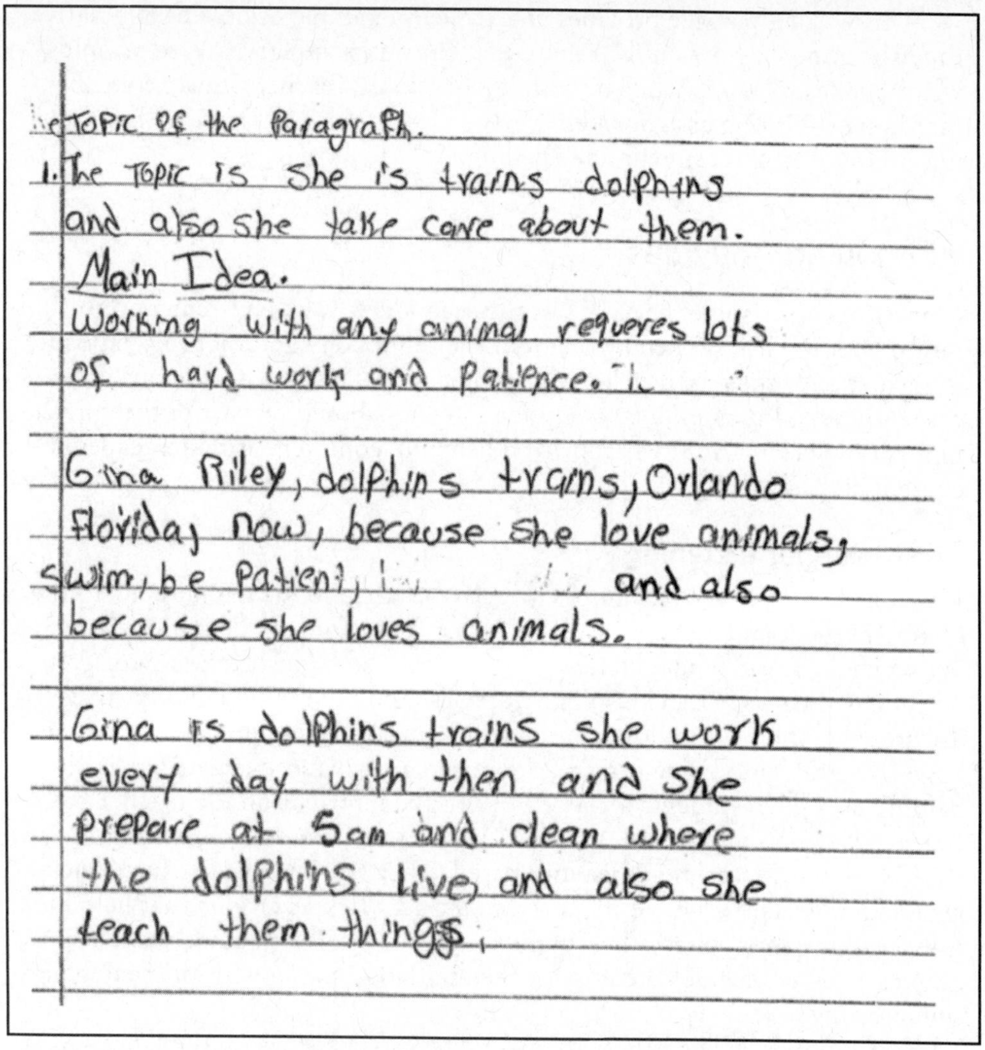

> Topic of the Paragraph.
> 1. The Topic is she is trains dolphins
> and also she take care about them.
> Main Idea.
> Working with any animal requeres lots
> of hard work and patience. it
>
> Gina Riley, dolphins trains, Orlando
> Florida now, because she love animals,
> swim, be patient, and also
> because she loves animals.
>
> Gina is dolphins trains she work
> every day with then and she
> prepare at 5am and clean where
> the dolphins live, and also she
> teach them things.

Figure 5.14   Sample Student Writing

Ernest Hemingway, a highly acclaimed author in the middle of the last century, was a prodigious writer while he was growing up, and even as a native English speaker, his writing had many errors. The following is an excerpt of a composition, recounting an ocean voyage he took with his father when he was in the sixth grade in 1911. In reading, note that there are punctuation, capitalization, and spelling errors:

My First Sea Vouge

I was born in a little white house on the Island of marthas vineyard in the state of massachuset . . . my father, the captain of the three masted schooner "Elizabeth" took me and my little Brother around the "Horn" with him to Australia . . . it [porpoise] tasted like pork only it was greesier . . . after a fine vouge and had just as good vouge going Back.

This writing passage provides an excellent example of how even a native English speaker who would go on to become an exemplary, award-winning writer makes mistakes while developing his skills. Teachers must remember that in most writing assignments, it is the message and expression that are important, not the grammar and spelling.

Listening Activities

Many teachers assume that ELLs at the **secondary level** have many opportunities to hear English spoken throughout the school day and that this exposure is adequate for them to develop **oral proficiency**. This is not necessarily the case, however. Instruction in listening strategies should be part of the curriculum and will result in ELLs' improved listening comprehension in academic content classes (NCLRC, n.d.).

Strategies for Listening

Listening strategies are techniques or activities that contribute directly to the comprehension and recall of listening input. Therefore, by definition, listening strategies must be taught. This can be achieved by instruction in discrete listening strategies, video listening strategies, and note-taking ability, as well as through applying top-down and bottom-up strategies and integrating metacognitive strategies. Using graphic organizers or advanced organizers is also helpful, as it gives students a framework of the information the teacher has predetermined as important and thus worth identifying while listening.

Top-down strategies are listener based. They tap into the listener's background knowledge of the topic, activating a set of expectations that help the listener to interpret what is heard and anticipate what will come next. Top-down strategies include listening for the main idea, along with predicting and summarizing.

Bottom-up strategies are text based. The listener relies on the language in the message, such as the combination of sounds, words, and grammar that creates meaning. Bottom-up strategies include listening for specific details, recognizing cognates, and recognizing word order patterns, word stress, and syllables.

To help ELLs extract meaning from a listening text, teachers should direct them to follow four basic steps (NCLRC, n.d.):

1. To figure out the purpose for listening, activate background knowledge of the topic and predict or anticipate content.

2. Attend to the parts of the listening input that are relevant to the identified purpose, and ignore the rest.

3. Use top-down and bottom-up strategies that are appropriate to the listening task, and use them flexibly and interactively.

4. Check comprehension both while listening and when the listening task is over.

Teachers can intermittently stop the listening exercise to emphasize segments of the listening text and then replay those segments for further examination. Also, helping ELLs integrate metacognitive skills while listening will help them gain confidence in their ability to understand content (Zainuddin, Morales-Jones, Yahya, & Ariza, 2002). Metacognitive strategies that can be taught along with listening skills include the following:

- Being able to connect to real-life situations

- Conducting critical analysis and questioning of ideas

- Self-evaluating a learning activity after completing it

- Recognizing the organization of information to skim and scan pages of text

- Developing mnemonic devices to remember details

- Self-correcting

Authentic materials and situations prepare students for the types of listening they will do outside the classroom. Using easily accessible listening programs allows students to practice skill development during one-way communication, such as listening to radio and television programs.

Planning Activities for Listening

As teachers design listening, or aural, tasks, they should keep in mind that expecting ELLs to have complete recall of information is unrealistic. Not even native English speakers have this level of recall. Listening exercises should be success oriented and build students' confidence in their listening ability.

Contextualized listening activities approximate real-life tasks and give listeners an idea of the type of information to expect and what to do with it before engaging in actual listening (NCLRC, n.d.). A beginning-level task might be to locate places on a map (one way) or exchange name and address information (two way). At an intermediate level, students might follow directions for assembling something (one way) or work in pairs to create a story to tell to the rest of the class (two way).

Each activity should focus on the improvement of one or more specific listening skills. Recognizing the goals of listening comprehension in each listening situation will help students select appropriate listening strategies:

- *Identification:* Recognizing or discriminating specific aspects of the message

- *Main idea comprehension:* Identifying the higher-order ideas

- *Detail comprehension:* Identifying supporting details

- *Replication:* Reproducing the message orally or in writing

A listening activity may have more than one goal or outcome, but teachers should be careful not to overburden the attention of beginning or intermediate listenerss (NCLRC, n.d.).

The activities conducted during prelistening may serve as preparation for listening in several ways. During prelistening, the teacher may build background knowledge, clarify any cultural issues, and provide opportunities for group or collaborative work. Sample prelistening activities include the following:

- Looking at pictures, maps, diagrams, and graphs

- Reading relevant materials

- Constructing semantic webs, which show how words and concepts are related
- Predicting the content of the listening text
- Going over the directions or instructions for the activity
- Doing guided practice

While-listening activities relate directly to the text, and students do them during or immediately after listening. Sample while-listening activities are as follow:

- Listening while looking at visuals
- Filling in graphs and charts
- Following a route on a map
- Checking off items on a list

Teachers should keep in mind these points when planning listening activities:

- If students are to complete a written task during or immediately after listening, allow them to read through it before listening.
- Keep writing to a minimum during listening.
- Organize activities so they guide listeners through the text.
- Before beginning the listening activity, use questions to focus students' attention on the elements of the text that are crucial to comprehension of the whole.
- Before listening, use predicting to encourage students to monitor their comprehension as they listen.
- Give immediate feedback, whenever possible.

Several online resources provide useful information and activities, as well. Randall's ESL Cyber Listening Lab (www.esl-lab.com) contains over 40 dialogues and general listening quizzes in the categories of easy, medium, and difficult. Students will enjoy listening to dialogues of the characters in these recordings of adult and children's voices. For each dialogue, students can answer prelistening questions, listen to the dialogue, read the script, and take a vocabulary quiz. The vocabulary quizzes include multiple-choice and short-answer questions, along with mixed-up sentences, vocabulary matching, and text completion items (similar to a cloze activity). Students can do all these activities independently, as their responses are evaluated interactively. Students can also retake the quiz and listen to the dialogue again, with or without the script. These activities can form the center of a block schedule (see Appendix B), as students rotate activities, keeping them on task and engaged with English language learning.

Another useful website is Interesting Things for ESL Students (www.manythings.org). Under the heading "Listening & Reading" are many fun activities for ELLs, such as word games, puzzles, quizzes, exercises, and much more.

Speaking Activities

Traditional classroom speaking practice often takes the form of drills. In contrast, the purpose of real communication is to accomplish a task, such as conveying a telephone message, obtaining information, or expressing an opinion. In real communication, participants must also manage uncertainty about what the other person will say. Finally, authentic communication can involve an **information gap**, with each participant having information the other does not (NCLRC, n.d.). To bridge that gap, participants may have to clarify their own meaning or ask for confirmation of their own understanding.

Cooperative learning groups promote oral language development and foster conversations about content among students in an informal and non-threatening setting. Students engage in discussion that focuses on the content task and allows for negotiating the meaning of content vocabulary. To create speaking activities that will develop communicative competence, instructors can incorporate a purpose and an information gap, allowing students to practice language use more freely.

Two common kinds of structured output activities are *Information Gap* and *Jigsaw*. In both these activities, students complete a task by obtaining missing information, as is necessary in real communication.

Information Gap

During Information Gap activities, students practice the features of grammar and vocabulary by discussing differences in the information provided. For

This student is giving an oral presentation of the information she and her fellow students gathered during a small-group activity.

instance, discussing differences in how certain activities are portrayed leads to the practice of verbs. Discussing differences in number, size, and shape leads to practice of adjectives, and discussing differences in position or location leads to practice of prepositional phrases.

One Information Gap activity involves students working in pairs to fill in the gaps in a schedule or timetable. The two partners have the same basic bus schedule but with different arrival and departure times missing. Without seeing one another's schedules, the partners must ask questions and determine how to fill in the blanks and complete the master schedule.

A second activity has two partners solve a problem or complete a process by compiling a set of directions. The partners have similar lists of procedures, but each is missing different details. The students must work together to fill in all the missing details. In another variation, students have pictures that are similar—for instance, pictures of two devices or machines that do the same task. Together, the partners must determine what the device or machine does.

Jigsaw

Jigsaw activities are elaborate Information Gap activities that are done with small groups of students (see Chapter 7). In a Jigsaw activity, panels of a comic strip or storyboard, pieces of a puzzle, or a series of related photos are distributed among members of a group. Together, group members must determine how to fit together all the pieces to create a whole picture or tell a complete story. Members cannot show one another the panels, pieces, or photos they have.

In one Jigsaw activity, a group of four students were given four panels (one panel per student) from a storyboard illustrating this narrative:

1. A girl is sitting at the computer with her books open, typing away on a final report.

2. She hears her mother calling from the other room to come to dinner.

3. As the girl starts to get up, the lights suddenly go out.

4. She exclaims "AAHHH! I forgot to save all my work!" as she drops her head into her arms on the table.

The four panels described here have a clear narrative line, so group members will likely agree on their appropriate sequencing. The Jigsaw task can be made more demanding, however, by using pictures that lend themselves to alternative sequences. In this case, partners will have to negotiate to agree on a satisfactory sequence.

When conducting Information Gap and Jigsaw activities, teachers should be conscious of the language demands they place on ELLs. If an activity calls for ELLs to respond orally using vocabulary or content they do not know, the teacher should conduct an initiating activity, perhaps brainstorming with students using a semantic web or other graphic organizer. When setting up the activity, the teacher should preview the language ELLs will need, determine what they already know, and supplement what they are able to produce.

These kinds of structured speaking activities can form an effective bridge between instructor **modeling** and communicative output, because they are partly authentic and partly artificial (NCLRC, n.d.). Like authentic communication, they feature information gaps that must be filled in for successful completion of the task. However, whereas authentic communication allows speakers to use all of the language they know, structured activities have students practice specific features of language and use only brief sentences, not extended discourse. Providing this structure controls the number of variables that ELLs must deal with when first exposed to new material. As they become comfortable, they can move on to more complex speaking activities.

Role-playing activities and discussions resemble real communication settings and allow students to practice using all the language they know. In role-plays, students are assigned parts or characters and put into situations they may encounter outside the classroom. Because role-plays imitate real life, the range of language functions that may be used is expanded considerably. Moreover, students explore relationships as they play their parts, requiring them to use language that is appropriate to the situation and the characters. Doing so allows them to practice and develop sociolinguistic competence.

Students usually enjoy role-playing, but those who lack self-confidence or have lower language proficiency may find it intimidating, at least at first. To conduct successful role-playing activities, teachers should follow these guidelines (NCLRC, n.d.):

- Prepare carefully.
- Set a goal or outcome.
- Give each student a role card that describes the person or part to be played.
- Keep the audiences for role-plays small.
- Give students time to prepare.
- Be present as a resource, answering students' questions as they arise.
- Do not correct students' pronunciation or grammar unless they specifically ask for this kind of help.
- Do not expect all students to contribute equally to the discussion or to use grammar accurately. Allow students to work at their own levels.
- Give and get feedback about the activities.

Given the wide variety of activities and tasks in middle and high school classrooms that involve providing information via oral communication, it is important for ELLs to have strong listening and speaking skills and strategies to access that information. Many students are confident of their listening and speaking abilities in their ELL classrooms and social settings; however, they are often less confident when it comes to comprehending oral information in their mainstream content area classes (Keefe, 2008).

To increase students' abilities, teachers should conduct explicit instruction of listening and speaking strategies (Chamot & O'Malley, 1994; Mendelsohn, 1994). Strategy instruction should follow these steps:

1. *Preparation:* Define the strategy.
2. *Presentation:* Model how the strategy is used.
3. *Guidance:* Guide students in practicing the strategy.
4. *Evaluation:* Give appropriate feedback.
5. *Expansion:* Provide opportunities for practice.

6. *Assessment:* Help students assess the effectiveness of their strategy use.

7. *Application:* Have students use the strategies in authentic tasks by encouraging them to apply the strategies in other classes.

By conducting well-prepared speaking activities such as role-plays, teachers can encourage ELLs to experiment and innovate with the language. Creating a supportive atmosphere will allow them to make mistakes without fear of embarrassment. This will contribute to students' self-confidence as speakers and motivate them to learn more.

References

Chamot, A., & O'Malley, J. (1994). *The CALLA Handbook.* New York: Addison-Wesley.

Chomsky, N. (1987). *The Chomsky reader.* New York: Pantheon Books.

Florida Department of Education (FLDOE). (1995). *Teaching excellence and cultural harmony: 1 and 2: Linguistics.* San Diego, CA: Jostens Learning.

Hoch, F. (2008). *Writing and English as a second language.* University of North Carolina LEARN NC. Retrieved August 3, 2008, from www.learnnc.org/lp/pages/672

Keefe, M. R. (Producer/Researcher). (2008). *Voices of immigrant ELL high school students* [Video]. Martin County School District, Florida, TV Production Classes.

Kent School District. Retrieved on September 21, 2007, from www.kent.k12.wa.us/curriculum/tech/unit_plan_2community.doc

Krashen, S. (1989). *Language acquisition and language education.* New York: Prentice-Hall.

Lange, E., & Park, J. (2009). Flash writing to develop students' overall writing skills. *Essential Teacher, 6,* 34–36.

Leavitt, H., & Sohn, D. (1985). *Look, think and write: Using pictures to stimulate thinking and improve your writing.* Lincolnwood, IL: National Textbook.

Mendelsohn, D. (1994). *Learning to listen: A strategy-based approach for the second language learner.* San Diego, CA: Dominie Press.

National Capital Language Resource Center (NCLRC). The essentials of language teaching. Retrieved October 20, 2007, from www.nclrc.org/essentials/listening/developlisten.htm

Yoon, B. (2008). Uninvited guests: The influence of teachers' roles and pedagogies on the positioning of English language learners in the regular classroom. *American Educational Research Journal, 45*(2), 495–523.

Zainuddin, H., Morales-Jones, C., Yahya, N., & Ariza, E. (2002). *Fundamentals of teaching English to speakers of other languages in K–12 mainstream classrooms.* Dubuque, IA: Kendall/Hunt.

Chapter 6

Math, Science, and Social Studies:
Challenges and Adaptations for ELLs

*L*anguage is a process of free creation; its laws and principles are fixed, but the manner in which the principles of generation are used is free and infinitely varied. Even the interpretation and use of words involves a process of free creation.

—Noam Chomsky

Given the increased levels of cultural and language diversity found in U.S. schools today, teachers need to be prepared to manage their classrooms in fair and cooperative ways. Teachers should aim to create a learning environment that promotes cultural understanding, encourages academic learning, and helps to prepare all students for the larger world of community and work. This chapter is devoted to discussing three aspects of teaching the content areas to **secondary-level** English language learners (ELLs):

1. The difficulties ELLs face in the content areas of math, science, and social studies

2. The adaptations teachers can make to provide comprehensible input for ELLs in content area classrooms

3. Sample lesson plans and activities in math, science, and social studies

This chapter begins with general descriptions of a variety of activities. These activities are then discussed in more detail as they are applied within sample lessons in math, science, and social studies (School District of Palm Beach County, n.d.).

Many of the activities involve teams competing against each other. For the teams to be manageable, they should have no more than five or six students each. When only two teams are needed for an activity, additional students can form a third group of audience members or judges. In succeeding rounds of the same activity, the audience members or judges should rotate positions with the team members.

Many of these activities integrate teaching concepts in the content areas of math, science, or social studies with teaching concepts in the language arts. For example, there is a math activity in persuasive writing that requires students to write a response to this prompt:

Usually, everyone likes to have more of something. Before you begin writing, think about what you want less of.

This writing prompt relates to the math concept of inequalities. Other examples of interdisciplinary assignments are the *Making Sense* activity, in which students must form complete sentences using science terms, and rewriting a paragraph of social studies content in the past tense. These kinds of activities reinforce language arts concepts by working with content area topics and vocabulary.

Since this chapter is devoted to preparing lesson plans, a brief discussion on **language objectives** is important and should not be overlooked. Along with the content objective, students need to understand the language of that objective. An example would be if the content objective is for small groups to decide whether they are *pro,* or *for,* a rule that talking on a cell phone while driving is safe or if the concensus of the group is *con,* or *against,* that rule. The meaning of the word *decide* should be explained, and the questions for students are: What does *decide* mean in these directions, and what are students to do with this issue? Other examples are if the content objective requires students to *formulate* a hypothesis before starting a science project or *justify* the action of the military during a certain time in history. Students provide a definition of the term *and* an explanation as to how the word relates to the objective of the lesson. Knowing the meanings of such terms is critical for ELL students to understand before starting and completing assignments successfully.

General Descriptions of Content Area Activities

Total Recall

Students form at least three teams. Then each team prepares three or more questions and answers based on a given passage in the textbook. Teams are also allowed to take notes about the text. Teams then take turns asking each other their questions. The same question cannot be asked twice.

Members of the responding teams are not allowed to raise their hands to indicate they know the answer to a question. The team asking the question will choose which team it wants to answer the question. If the chosen team does not answer correctly, it loses a point and the team asking the question gets a point.

When a team's answer has been ruled incorrect, it can challenge the team that asked the question. The challenging team must prove that its answer is correct or that the questioning team's answer is incorrect. The challenging team does not need to prove both. The other teams in the competition can join the challenge on either side, but they must do so immediately. Once the teams have taken sides on a challenge, they consult the textbook to determine the correct answer (or answers, in some cases). Each team on the side with the correct answer gets two points.

True or False

Students form teams and create three statements about the assigned text or topic: true, false, or a combination of the two. To begin the competition, a member of the first team reads a statement aloud. Members of the other teams listen and record on a chart whether they believe the statement is true, false, or some of both. The questioning team decides which responses are correct. Each team with a correct answer earns one point. In the case of a disagreement, students follow the challenge procedure of the *Total Recall* activity.

Judgment

Working in teams, students copy or create five sentences from or about the reading selection that they believe are a combination of fact and opinion. Each team records its sentences on five separate strips of paper—one sentence per strip. Teams then swap sentence strips.

Each team writes its own team name on the backs of the strips. Team members then read each sentence and judge it to be a fact or opinion. As appropriate, teams put their sentence strips in "Fact" and "Opinion" envelopes, which the teacher has provided at the front of the classroom.

When all the teams have finished reviewing their sentence strips, the teacher takes them from the "Fact" and "Opinion" envelopes and reads them aloud, one at a time. As a class, students decide if each sentence was placed correctly. If it was, the team who evaluated the sentence gets a point. If it was not, that team loses a point.

This game can be adapted to focus on cause/effect, reality/fantasy, or inferred/explicit in evaluating the sentences.

Opinion/Proof

This is a good prewriting activity. To begin, the teacher introduces the concept by having students read a selection about which opinions can be formed. The teacher draws a vertical line on the board to create a simple two-column table. At the top of the lefthand column, the teacher writes "Opinion," and at the top of the righthand column, "Proof."

The class discusses the selection. In the "Opinion" column, the teacher records students' opinions of the selection. For each opinion, students should offer a number of factual statements from the selection that supports the opinion. The teacher should record these statements in the "Proof" column.

Consider the following example:

Opinion	**Proof**
Napoleon was a great leader.	He ended the revolution.
	He drew up a new constitution.
	He established fair taxation.

Wrong Word

The teacher reads aloud to students a sentence containing a wrong word, such as either of the following:

1. <u>Contribution</u> is the method of calculation. (Computation)
2. <u>Arithmetic</u> is math that deals with general statements of relations and that uses letters and symbols to represent sets of numbers and values. (Algebra)

In each case, the underlined word is incorrect and should be replaced with the word shown in parentheses at the end of the sentence. Working in teams, students must decide which word is wrong and fix it. Each team gets a point for each correction it makes.

This activity can be adapted by having teams provide sentences with incorrect words for the other teams to correct.

Jeopardy

To prepare, the teacher makes a chart with pockets out of posterboard (or some facsimile thereof) and envelopes. The chart should have nine pockets arranged in three rows—three pockets per row. Above the top row of pockets, the teacher writes A, B, and C, labeling the three columns of the chart. Along the left side, the teacher writes 2, 3, and 4, labeling the three rows of the chart. (These numbers reflect point values.)

The teacher also creates a series of cards containing definitions of vocabulary words from the students' reading (i.e., not the words themselves). The words being defined should be of three difficulty levels: easy, medium, and difficult. On a separate sheet or series of cards, the teacher records the word that corresponds with each definition.

In the top row of pockets, the teacher places three cards containing the definitions of "easy" vocabulary words. (The students should not see the cards.) In the second row of pockets, the teacher places three cards containing definitions of "medium" words, and in the third row, three cards containing definitions of "difficult" words.

To play the game, student teams take turns picking pockets and identifying words from the definitions. A member of the first team picks a pocket from the chart—2/C, for example. Then the student reads the definition on the card—for instance, "This damages or kills organisms." The student, with the help of his or her team, responds by identifying the word being defined but stating it in question format—in this case, "What is a virus?" If the student provides the correct vocabulary word, his or her team gets 2, 3, or 4 points, depending on the word's level of difficulty (per the three rows of the chart).

If the student's answer is incorrect, the next team tries to identify the word but for 1 point less than the previous team would have earned. For example, if the first team guessed incorrectly for a word worth 3 points, then the next team would get 2 points for answering correctly. If that team also guessed incorrectly, the next team would get 1 point for answering correctly. If no team answers correctly before the point value is reduced to 0, then each team loses 1 point.

Student-Developed Tests

Student groups write portions of the test and hand them in to the teacher. The teacher then creates a comprehensive test for all students to take.

Studying for Tests in Groups

The teacher forms groups of students and allows them one full class period to study for a test. Students do not have to study in their assigned groups but can be provided an incentive to do so. The teacher may propose that if all group members score above 80 percent, he or she will increase their scores by the difference between 80 and the lowest percentile score. For example, if the lowest score in the group is 82 percent, everyone in the group will get an extra 2 percentage points added to his or her score.

Team Spelling Tests

The teacher selects 10 to 15 vocabulary words from students' reading and writes them on the board, overhead or electronic display. Working in teams, students study the words for three to five minutes. At the end of study period, the teacher hides the words from view.

Each team gets out one pencil and one sheet of paper. A team member writes the team's name at the top of the paper and writes the numbers 1 to 10 (or up to 15, depending on the number of words) down the left side of the paper. The teacher then reads aloud the vocabulary words in the manner they would be read during a traditional spelling test: stating each word slowly and clearly, using it in a sentence, and then repeating it. The teacher allows ample time between words for students to write down their spellings.

In each team, members work together to spell each word. The first team member writes word number 1 on the team's paper and then passes the paper and pencil to the second team member, who writes word number 2. The paper and pencil are passed from student to student until all the spelling words have been completed. (Each team member will likely write out two or three words, depending on the size of the team.) Teams exchange papers and check one another's spellings. Each team gets 1 point for each correctly spelled word. The spelling test can be made more challenging by asking teams to define each word or write a sentence using it.

Interviews

The teacher plays the role of an expert or well-informed person on a specific topic. Students play the roles of journalists and interview the teacher.

To begin, the teacher assigns the students to groups and distributes a set of interview questions among them. One student from each group then interviews the teacher, asking him or her the questions in the sequence indicated. As the teacher answers the questions, the other group members take notes.

Students can save their notes for use in follow-up writing activities.

Making Sense

Working in teams, students write statements about a topic using a set of provided information that includes names, places, dates, and so on. For example, using this information—1863/War/Lincoln/Pennsylvania/Address—students will write a statement such as, *In 1863, during the Civil War, President Lincoln went to Pennsylvania and delivered the Gettysburg Address.* This can be done as an initiating or review activity.

Cubing

Cubing involves creating a three-dimensional cube that has choices of activities on it (Turville, 2007). Each face of the cube describes an activity that students can complete to achieve specific learning goals. The activities on the cube can be somewhat generic or topic specific.

Each student in the group describes an aspect of the topic on a piece of paper, making one side or face of the cube. One member of the group draws lines on a large piece of posterboard, sectioning spaces into six equal-sized faces of the cube (see Figure 6.1). Then the posterboard is cut or folded along those lines, then taped, stapled, or glued to form the cube. Each face of the cube should accommodate the paper each student in the group has used to describe a learning goal of the topic. Those papers are then glued to each face of the cube, creating a cube of activities on the topic. (See also Figure 6.5 for another example of a Cubing activity.)

Cubing is often used at the end of a unit of study, when students have developed a common language and under-

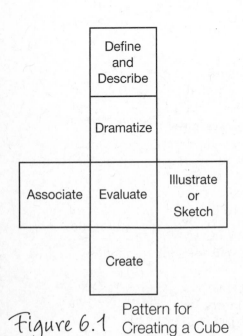

Figure 6.1 Pattern for Creating a Cube

Student Glossary (Any Content Area)		
Word	Definition	Picture
English_____ Native Language _____	Text definition:_____ _____ Your sentence:_____ _____	
English_____ Native Language _____	Text definition:_____ _____ Your sentence:_____ _____	
English_____ Native Language _____	Text definition:_____ _____ Your sentence:_____ _____	

Figure 6.2 Student Glossary

standing of a topic and can do projects of interest to them. Cubing also can be used to create situational interest because of the novelty of this activity. By allowing students to choose the task that interests them the most, this activity allows for personal input.

Student Glossaries

Students can create their own glossaries of terms by using the graphic organizer shown in Figure 6.2. Students jot down the word in both English and their native language and then add a definition of the word, a sentence using it, and a picture of it.

Including the native language form of the word both validates and encourages use of students' first languages (L1s). Including a picture helps students recall what the term means, much like a mnemonic device.

Challenges for ELLs in Mathematics

Mathematics is not just arithmetic. For English language learners and teachers, math poses considerable challenges. Problem solving involves not just language but a thought process. Teachers may find that ELLs use different processes to arrive at answers. Also, students from other **cultures** may be less concerned about the thought process they followed and more concerned with getting the correct response, which will make them unable to justify their answers. Many teachers do not validate ELLs' thought processes and prior mathematical knowledge.

Here are some of the difficulties ELLs face when learning mathematics:

- The formation of numbers and conventions such as use of a decimal point and comma vary from culture to culture.

- Students have no experience with the measurement system used in the United States.

- Many students have never seen or worked with manipulatives, such as algebra tiles, and may not take a lesson using them seriously.

- Students may have learned math by rote memory, without understanding the underlying concepts.

- Math is not spirally taught in many cultures, so students may not know a lot about geometry, for example.

- Estimating, rounding, and geometry are not often taught as early in other countries as in the United States.

- Mathematical terms do not always translate well from one language to another.

- In some countries, the math curricula involves primarily calculation.

- Word problems may not be introduced until much later in students' education.

- Students may be used to doing mental math. They may not show their work, or they may show their work in different ways (Haynes & O'Loughlin, 2003).

Adaptations in Math Instruction

Many secondary school teachers believe that because math is a universal language, it is easier to teach to ELLs than other academic subjects (Balderrama & Diaz-Rico, 2006). In fact, mathematics has a unique language (Keefe, 2008), and ELLs must learn this language to be successful in this content area. Universal math concepts are inherent and imbedded in math. Therefore, how these concepts are represented is culturally based. For example, in the United States, the units of measurements are inches, feet, yards, and miles, whereas in many other countries, the metric system of measurement is used, which is based on the power of 10. By being aware of these differences, teachers can mediate ELLs transition in learning a new language to express mathematical concepts.

Here are some strategies teachers can incorporate in their instruction of ELLs:

- Use math as it applies to everyday, real-life situations; doing so makes it meaningful and helps students internalize and retain math concepts.

- Use manipulatives to help make abstract concepts more concrete, and provide a context that makes conceptual understanding easier so students can see connections between different representations of mathematical ideas.

- Plan activities that facilitate, explore, and investigate math concepts; that promote the construction of math knowledge; and that nurture students' curiosity.

- Drill and practice should not be the staple of a math curriculum. Instead, provide math problems that may have various correct solutions and for which answers can be presented in multiple ways (Balderrama & Diaz-Rico, 2006).

This math teacher is using the SMART Board technology to deliver the lesson, while students use algebra tiles, a type of manipulative, at their desks.

Communication and Literacy in Math

Communication in mathematics class has the potential to facilitate students' understanding and develop their computational fluency. However, the practice of discussing ideas in English may place ELLs at a distinct disadvantage. Schleppegrell (2007) suggests that a focus on language is critical for students' learning in the classroom, that both students and teachers should use math language, and that instruction should assist students to move from everyday language to the more formal language of math.

Research in mathematics education has identified specific instructional features that promote conceptual understanding of mathematics and are associated with higher levels of performance (Torres-Velasquez & Lobo, 2004/2005). One such feature is communication. Many researchers of mathematics learning have found that students benefit from communicating their mathematical ideas (Garrison & Cooper, 1999; Gutiérrez, 2002; Lager, 2006; Schleppegrell, 2007). Teachers prompt students to articulate their various problem-solving strategies when they ask effective questions, which can also create a cross-pollination of ideas (Bresser, 2003). By engaging in shared dialogue, students begin to build computational fluency and become flexible problem solvers.

What happens, however, when ELL students are expected to communicate mathematical ideas in English? English language learners can become confused by the various meanings of mathematics terms. For instance, terms such as *table, column, whole,* and *sum* have different meanings in math usage versus everyday usage. Similarly, mathematical operations can be expressed using a variety of terms, such as *plus, and, add, sum,* and *combine.* Even a simple word such as *left,* as in "How many are left?" can be confusing for ELLs, given the commonly used directional meaning of the word, as in "Stay to the left" and "Raise your left hand." A symbolic statement, such as $12 - 7 = 5$, can be expressed verbally in several ways, such as "Seven from twelve leaves five" and "Twelve take away seven is five." Teachers must be keenly aware of these differences in having mathematical conversations with ELLs.

Participating in mathematical discussions can also help ELLs become flexible problem solvers. Such discussions make students aware of the numerous strategies for finding an answer. When these discussions involve ELLs, teachers must provide extra support. That support can be provided by creating a safe environment for expressing ideas, **modeling** mathematical talk, asking questions and using prompts, providing mathematics games that have students converse in small groups, and moderating discussions to make sure that the talk is productive and focused on mathematics (Bresser, 2003). When teachers facilitate productive talk during math classes, they accomplish two valuable goals: computational fluency and English language development.

Consider what is involved for an ELL student to solve a word problem. Here is a typical problem that students encounter on state tests:

> The Usman School plans to have the school library carpeted. The room is in the shape of a rectangle and measures 20 feet by 28 feet. The carpet costs $22.50 per square yard, including installation. Determine how much it will cost to have the library carpeted.

For a student to solve this problem, he or she must recognize that because the carpet is priced by the square yard, the measurements in feet need to be converted to yards (by dividing by three). Then, to find the total square yardage of the library floor, the student must multiply the two dimensions of the room (base times height). Finally, to find the cost, the student must multiply the square yardage of the floor by the cost of the carpet.

All these calculations involve just the math concepts. A student who is an English language learner must also understand that having a room *carpeted* means "putting down a rug that covers the total area of a room." The student must also understand that the word *installation* means "the act of setting up or putting in something"—in this case, carpet.

Students need to read and understand three types of vocabulary:

1. *Math* vocabulary, including terms such as *square yard* and *rectangle*

2. *Procedural* vocabulary, including terms such as *determine, explain, calculate, sketch a graph,* and *show your work*

3. *Descriptive* vocabulary, including terms such as *installation,* which test writers use to provide a context for math problems (DiGisi & Fleming, 2005)

Students also need to know strategies that can help them read the complex questions that often appear in word problems. These multistep questions ask students to apply their mathematical understanding and require demonstrating several math skills.

In addition, ELLs need to know how to show their work on open-response questions in order to get full credit. For example, in problems that say "Explain your answer" and "Show your work," students need to know that getting full credit requires labeling all their work, describing the steps they used to solve the problem, and clearly identifying their answer. They do not have to write complete sentences. This is critical for ELLs who have a good understanding of math concepts but not the necessary academic math vocabulary in English.

Math teachers should design their courses to meet these three goals:

1. To teach students to recognize the types of vocabulary used in math questions and to reinforce that vocabulary

2. To provide students with strategies for reading math problems and questions and determining what they need to do

3. To give students practice in explaining their thought processes and showing their work (DiGisi & Fleming, 2005)

One helpful strategy for teaching math vocabulary is to post academic math terms on the wall, where students can refer to them. Students are accustomed to seeing so-called word walls in elementary school and will also find them helpful at the secondary level. In addition, math teachers can encourage students to label all their answers, so they will be familiar with saying, writing, and reading words such as *square feet, calculations,* and *equation.* Students can also write math reflections, in which they describe their understanding of concepts, such as interior angles, the area of a parallelogram, and positive and negative integers. This type of writing helps students develop and practice math vocabulary.

English language learners need to be taught procedural words, which are not essential for solving math problems. Knowing the meanings of words such as *estimate, compute, describe,* and *sketch* is critical to understanding and solving math problems, as well as problems in science and social studies. Showing and explaining examples of students' handwritten solutions, which reflect a range of scores, allows ELLs to see what a complete answer looks like. Answering language- and math-specific questions slowly also ensures that students understand each step.

Students who are new to American culture may be unfamiliar with descriptive words, such as *granola bars, carpet, bounce,* and *balloons,* which are meant to make math questions interesting but are not essential to solving them (DiGisi & Fleming, 2005). Students can answer a question like "Make a *bar* graph that shows the number of granola *bars* each student ate" even if they do not know the meaning of *granola bars.* Students can cover up the words *granola bars* and realize that if they understood the question is asking them to compare quantities by making a graph, they can answer it. Similarly, when a question mentions *a box of granola bars,* students can skip the word *granola* and still solve the problem.

Students become empowered when they realize they do not have to skip a question just because they do not understand every word in it. To reinforce this strategy, teachers and students can practice reading problems and crossing out those words that are unnecessary for producing a solution. Another strategy is to look for **cognates,** which are words that have similar sounds and spellings in English and other languages.

Teachers should reiterate to students that they must be aware of the units of measurement in a problem. Doing so will remind them that they may need to do conversions, such as changing feet to yards. Since many math problems require students to work through a progression of steps, students should also be encouraged to read every problem at least twice.

Teaching students to visualize what the problem is asking can be very helpful, as well. For example, if a problem involves a square that measures 8″ × 8″, the teacher can make such a square out of construction paper so students can see the size. If a problem involves determining the perimeter of a football field, students can draw a field on paper and write in the measurements. Teaching students to create a table out of the information provided in a problem can also help clarify what is being asked.

All these techniques help students realize that they have to read actively and think about the parts of the problem, even though it may contain only a few sentences.

Algebra—Inequalities

Vocabulary

inequality	disjunction	conjunction	at least
at most	fewer than	no more than	no less than
compound inequality	compound sentence		

Summary

1. Inequalities are solved just like equations. When the coefficient of the variable (i.e., the number in front of the variable) is negative, everything is multiplied (or divided) by that negative number. For example, consider the equality $-4x < 12$. To determine x, divide each side by -4 or multiply each side by $-1/4$. The solution is $x < -3$. If the coefficient is negative and the variable is positive, do not change the $<$ or $>$ sign: $5 + x > 4x > -1$.

2. A compound sentence is two sentences rewritten as one using *and* or *or*.
   A conjunction is a compound sentence using *and*.
   In a true conjunction, *both statements are true*.

$$3 + 3 = 6 \text{ and } 7 - 2 = 5$$

   In a false conjunction, *one or both statements are false*.
   A disjunction is a compound sentence using *or*.

$$3 + 3 = 6 \text{ or } 7 - 2 = 5$$
$$3 + 3 = 6 \text{ or } 7 - 2 = 8$$

   A disjunction is true if *one or both statements are true*.
   A compound inequality can have either *and* or *or*.

$$r > 4 \text{ and } r < 15$$

   This inequality can also be written as $4 < r < 15$. This means r is between 4 and 15. Here is a compound inequality that uses *or:*

$$r > 2 \text{ or } r < -8$$

   It is not possible for r to be both greater than 2 and less than -8, so one or the other is true. This means r is not between -8 and 2.

3. If an inequality has an absolute value, two answers can sometimes be determined. Two inequalities must be solved for absolute value problems:

$$|x| > 3$$
$$x > 3 \text{ or } x < -3$$

   If the symbol in the original problem is $<$ or $\leq$, then the word to be selected is *and*. If the symbol in the original problem is $>$ or $\geq$, then the word to be selected is *or*. Here is another example:

$$|x + 2| > 4$$
$$x + 2 > 4x + 2 < -4$$

   There are two answers: $x > 2$ or $x < -6$. It is impossible for x to be both greater than 2 and less than -6, so the answer is a disjunction: x is greater than 2 or x is less than -6.

4. If the absolute value is equal to a number, solve two equations. Both answers are correct:

$$|x + 3| = 5$$
$$x + 3 = 5 \quad x + 3 = -5$$
$$x = 2 \quad x = -8$$

Word Bingo

Write the vocabulary words on the board. Choose vocabulary words from the unit summary or from students' classroom texts. Be sure to coordinate the Bingo vocabulary with the material you will be reading to students. You can also include words from previous lessons.

Give each student a blank card with as many squares as there are vocabulary words on the board. Have students write the words anywhere on the card, one word per space. Each card should look different.

Here are some vocabulary words for this topic:

just like	at least	at most	except when
compound inequality	variable is	everything	do not change
true conjunction	false conjunction	compound sentence	are true
could have	greater than	less than	conjunction
disjunction	fewer than	inequality	not less than

Dictation

Tell students to write the sentences using words instead of symbols:

1. Five is less than nine.
2. *x* is no more than four.
3. *y* is at most twenty-three.
4. *z* is greater than five and less than nineteen.
5. *a* is at least one.

Prereading

Use the paragraph below for the prereading text:

Inequalities can sometimes be solved like equations. A compound sentence is two sentences rewritten as one. A conjunction is a compound sentence using *and*. A disjunction is a compound sentence using *or*. A compound sentence in math can have equations or inequalities. Absolute value equations and inequalities may have two answers. Knowing how to solve problems with more than one answer helps us use math in everyday life.

Persuasive Writing

In this writing activity, remind students to budget their time. Using the **process writing** approach, they should spend approximately 10 minutes on brainstorming and prewriting, 20 minutes on drafting, and 10 minutes on editing. Record the time and give students the command to begin.

Here is a sample prompt:

Usually, everyone likes to have more of something. Before you begin writing, think about what you want less of.

Wrong Word

Have students identify and correct the wrong words in these sentences:

1. A conjunction is a compound sentence using *or*.
2. A disjunction is a compound sentence using *and*.
3. A compound inequality can have *and* or *but*.
4. In an absolute value equation, there can be three answers.
5. *At least* and *no more than* mean the same thing.

(continued)

Jeopardy

Set up the game chart using this information:

Answer	**Question**
$3 < x < 10$	What is a compound inequality?
Five is less than 10, and 10 is equal to two.	What is a compound sentence?
$y \leq 2$	How is "No more than 2" expressed?
$x = 8$ and $x < 9$	What is a true conjunction?
$|x| = 3$	How is "$x = 3$ and $x = -3$" expressed?

Fill in the Blanks

Have student use these words to fill in the blanks in the statements below:

one   both   inequalities   disjunction   conjunction   equalities   rewritten

1. _____ can sometimes be solved like equations.
2. A compound sentence is two sentences _____ as one.
3. A _____ is a compound sentence using *and*.
4. A _____ is a compound sentence using *or*.
5. A compound sentence in math can have _____ or inequalities.
6. In a true conjunction, _____ sentences are true.
7. In a false conjunction, _____ or both sentences are false.

True/False

Ask students to indicate if each of the following statements is true (T) or false (F). Then ask students to correct each false statement, rewriting it on the line provided.

_____ 1. Inequalities are solved like equations except when the variable is *x*.

_____

_____ 2. This is a compound sentence: "We have one dog. We have two cats."

_____

_____ 3. Fifty-four is greater than forty-five and less than nineteen.

_____

_____ 4. Absolute value equations and inequalities may have many answers.

_____

_____ 5. A disjunction is a compound sentence using *and*.

_____

Source: www.palmbeach.k12.fl.us.

Graphic Organizers for Math

Figures 6.3, 6.4, and 6.5 are graphic organizers that can be used in math activities. Figure 6.3, a sample of the Frayer model organizer, can be used with ELLs to build background knowledge. Figure 6.4 is a grid students can use to plot points and make graphs. Figure 6.5 is a sample math task cube.

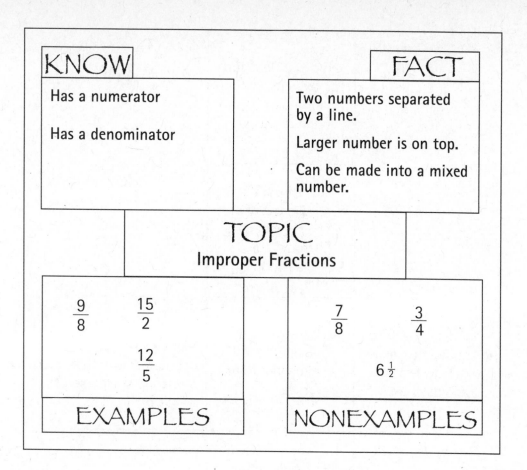

Figure 6.3 Sample of the Frayer Model Organizer

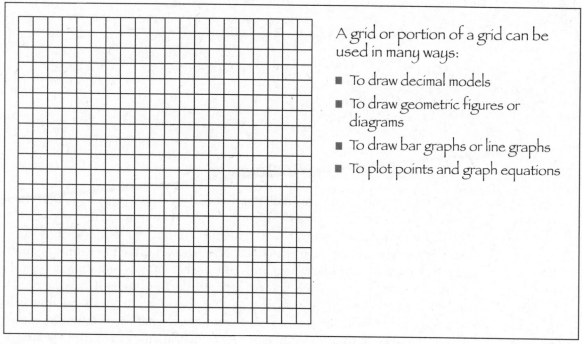

A grid or portion of a grid can be used in many ways:

- To draw decimal models
- To draw geometric figures or diagrams
- To draw bar graphs or line graphs
- To plot points and graph equations

Figure 6.4 Sample Grid

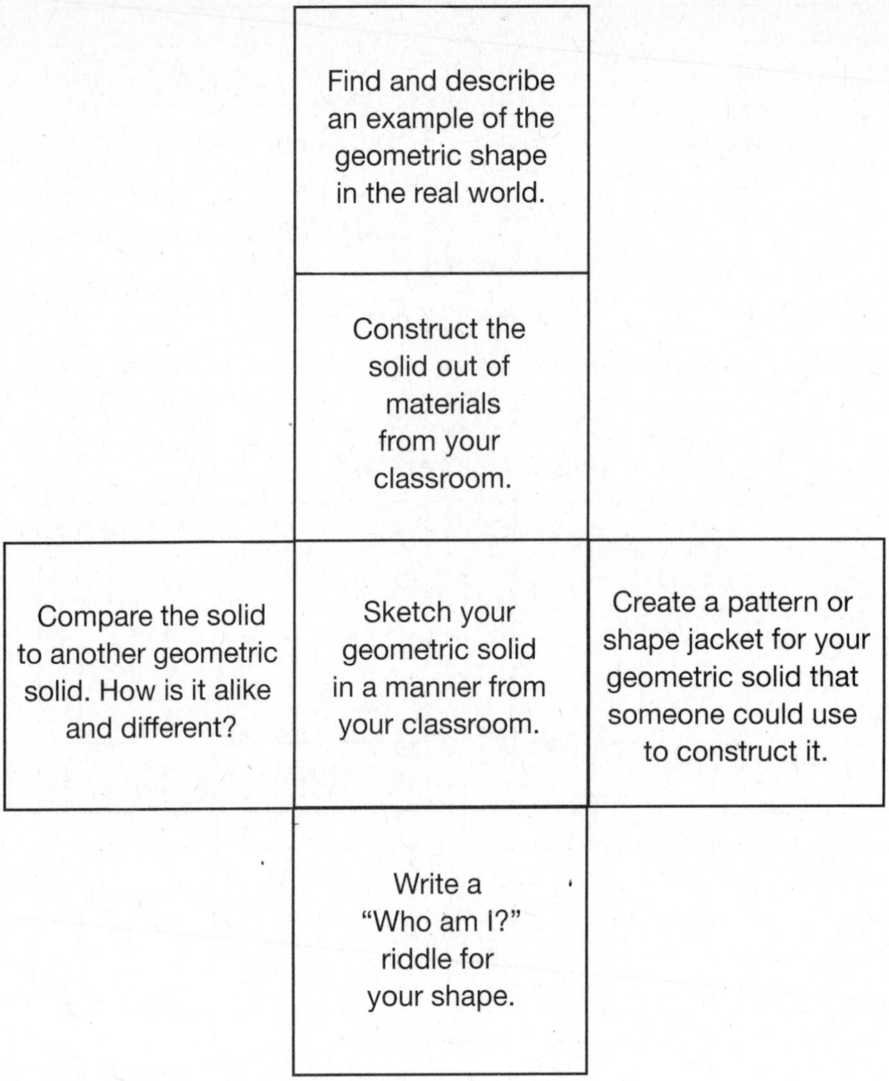

Find and describe an example of the geometric shape in the real world.

Construct the solid out of materials from your classroom.

Compare the solid to another geometric solid. How is it alike and different?

Sketch your geometric solid in a manner from your classroom.

Create a pattern or shape jacket for your geometric solid that someone could use to construct it.

Write a "Who am I?" riddle for your shape.

Figure 6.5 Sample Math Task Cube

Source: Turville, 2007.

Challenges for ELLs in Science

Several aspects of science are challenging for ELLs. One difficulty is that the language used to explain specific scientific terms is complex. The use of terms such as *formulate, categorize, rearrange,* and *separate* compounds ELLs' difficulty in understanding scientific concepts. A second difficulty is that many ELLs lack background knowledge in science. They may be unfamiliar with the nature of scientific procedures and equipment. Finally, students may face cultural challenges. For instance, what might be considered a hands-on approach in an American classroom might be different from what they recognize. Similarly, drawing conclusions on their own may be difficult for ELLs. In their native cultures, students may not have been trained to make guesses.

Displaying scientific equipment in class will help make science more relevant and comprehensible for ELLs, who may have limited background knowledge and experience in science.

English language learners may face these challenges when studying science:

■ Science vocabulary presents difficulties. Even some simple words may have alternative meanings in science—for example, *volume* to mean both "measurement" and "level of sound."

■ Material is covered too rapidly for some students.

■ Directions are often complicated and have multiple steps.

■ Science textbooks are often *text heavy.* In addition, they are often written in the passive voice and use complex sentence structures.

■ Diagrams and other visuals in texts and other materials may be complex and difficult to understand.

■ Work is often done with partners or in groups, to which students may be unaccustomed.

■ Science labs, equipment, and procedures (including the scientific method) may be unfamiliar to students (Haynes & O'Loughlin, 2003).

Adaptations in Science Instruction

In the science classroom, the teacher should create a low-anxiety environment. In such a classroom, students will be encouraged to use language freely and take risks, making errors and mistakes in their work as scientists. Students should know that in science, as in language, making mistakes is part of the learning process. In fact, errors in scientific work have led to major discoveries.

Here are some suggested adaptations for teaching science to ELLs:

- Use supplementary textbooks written at a simpler level, along with books about science written in students' native languages.
- Explicitly teach scientific vocabulary and make connections among concepts.
- Clarify how some words have different meanings in different contexts.
- Build vocabulary by playing word games.
- Allow students to use visual and native language dictionaries.
- Explicitly teach how to use the textbook with activities such as *Text Quests*.
- Model how scientific writing is different from other writing.
- Provide charts of the steps to follow in conducting experiments and writing reports.
- Model how to describe observations orally.
- Have students create diagrams of the steps followed after observing an experiment or demonstration (Balderrama & Diaz-Rico, 2006).

Teaching Science to ELLs

Initiatives for the reform of science education promote a vision of science for all students. The National Science Teachers Association (NSTA, 2006) asserts that all students, including those identified as ELLs, can and should have every opportunity to learn and succeed in science. Teachers play a critical and central role in this process; it is important for school systems to devote time and resources to effective professional development for all K–12 teachers of science, including those who teach ELLs. However, research indicates that many science teachers have not developed the teaching strategies needed to support the learning of ELLs in **mainstream classes**.

In one study, Sandefur, Watson, and Johnston (2007) considered literacy development, the science curriculum, and adolescent ELLs. These researchers constructed a "top 10" list of literacy strategies to support ELL students' academic development in the science classroom. One of the recommended strategies is Trade the textbooks for trade books. Well-written picture books, containing diagrams that focus on science, are appealing to adolescent learners due to their outstanding photography and easy-to-read text. Another recommended strategy is to "frontload" the reading event. As discussed elsewhere, this is synonymous to *Teaching the Text Backward* (see Chapter 1). Using a graphic organizer, students can chunk the information from the text into shorter, more manageable pieces. They can then share the information with others in the group and collectively build background knowledge. Two other strategies—"Name that text structure" and "Death to the questions at the end of the chapter and other worksheet-like activities"—involve exercises that assist students in comprehending the text when used with a graphic organizer such as *What Does Your Textbook Say?* or *Compare and Contrast*. Answering end-of-the-chapter questions is of limited value, considering that there are far more real-world, authentic writing situations students could experience, such as writing in a learning log or recording ideas and questions on sticky notes while reading through the text. Teachers' and students' use of these strategies provides **scaffolding**, helping ELLs achieve independence and enriching the print experiences of mainstream students.

A report prepared by Janzen (2008) discusses a long-term project called Chèche Konnen, which means "search for knowledge" in Hatian **Creole**. The goal of Chèche Konnen is to provide ELLs access to science learning by engaging them in authentic science activities. As described by Rosebery, Warren, and Conant (1992), scientists pose their own questions; plan and implement research to explore their questions; build and revise theories; collect, analyze, and interpret data; and draw conclusions and make decisions based on their research.

In one example of the work of Chèche Konnen, Hudicourt-Barnes (2003) describes the discussion in a middle school classroom in which students make use of a Haitian style of conversation called *bay odyans*. In bay odyans, one participant begins with a statement; another challenges the statement, often in a dramatic manner designed to entertain listeners; and then the two argue. Hudicourt-Barnes suggests that when a particular style of bay odyans known as *diskisyon* is used in the classroom, the teacher does not act as the single source of information about science. Moreover, students can use their communication skills to expand their understanding in ways that resemble the behaviors of practicing scientists.

Research by Buck, Mast, Ehlers, and Franklin (2005) has identified three strategies found effective in creating a mainstream science classroom conducive to the needs of ELLs:

1. *Authentic visuals:* The use of pictures, books, and other graphics creates an authentic context that does not depend heavily on language. The use of these visuals also provides students with a variety of cues within activities. In the research, one particularly effective activity involved the use of models of human bones, which were exact replicas, along with picture books of bones. In this research project, the average grade for ELLs on the subsequent assessment was a B, which was the same average grade for the non-ELLs. In this study, the concepts conveyed via authentic visuals were mentioned by students in the interview process and were most often responded to correctly on classroom-based assessments of ELLs (Buck et al., 2005).

2. *Hands-on activities:* English language learners benefit from doing hands-on activities in which students are involved in the planning. Researchers' initial observations verified that ELLs were actively engaged during the time spent in hands-on activities; in contrast, students were mostly engaged in off-task behavior during the time the teacher spent on an overhead (Buck et al., 2005).

3. *Cooperative learning groups:* Researchers found that establishing workable **cooperative learning** groups was the most effective method for ensuring learning by ELLs. However, using cooperative learning groups required a lot of time in planning and organizing materials. To produce maximum learning in these groups, rules and roles must be established and practiced regularly (Buck et al., 2005).

Strategies found ineffective for ELLs included the use of symbolic visuals, complex games, and a demonstration of notetaking using an overhead. In one section of students with whom the notetaking demonstration was used extensively, the average test score for non-ELLs was B+ and for ELLs, D– (Buck et al., 2005).

An important outcome of the Buck et al. (2005) study was that non-ELLs increased their understanding of course objectives in a classroom that was actively being restructured to better meet the needs of the ELLs. This outcome demonstrates that the measures taken to create more inclusive classrooms are not detrimental to nontargeted, non-ELL students. Clearly, this is an important consideration when including ELLs in mainstream classrooms.

Biology I—Viruses, Monorans, and Protists

Vocabulary

host	moneran	protozoan	insect
nitrogen	immune system	nonliving	recycle
fission	parasite	algae	bacteria
virus	mitosis	antibiotics	plankton

Summary

Viruses: Viruses are things that can damage or kill organisms, but they are not classified into any kingdom. Many biologists do not consider viruses living things. Viruses are considered parasites. They use the living cells and damage them. They need a host cell for reproduction. There are many viral diseases that affect our lives. Viruses can be spread in many ways. Some are carried by insects. Others are found on food or in water. Many viruses can become airborne. Many viral diseases can be prevented with vaccines. There are now vaccines for many diseases, and scientists are working to develop more.

Monerans: The kingdom Monera includes the oldest and most common organisms on Earth: bacteria. Bacteria do not have a nucleus protecting their DNA, making them prokaryotic. Monerans carry out all the processes of living things. Some bacteria are producers, some are consumers, and many are decomposers. Bacteria that are decomposers are some of Earth's best recyclers. When an animal dies, bacteria break down the body into useable parts, such as nitrogen, carbon dioxide, and minerals. Many bacteria are helpful. Bacteria reproduce by a process called *binary fission.* Bacteria can also reproduce by way of *conjugation.* When bacteria get bigger, they can reproduce again. Most food spoilage is caused by bacteria. Bacteria are found everywhere. They can be in the air, in the water, and on food.

Protists: The kingdom Protista contains a wide variety of organisms. It is the classification for organisms that do not fit in any other kingdom. All protists have nuclei. Some protists are unicellular, and some are multicellular. Some protists are like plants, some are like animals, and others are like fungi. Plantlike protists are called *algae.* Animal-like protists are called *protozoans.* Examples of protozoans are amoebas and paramecium. Most protozoans live in the water, eating bacteria, plankton, and other organic matter. Many human diseases, including malaria, are caused by protozoans.

Word Bingo

Write the vocabulary words on the board. Choose vocabulary words from the unit summary or from students' classroom texts. Be sure to coordinate the Bingo vocabulary with the material you will be reading to students. You can also include words from previous lessons.

Give each student a blank card with as many squares as there are vocabulary words on the board. Have students write the words anywhere on the card, one word per space. Each card should look different.

The following sample Bingo vocabulary words are from the unit summary:

organisms	processes	parasites	plankton
bacteria	airborne	protozoans	human
viral diseases	algae	amoebas	kingdom
reproduce	useable	vaccines	prevented
similar	paramecium	organic matter	
biologists	binary fission	multicellular	
damage	decomposers	insects	

Team Spelling Test

Use the following words for the test. Give students the singular form, and have them write the plural form.

virus	viruses	phyla	phylum
fungus	fungi	bacterium	bacteria
flagellum	flagella	symbiosis	symbioses
colony	colonies	cilium	cilia
paramecium	paramecia	category	categories

Interview

You are to play the role of a bacterium. Have the student interviewers ask you these questions:

1. What are you? (bacterium)

2. How can you be helpful to humans? (help to produce foods and medicines)

3. What else do you do? (break down pollutants)

4. What are some of the bad things you can do? (spoil food, poison water, cause disease)

5. What important jobs do you have? (acting as a decomposer and assisting in the breaking down and recycling of dead matter)

Prereading

Use the paragraph below for the prereading text:

Viruses are things that can damage or kill organisms. Biologists do not consider viruses living things. There are many viral diseases that affect people, animals, and plants. Vaccines have been developed to prevent some of these diseases.

The kingdom Monerans includes bacteria. Some bacteria are producers, some are consumers, and some are decomposers. Many bacteria are helpful in the preparation of foods and medicines. Some are harmful, causing food to spoil.

Protists have a nucleus. Some are animal-like and some are plant-like. Algae are plant-like protists. Protozoans are animal-like protists. Protozoans cause diseases.

(continued)

Opinion/Proof

Allow teams of students to write their own opinions and support them with proofs. Share this example:

Opinion	*Proof*
Bacteria are very helpful.	Some are decomposers that recycle dead matter into useable parts.
	Some flavor food and help in the production of foods.
	Some are used in industry.
	Some help clean up oil spills in the ocean.

Wrong Word

Have students identify and correct the wrong words in these sentences:

1. Viruses are considered living because they do not need energy.
2. Many common diseases are caused by vaccines.
3. Bacteria help in the cooking of food.
4. The process of heating milk before packaging is called *refrigeration.*
5. Most protozoans live in the air and eat bacteria, plankton, and other organic matter.

Jeopardy

Set up the game chart using this information:

Answer	*Question*
Viruses	What are things that can kill or damage organisms called?
Bacteria	What are the oldest and most common organisms called?
Algae	What are plantlike protists called?
Host cell	What do viruses need for reproduction?
Binary fission	How do bacteria reproduce?

Classification

Ask students to classify items under the following headings:

Monerans	*Protists*	*Diseases*
bacteria	algae	dysentery

Making Sense

Working in teams, have students write statements using the sets of information you provide. For example, using this information—Viruses/things/can damage/kill/organisms—students will write a statement such as this:

Viruses are things that can damage or kill organisms.

Here are additional sets of information:

1. Vaccines/made from/viruses/ reproduce
2. Bacteria/decomposers/break down/dead matter/recycle/parts
3. Refrigeration/cooking/slows down/ destroys/bacteria
4. Algae/plantlike releases/oxygen/found/environment
5. Protist/reproduce/process/mitosis/make copies/itself

Practice/Reading Comprehension

Have students reread the summary at the end of a section or chapter in their textbook. As they read, have them locate sentences that are fact and sentences that express an opinion. Here is an example of each:

Fact: Bacteria are producers, consumers, and decomposers.

Opinion: Bacteria are helpful.

Ask students to find five sentences that are fact and five that are opinion and write them on the lines below.

Fact

_____

_____

Opinion

_____

_____

Source: www.palmbeach.k12.fl.us.

Graphic Organizers for Science

Figures 6.2 to 6.4, and Figures 6.6 through 6.10 are samples of graphic organizers that can be used with science content. These tools are effective because they allow ELLs to chunk the significant information, which can be placed in a **portfolio** and referred to during independent work. Charting, graphing, and illustrating information helps students focus on key content in a visual manner, avoiding linguistic complexity.

Matrix grids have wide application (see Figure 6.6). They are used to visually compare key variables across several categories—for instance, to compare characteristics or qualities or a set of substances. A matrix can be filled in with plus or minus signs, number denoting specific amounts or percentages, or short descriptive words.

Figure 6.7 is a sample of a RAFT chart. The acronym RAFT stands for Role, Audience, Format, and Topic (Santa, 1988). Originally used for writing assignments in the language arts, the RAFT format has been adopted by those

Specimen	Luster	Cleavage	Hardness	Color
A				
B				
C				

Figure 6.6   Sample Matrix Grid

Insect Life Cycle

Role	Audience	Format	Topic
Egg	Adults	Create a poem	I've got potentiality!
Larva	Other larva	Create a short play	I don't want to grow up!
Adult	Larva	Develop a chart	I'm tired of all this responsibility!
Pupa	Adults	Write a song or rap	Please release me, let me go!

Figure 6.7   Sample RAFT Chart

Observations in Science

What can you tell me about _____?

What is it?	From what material is it made: wood, plastic?	Color	Shape	Size	Weight	Measurement	Living or nonliving

Figure 6.8   Sample Observations Organizer

who teach differentiated instruction. It provides choices for students and can be formatted so the choices are more engaging. RAFT charts can be particularly effective in helping students explore various points of view.

Figure 6.8 is a sample of an Observations Organizer, which students can complete and then place in their portfolios or science notebooks for future reference. Students can complete several of these organizers to document observations of several items; this collection of data can then be used to complete a Compare/Contrast Organizer (see Figure 6.9).

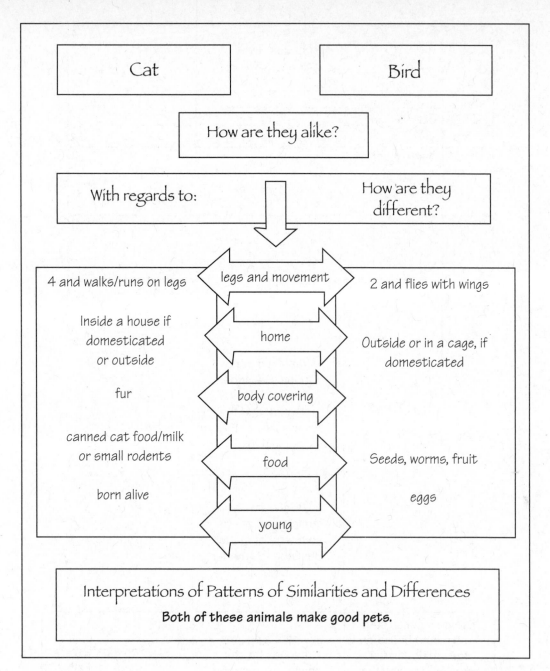

Cat		Bird

How are they alike?

With regards to:		How are they different?
4 and walks/runs on legs	legs and movement	2 and flies with wings
Inside a house if domesticated or outside	home	Outside or in a cage, if domesticated
fur	body covering	
canned cat food/milk or small rodents	food	Seeds, worms, fruit
born alive		eggs
	young	

Interpretations of Patterns of Similarities and Differences
Both of these animals make good pets.

Figure 6.9 Sample Compare/Contrast Organizer

Figure 6.10 shows a sample tool students can use in doing research. Two cards can fit on one notebook page. This organizer, like most of the sample graphic organizers in this book, can be used in the other content areas, not just science.

Figure 6.11 is a sample of a science task cube. It can be used to elicit ELLs' creative perspectives in learning content by exercising the different learning channels, or modalities, by which students learn and develop long-term comprehension.

RESEARCH
Source Card
(Book, Magazine, Website)

Author _____

Title: _____

Publication Name & Date _____
  Or Website

Notes in your own words:

Quotes:

Figure 6.10

Sample Research
Organizer

	Create a song or rap that describes the type of matter selected, and the movement of the molecules.
	Write a birth announcement for your type of matter. Describe the matter in detail.
Create a comic strip with a hero based on the type of matter selected. Be sure that your comic strip discusses the movement of the molecules in that state.	Create a play or reader's theater based on your type of matter. Tell about your molecular movement.
	Write a "Who am I?" riddle for your kind of matter.

Design a pattern or "shape jacket" for the type of matter.

Figure 6.11

Sample Science
Task Cube

Challenges for ELLs in Social Studies

Social studies and U.S. history provide overwhelming challenges to ELLs. The primary challenge is that these students have limited background knowledge of the United States and its history, geography, and current events. Many students will memorize information for a test, but because the information has no relevance for them, they will quickly forget it.

The language of social studies also poses a challenge for ELLs. Schleppegrell, Achugar, and Orteiza (2004) recommend that social studies teachers explicitly teach ELLs the grammatical features of history language to develop their proficiency in reading and writing. In one example of applying this recommendation, the researchers explain how students can be taught to identify different types of verbs while reading textbook passages. The researchers connect this analysis to the critical questions teachers and students ask in history classes—for instance, Whose views are presented in the text?, What are those views?, and Do the individuals agree or disagree?

English language learners face these difficulties when studying social studies:

- Students cannot apply higher-order thinking skills for reading and writing.

- Students are not familiar with vocabulary about historical events, government processes, and so on.

- Social studies textbooks often contain complex sentences, are written in the passive voice, and make extensive use of pronouns.

- Students may not be accustomed to voicing their personal opinions.

- Concepts such as privacy, democracy, rights of citizens, and free will may not exist in students' native cultures.

- Students may not understand the concept of movement within the socioeconomic and political structures in American society.

- Students are unaccustomed to being asked to state an alternate view about conditions in another country.

Having students work in small groups is an effective approach to social studies instruction, as it encourages peer interaction, critical thinking, and the use of both social and academic English.

- The American approach of teaching history as a timeline of events may be foreign to students who have learned history by studying dynasties or periods (Haynes & O'Loughlin, 2003).

Adaptations in Social Studies Instruction

Social studies is a rich area of study, as its concepts are rooted in history, civics, philosophy, economics, anthropology, sociology, and political science. The social studies curriculum thus requires a high level of literacy and depends a great deal on language. Unfortunately, the language in many textbooks is not **contextualized,** and the way topics are presented at the secondary level does not often reflect ELLs' personal experiences (Balderrama & Diaz-Rico, 2006). History poses particular challenges to ELLs and requires teachers to adapt and illustrate the information that native English speakers know from their everyday experiences of living in the United States.

Social studies textbooks are vocabulary heavy. They are replete with specialized language, including not only terms about historical events and government processes but also many names of people and places. Examples of low-frequency vocabulary terms include *proletariat* and *oligarchy* in world history and *carpetbagger* and *antebellum* in U.S. history. Reading history texts is difficult even for native English speakers, because the materials contain long sentences with multiple embedded clauses. Other challenges for ELLs include their lack of prior exposure to the elementary school social studies curriculum and their lack of a rudimentary understanding of the cultural context in which social studies knowledge is constructed (Haynes & O'Loughlin, 2003).

The challenge faced by high school social studies teachers, who derive their content from a range of academic areas, is to reduce the **cognitive demand,** or load. Finding ways of doing so without "dumbing down" the content can be particularly challenging.

Here are some suggestions for adapting social studies instruction for ELLs:

- Re-enact historical events using role-playing, which is appealing to adolescents.

- Use collaborative projects and assignments, in which students solve problems together as they use content-related vocabulary in a low-anxiety environment.

- Have students write "What If?" stories, in which they use language to make predictions about history or suggest how the course of history might have had a different outcome.

- Present information in alternative formats, such as graphic organizers, maps, tables, charts, and graphs. Doing so identifies key concepts, reduces the level of verbiage, and models the different means historians use to gather evidence.

- Engage students in practicing metacognitive skills, such as knowing how and where to find information in the text by using *Text Quests*.

- Incorporate movies, news clips, and video streams that reflect actual events in history (Balderrama & Diaz-Rico, 2006).

Making Social Studies Meaningful to ELLs

A study conducted by Ahmad and Szpara (2006) focused on how to develop an effective learning environment for teaching secondary-level social studies to a sheltered population of ELLs. These researchers proposed a three-part approach to meeting the needs of ELLs in mainstream classes in social studies:

1. Provide social and cultural supports during students' process of **acculturation.**

2. Provide explicit instruction in the academic strategies necessary for successful comprehension of in-depth content.

3. Make the social studies curriculum more accessible through a range of strategies for reducing cognitive load without reducing content.

Compared to the other content areas, math and science, the social studies present a second, uniquely embedded challenge for ELLs. As Ahmad and Szpara (2006) point out, not only are ELLs learning a new language and culture in the social studies classroom, but they are also learning a different interpretation of historical events, developing a different conception of government, and learning a different philosophy of citizenship.

Learning social studies lessons requires strong English language proficiency. Given this, ELLs may passively memorize facts and terms to pass a test. Doing so contributes little to their intellectual and social growth, however.

Cultural literacy also poses a unique challenge for both ELL teachers and students in the social studies classroom (Ahmad & Szpara, 2006). Newcomers to the United States are not familiar with the rituals of their newly adopted culture. However, the social studies curriculum is inherently culture specific. Mainstream social studies classes discuss topics that native-born American students have been studying since the elementary grades. It may not be accurate to assume that ELLs have no prior knowledge about the United States. However, it is reasonable to assume that ELLs' experiences with American culture may be potentially skewed, stemming from the views of their home cultures and educational systems.

The prior educational experiences of ELLs may not have prepared them for practices that are common and appropriate in a typical American history or government classroom, such as questioning authority, stating opinions without fear of reprisal, and asserting points of view on controversial issues. Students' lack of experience with these practices, combined with their lack of English verbal skills, may prevent them from expressing themselves openly or disagreeing with an authority figure, such as a teacher.

The National Council for the Social Studies (2008) suggests that social studies draw its content from the social sciences, natural sciences, and humanities and identifies several specific topics, such as the Bill of Rights, how a bill becomes law, voting and elections, foreign policy, and the role of the media. Students who were born and brought up in American society have been exposed to many of these topics, even before they entered elementary school, through the process of socialization. In contrast, ELLs who enter the U.S. educational system at the secondary level begin to learn basic facts about the U.S. government as teenagers. Many of these students belong to immigrant families that are just beginning to **assimilate** into the dominant culture. These families may not be prepared to provide the intellectual support their children need in completing social studies assignments.

Social studies teachers need to adapt the curriculum for their ELL students. Ways to reduce the cognitive load of social studies content are included in the list that follows.

- Incorporate primary source materials or realia, such as a copy of the U.S. Constitution, into instruction.

- As much as possible, provide students with linguistically lighter texts that correspond to the regular grade-level textbooks.

- Provide online newspapers in students' home languages, and have students compare their coverage of issues to the coverage in American newspapers.

- Start each lecture with an active review of the content, and end it with a summary of key points.

- Provide adequate wait-time after asking a question, allowing students a period of silence in which to understand what is being asked and to formulate a response.

- Try to avoid the use of colloquialisms, idioms, and slang. If they come up in the context of reading or discussion, explain their meanings.

- Encourage students to translate texts in class or in small groups. (Consult the website www.freetraslation.com for this purpose.) Also have students develop vocabulary lists over time.

- Condense high-level content to key information using bulleted lists, highlighted text, and so on.

- Use graphic organizers as much as possible to identify key content. Important information should be written down and emphasized to ensure students' understanding.

- Provide hands-on learning opportunities, such as taking surveys and enacting the TV news.

- Give demonstrations. For instance, show how a printing press works using stamps and an ink pad, or show how the system of checks and balances work in U.S. government by creating the same system in the classroom and debating the issue (Ahmad & Szpara, 2007).

Salinas, Franquiz, and Guberman (2006) report that student teachers used graphic organizers to help students make sense of questions and organize ideas about their conclusions. For example, in a unit on the role of women in social movements, after presenting a historical nineteenth-century photo and a contemporary photo of assembly line workers in the United States as pertinent primary sources, the teacher used a Venn diagram to record students' understanding of differences and similarities between the two time periods. (See the section on graphic organizers later in this chapter.) Also, the teacher provided the children's book *Si, Se Puede!* (*Yes, We Can!*), a bilingual story by Diana Cohn that is set against the backdrop of the successful Justice for Janitors strike in Los Angeles in 2000. Reading this story provided ELLs an opportunity to learn terms such as *rally, union,* and *strike,* which were unfamiliar to them.

In courses on world history, a lesson on roman numerals might be conducted as an anticipatory activity. English language learners will then understand this numbering system when they encounter Roman numerals in their reading. (Note the use of roman numerals in referring to Charles V and Philip II in the Summary section of the following lesson.)

World History—The Rise of Nations

Vocabulary

principle	defeat	limited constitutional monarchy
channel	monarch	throne
common law	parliament	inherit
constitution	divine right	Hapsburg

Summary

The Rise of Nation States (1500–1800 CE, or common era): A family of kings from Germany called the Hapsburgs took over most of Europe in the early 1500s. In 1516, a Hapsburg king named Charles V inherited the Spanish throne and was named the Holy Roman Emperor for all of Europe. Charles V also became king of the Netherlands (Holland), Germany, Hungary, and Italy. In 1556, Charles V gave Spain, the Netherlands, and Italy to his son Philip II. Charles gave Austria to his brother Ferdinand.

Philip II began many wars with other countries. He was defeated by England when many of his ships were sunk in the English Channel during a storm. With this defeat, Spain's power in Europe was weakened. By the early 1600s, most of the wars in Europe were over. France and England began developing strong national governments.

England formed a parliament. A *parliament* is a group of people who have the right to make laws and limit the power of the king. The English king had to have the permission of parliament to do many things. This is called a *limited constitutional monarchy*. The king ruled, but his power was limited by the English constitution. The English constitution was a collection of ideas, laws, principles, and common law.

At the same time, the French kings were becoming very powerful. The French people believed in the divine right of kings. They believed that God gave the French kings the right to rule. Louis XIV was the most powerful of the French kings. He did not call the Estates-General for advice or permission. The Estates-General was the same as the English parliament. After the death of Louis XIV, the power of the kings weakened and the people looked for ways to make the government stronger.

Follow Directions

Have each student write the following sentence on a sheet of paper:

In 1516, a Hapsburg king named Charles V inherited the Spanish throne and was named the Holy Roman Emperor for all of Europe.

Next, have students mark up the sentence by following these directions:

Directions:

1. Draw a circle ◯ around each noun (person, place, or thing).
2. Draw a box ☐ around the date.
3. Draw a <u>line</u> under the prepositional phrase.
4. Put a star ☆ over the king's title.
5. Write what kind of a sentence it is: declaration, question, or command.
6. Divide the sentence into two separate sentences.

(continued)

Interview

You are to play the role of Elizabeth I of England. Put together an interview committee of several students, and provide them with the questions below. Have students take turns asking the questions.

1. Where did you rule as queen and when? (England, 1558–1603)

2. For what was your reign known? (It was a great cultural period.)

3. Why? (Poets and writers praised Elizabeth, and the theaters thrived.)

4. Why did your people respect you? (I was interested in their welfare.)

5. What was it like being a queen in Europe surrounded by mainly kings? (It was difficult to be the only woman ruler among so many men.)

Wrong Word

Have students identify and correct the wrong words in these sentences:

1. Charles V was king of England.

2. Spain was defeated by France in the English Channel.

3. The French believed that Philip II gave kings the divine right to rule.

4. Louis XIV always called on the Estates-General for advice.

5. After the death of Louis XIV, the power of kings was stronger.

Jeopardy

Set up the game chart using this information:

Answer	*Question*
Charles V	Who was the first Hapsburg king?
Parliament	What kind of governing body did England develop to make laws?
Limited constitutional monarchy	What kind of government did England have?
Divine right of kings	On what idea did the French base their belief that kings had the right to rule?
God	From whom did the French think the kings' power came?

Sentence Builder

For each of the following items, help students build the sentence by adding the information provided in parentheses:

1. Philip II was defeated by England. (in the Channel)

   Philip II was defeated by England in the Channel. (Armada)

   Philip II's Armada was defeated by England in the Channel. (English)

   Philip II's Armada was defeated by England in the English Channel.

2. The parliament is a group of people. (English)

   The English parliament is a group of people. (who make laws)

   The English parliament is a group of people who make laws. (limit the power of kings)

   The English parliament is a group of people who make laws and limit the power of kings and/or queens.

3. Louis XIV did not call on the Estates-General. (the French king)

   The French king, Louis XIV, did not call on the Estates-General. (for advice)

   The French king, Louis XIV, did not call on the Estates-General for advice. (or permission)

   The French king, Louis XIV, did not call on the Estates-General for advice or permission.

Rewrite the Paragraph

Have students rewrite the following paragraph entirely in the past tense:

> The Hapsburgs take over most of Europe in the 1500s. Charles V inherits the throne of Spain and becomes the Holy Roman Emperor. He rules the Netherlands, Germany, Austria, Hungary, and Italy. His son Philip II sends a group of ships that he calls an Armada and fights England in 1888 CE. His ships sink, and Spain's power is weakened. Governments are becoming stronger. England forms a parliament to help make laws. France forms an Estates-General, but Louis XIV does not listen to them. He believes that his power comes from God and that he does not have to listen to the people.

True/False

Ask students to indicate if each of the following statements is true (T) or false (F). Then ask students to correct each false statement, rewriting it on the line provided.

_____ 1. A parliament is a group of people who teach the law.

_____

_____ 2. The family of kings from Germany were called the Germanias.

_____

_____ 3. Charles V inherited the throne of England.

_____

_____ 4. The Spanish Armada was sunk in a storm.

_____

_____ 5. Phillip II sent the armada to a war with England.

_____

(continued)

Sample Social Studies Lesson (continued)

Sentence Writing

Have students write a sentence using each of the following words. All the sentences should be written in future tense.

1. defeat

____

2. develop

____

3. make

____

4. limit

____

5. decide

____

Complete the Table

Create a table based on Figure 6.12 and distribute to students, one per student. Then review the following terms and descriptions. Have students place the letter of each term or description in the most appropriate place in the table.

A. Louis XIV
B. Spent too much on court ceremonies and left the country badly in debt
C. Versailles
D. Parliament
E. The Fronde, a series of uprisings by nobles and peasants in 1648 and 1653
F. A warm water port on the Black Sea
G. Seized her husband's throne and ruled as empress

MONARCHS	Person	Event	Place
Russian Tzars and Tzarinas			
French Monarchs			
British Monarchs			

Figure 6.12

Synonyms

Ask students to rewrite each of the following sentences by replacing the *italicized* word with a synonym. Students can also make other changes, as needed, for grammatical accuracy.

1. The Hapsburgs *came* from Germany.

_____

2. A government that *limits* the king's power is called a limited constitutional monarchy.

_____

3. The most *powerful* French king was Louis XIV.

_____

4. Philip II's armada was *destroyed* by a storm.

_____

5. After the death of Louis XIV, the power of kings *weakened*.

_____

Source: www.palmbeach.k12.fl.us.

Graphic Organizers for Social Studies

Figures 6.13, 6.14, and 6.15 are samples of graphic organizers that can be used, respectively, to identify people and places, to sequence and compare how concepts are alike and different, and to integrate parts of speech with social studies content.

Figure 6.15, the *What Does Your Textbook Say?* organizer, is used to record details about a picture in the chapter being studied. Students can consult their dictionaries to identify the subjects/nouns, pronouns, adjectives, verbs, and adverbs represented in the picture while using content area

Actors and Receivers

Actors	Action	Receiver/Goal
The colonies	Seceded	from England
The patriots	Fought the first battle	against the British in Lexington, MA

Figure 6.13 Sample Graphic Organizer

language. Then students can construct sentences using the words they identified, a task that incorporates the language arts. Not only can ELLs accomplish this activity, but doing it keeps them engaged with the content and using the same text as native English speakers. This aspect alone eliminates the negative effect on ELLs of having to use a more elementary text or doing a different activity from the native English speakers.

The value of the Venn diagram cannot be overestimated (see Figure 6.16). It is both versatile and capable of tapping higher-level thinking skills. It asks students to analyze and discern the similarities and differences of topics or concepts to judge their application.

Sequence Notes

Sequence notes are used to help you track a series of steps, stages, or events in a process.

1. In the first box, write what happens first in the process.
2. List the next steps in order in the next boxes.
3. In the last box, list the final step in the process or series.

Topic Title: The Cold War

The Korean War begins.
The Soviet Union and the United States develop missiles to carry nuclear weapons.

The Berlin Wall in Germany becomes a symbol of the cold war.
The Cuban missile crisis occurs.

The United Sates begins bombing North Vietnam and sends troops into battle in South Vietnam.
President Nixon visits China.

President Reagan and President Gorbachev sign a treaty limiting medium-range missile deployment.
The Soviet Union's communist government collapses.

Figure 6.14   Sample Sequence Notes Graphic Organizer

What Does Your Textbook Say?

Textbook page #_____ or Picture #_____

Using your dictionary, identify the items in the picture in your textbook.

Nouns or Subjects	Pronouns	Adjectives	Verbs	Adverbs

Use the words in the boxes to write three (3) sentences describing the picture.

1. _____

2. _____

3. _____

Figure 6.15   Sample *What Does Your Textbook Say?* Graphic Organizer

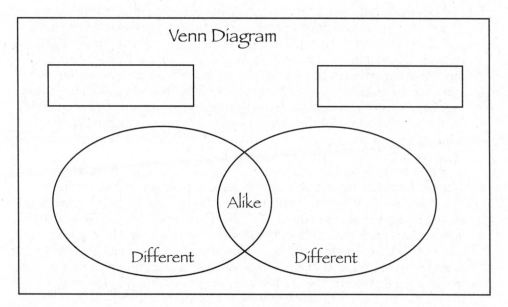

Venn Diagram

Alike

Different   Different

Figure 6.16   Sample Venn Diagram

Summary

Much of what has been discussed in this chapter can be summed up by the research of Janzen (2008):

> The language of academic texts, both the ones students read and the ones they produce, has distinctive features and meanings that may present a contrast to the language used in informal spoken **interaction; academic language** can also differ from one discipline to another. The academic uses of language as well as the meaning of individual words need to be explicitly taught for students to fulfill the genre or discourse requirements privileged in academic settings and to understand the material they encounter in, for example, history textbooks or mathematical word problems.
>
> Language can play a critical role in enabling students to reach deeper levels of comprehension in several other ways. When teachers ask students to articulate their thinking processes, share ideas in groups, or think through new ideas verbally or in writing, students are extending their engagement with and understanding of new information. The language of oral interaction does not necessarily have to be English, a point mentioned in the fields of math and elementary science teaching. Finally, as a prerequisite for instruction, teachers must thoroughly understand how the language of their disciplines construes meaning and must use academic language in clear and consistent ways in the classroom.
>
> A second theme, explicit instruction in cognitive behaviors such as learning or reading strategies, is less visible across the disciplines than are linguistic topics. A third theme, professional development, receives some attention in the literature. Several researchers have suggested that teachers need extended time for professional development so that they can achieve a variety of objectives: (a) learn about the language of their discipline in depth, (b) become accustomed to integrating language and content instruction, (c) understand their attitudes toward cultural diversity and their assumptions about ELLs, and (d) successfully adapt the knowledge base they acquired in training to actual teaching. A further challenge in the area of professional development is that content area teachers do not necessarily have either defined obligations or opportunities to learn about working with ELLs. In school settings, mechanisms may not exist for content area teachers to receive training, and, even when training occurs, teachers may not implement the **accommodations** they have learned about, as one investigation found (Brown & Bentley, 2004). Power differentials and different disciplinary epistemologies also prevent meaningful in-service cooperation between ESOL and content area teachers to the detriment of the students being served.
>
> Students at the middle and high school levels are less likely to receive targeted language instruction than are elementary school learners (Ruiz de Velasco & Fix, 2002). Moreover, the proportion of foreign-born immigrant children is greater in high school (7%) than elementary school, and it is at least probable that foreign-born children require more assistance in language learning than do U.S.-born children. More research can investigate how to assist teachers, administrators, and native-English-speaking students alike in viewing the presence of ELLs and their differing cultural practices as a resource, not simply as a problem to be dealt with or ignored.

References

Ahmad, I., & Szpara, M. (2006). Making social studies meaningful for ELL students: Content and pedagogy in mainstream secondary school classrooms. *Essays in Education, 16*, 1–14.

Ahmad, I., & Szpara, M. (2007). Supporting English language learners in social studies class: Results from a study of high school teachers. *Social Studies, 98*(5), 189–195.

Balderrama, M., & Diaz-Rico, L. (2006). *Teaching performance expectations for educating English learners*. Boston: Allyn & Bacon.

Bresser, R. (2003). Helping English-language learners develop computation fluency. *Teaching Children Mathematics, 9*(6), 294–299.

Brown, C. L., & Bentley, M. (2004). ELLs: Children left behind in science class. *Academic Exchange Quarterly, 8*(3), 152–158.

Buck, G., Mast, C., Ehlers, N., & Franklin, E. (2005). Preparing teachers to create a mainstream science classroom conducive to the needs of English-language learners: A feminist action research project. *Journal of Research in Science Teaching, 42*(9), 1013–1031.

DiGisi, L., & Fleming, D. (2005). Literacy specialists in math class! Closing the achievement gap on state math assessments. *Voices from the Middle, 13*(1), 48.

Garrison, L., & Mora, J. (1999). Adapting mathematics instruction for English language learners: The language-concept connections. In *Changing the faces of mathematics: Perspectives on Latinos* (pp. 35–48), Ortiz-Franco, L., G. Hernandez, & Y. De la Cruz (Eds.). Reston, VA: National Council of Teachers of Mathematics.

Gutiérrez, R. (2002). Beyond essentialism: The complexity of language in teaching mathematics to Latina/o students. *American Educational Research Journal, 39*(4), 1047–1088.

Haynes, J., & O'Loughlin, J. (2003). *Challenges for ELLs in content area learning*. Paper presented at the 2003 TESOL Annual Convention, March 25–29, Baltimore, MD. Available online at www.everythingesl.net/inservices/challenges_ells_content_area_l_65322.php

Hudicourt-Barnes, J. (2003). The use of argumentation in Haitian Creole science classrooms. *Harvard Educational Review, 73*(1), 73–93.

Janzen, J. (2008). Teaching English language learners in the content areas. *Review of Educational Research, 78*(4), 1010–1039.

Keefe, M. R. (Producer/Researcher). (2008). *Voices of immigrant ELL high school students* [Video]. Martin County School District, Florida, TV Production Classes.

Lager, C. A. (2006). Types of mathematics-language reading interactions that unnecessarily hinder algebra learning and assessment. *Reading Psychology, 27*, 165–204.

National Council for the Social Studies. (2008). Retrieved September 21, 2008 from www.socialstudies.org/standards

National Science Teachers Association (NSTA). (2006). NSTA Position Statement: Professional Development in Science Instruction. Retrieved on September 21, www.nsta.org

Rosebery, A. S., Warren, B., & Conant, F. R. (1992). *Appropriating scientific discourse: Findings from language minority classrooms*. Santa Cruz, CA: National Center for Research on Cultural Diversity and Second Language Learning.

Ruiz de Velasco, J., & Fix, M. (2002). Limited English proficient students and high-stakes accountability systems. In D. M. Piche, W. I. Taylor, & R. A. Reed (Eds.), *Rights at risk: Equality in an age of terrorism*. Washington, DC: Citizens' Commission on Civil Rights.

Salinas, C., Franquiz, M., & Guberman, S. (2006). Introducing historical thinking to second language learners: Exploring what students know and what they want to know. *Social Studies, 97*(5), 203–207.

Sandefur, S., Watson, S., & Johnston, L. (2007). Literacy development, science curriculum, and the adolescent English language learner: Modifying instruction for the English-only classroom. *Multicultural Education, 14*(3), 41–50.

Santa, C. (1988). *Content reading including study systems*. Dubuque, IA: Kendall/Hunt Publishing.

Schleppegrell, M. J., Achugar, M., & Orteiza, T. (2004). The grammar of history: Enhancing content-based instruction through a functional focus on language. *TESOL Quarterly, 38*(1), 67–93.

Schleppegrell, M. J. (2007). The linguistic challenges of mathematics learning and teaching: A research review. *Reading and Writing Quarterly, 23*, 139–159.

School District of Palm Beach County. (n.d.). Information retrieved January 12, 2009 from www.palmbeach.k12.fl.us

Torres-Velasquez, D., & Lobo, C. (2004/2005). Culturally responsive mathematics instruction. *Teaching Children Mathematics, 11*(5), 249–255.

Turville, J. (2007). *Differentiating by student interest: Strategies and lesson plans*. Larchmont, NY: Eye on Education.

Chapter 7

Peer and Cooperative Learning Structures

*L*anguage is a city to the building of which every human being brought a stone.

—Ralph Waldo Emerson

Small-group instruction has been proven one of the most successful approaches for working with English language learners (ELLs) (Kendall, 2006). Student-to-student teaching and learning is also effective with both ELLs and native-speaking students.

Using a **heterogeneous grouping** approach, teachers form groups of students of different languages and ability levels. These student teams maximize communication by creating an environment where negotiation of meanings in the second language (L2) takes place.

At times, however, ELLs will gain from being grouped according to their language needs, depending on the instructional objectives. When students with the same first language (L1) are in the same class, **homogeneous grouping** may be beneficial, in which groups comprise students with similar language and ability levels. Doing so is particularly beneficial at the early stages of language development. Since ELLs' cognitive processes are carried out in their L1s, a group of like-language users can have a discussion at a deeper level.

Group work, or **cooperative learning,** has these characteristics (Koutselini, 2008):

- Encourages risk taking

- Shifts the focus of learning from the specific language being practiced to the completion of a given task

- Allows for frequent teacher comprehension checks and direct teacher-to-student **interaction**

- Provides for face-to-face peer interaction and helps build peer relationships

- Revolves around specific tasks that lead to peer teaching

- Guides students to work together to negotiate both linguistic and content area information

- Encourages the use of both **social language** and **academic language**

- Involves the use of specific language to accomplish a task

- Leads to positive interdependence

- Allows students to be engaged and motivated by the content

- Encourages students to work collaboratively to solve problems, formulate opinions, and interpret text

- Is student centered and empowers students to take an active role in the learning process

Because ELLs have widely different educational backgrounds and experiences, it is important to explain to them the value of small-group work.

Students engage in problem solving in a cooperative learning group. Peer learning is an effective instructional tool and an example of best practices for working with ELLs.

Managing Peer and Cooperative Learning

Rules and Roles

Somewhere on the walls of the classroom, the teacher should post a set of rules for cooperative learning groups. The rules should be specific, such as the following:

- No dominators.
- Allow each person to contribute to the discussion.
- Be respectful of others' views by not making fun of or criticizing their responses.
- Group members must come to a consensus or agreement.

Highlighting these specific rules before students engage in group assignments and **role-playing** the right and wrong behaviors for group work will reinforce the purpose and set the stage for organized, well-managed group activities. Asking for students' suggestions in developing these rules may also reinforce their understanding of purpose and willingness to cooperate.

When assigning a group activity, teachers need to communicate the following to students:

1. *Clear objectives:* What is the purpose of this activity? What can students learn from it? Does the activity mimic a real-life experience students may encounter?

2. *Clear goals:* What are group members expected to achieve by the end of the activity? Will group members need to present their findings? Write something? Illustrate something? Research something?

3. *Roles for group members:* What is each student expected to do in the group? Students who have had limited or no experience working effectively in a cooperative learning setting will need specific descriptions of member roles. For example, members' roles could be timekeeper, reporter, materials manager, journalist, researcher, writer, illustrator, ambassador, director, monitor, messenger, secretary, data collector, and so on. Short descriptions of the responsibilities of all the roles should be posted on or near the rules.

4. *Time management:* How long will students work on this project? How long will the discussion be? What are students expected to accomplish during class time? What parts of the assignment need to be completed by what times?

If students are given the parameters of cooperative learning and have the opportunity to practice working in this kind of environment, they will develop several skills. For instance, students will learn how to arrive at a consensus, how to respectfully disagree with someone else's beliefs or findings, and how to be diplomatic in communicating with others. In addition, student will learn how to solve problems as a team, how to negotiate answers from different perspectives, and how to apply communication and coping skills. By working in groups, students will also become more willing to participate and engage in the material (Schaetzel, 2003).

Documentation Tools and Graphic Organizers

The forms shown in Figures 7.1 and 7.2 are excellent tools for documenting group work activities. The Group Member Assignments handout (Figure 7.1) describes roles students might play in small-group work, such as connector, word wizard, and passage picker (Daniels, 2001). The Group Work Evaluation Form (Figure 7.2) can be completed by group members upon completion of a given activity.

The **graphic organizers** shown in Figures 7.3, 7.4, and 7.5 can be used to increase students' focus on the content and to reduce the linguistic load of reading selections. Figure 7.3, which is an expanded KWL-type chart, can be used with any content area as either an initiating or closing activity. Figure 7.4 can be used to help ELLs identify a problem along with evidence of it and possible solutions and results. Figure 7.5 is another type of problem/solution graphic organizer.

Group Member Assignments

Connector

You are the connector. Your job is to find connections between the book/chapter and the real world. This means connecting the reading to:

-your own life   -other people or problems   -other writings on the same topic

-happenings in school/neighborhood   -similar events at other times and places

Some things today's assignment reminded me of

were...._____

_____

Word Wizard

Your job is to look for special words in the chapter/story. Words that are:-new

          -important-different   -interesting-hard   -strange

When you find a word that you think you want to talk about, mark it with a Post-it note.

Word   Page   Definition/Meaning

____   ____   _____

____   ____   _____

____   ____   _____

When your group meets, help your group members talk about the words you have chosen.

Things you can discuss:

Does anyone know what this word means?

How does this word fit in the chapter/story?

Can you draw the word?

Passage Picker

You are the Passage Picker. Your job is to pick parts of the chapter/story that you want read aloud in your group. You would pick:

-an interesting part   -a good description   -some good writing

Be sure to mark the parts you want to share with a Post-it note or bookmark.

Page   Paragraph   Why I chose this passage

____   ____   _____

____   ____   _____

____   ____   _____

Figure 7.1   Group Member Assignments Handout

Group Work Evaluation Form

Group Members:_____ Date:_____

Name of Activity:_____

	Very True	True	Not sure	Not Really	Did Not Do
GROUP CONTRIBUTION					
All members contributed toward activities					
Members completed assignment within time allotted					
Group stayed on task, members were not distracted					
Cooperation increased knowledge of topic					
All members agreed to a common solution					
INDIVIDUAL CONTRIBUTION					
I encouraged shared ideas					
I listened attentively to others					
I showed respect to feelings of others					
I completed my role in the group activity					
EVALUATION/ PROBLEM –SOLVING					
All members were involved in problem-solving					
All members shared ideas and conclusions					
Group actively worked toward a common goal					

Figure 7.2 Group Work Evaluation Form

Reflections – KWL & More

Name _____ Group _____ Date ____

Inquiry Based Instruction Topic _____

What I know.....	What I want to know.....	Why is this learning important?	What I learned.....
What thoughts did I have?	What learning process was used?	My original thoughts changed....	How did I work in my group?

Figure 7.3 Expanded KWL Chart

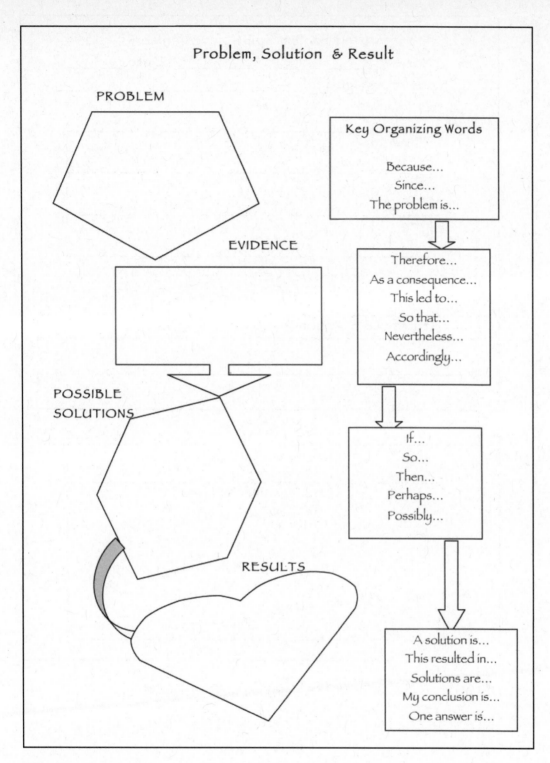

Problem, Solution & Result

PROBLEM

EVIDENCE

POSSIBLE
SOLUTIONS

RESULTS

Key Organizing Words

Because…
Since…
The problem is…

Therefore…
As a consequence…
This led to…
So that…
Nevertheless…
Accordingly…

If…
So…
Then…
Perhaps…
Possibly…

A solution is…
This resulted in…
Solutions are…
My conclusion is…
One answer is…

Figure 7.4 Graphic Organizer

Problem Solution Organizer

Name _____ Date _____

Name of Assignment _____

Who	
What	
Why	

Attempted Solution	Result

End Result/Outcome
What happened?

Figure 7.5 Problem/Solution Graphic Organizer

Types of Group Work

The following sections describe types of group work found effective with ELLs in content area classrooms (FLDOE, 2003).

Think-(Write)-Pair-Share

1. The teacher chooses a topic or question.

2. Students think individually. They may write a few notes to record their thoughts.

3. Pairs of students discuss their ideas and may agree on a response to share with the whole class.

4. The whole class shares ideas.

This approach to group work has several benefits for ELLs. It gives them time to think in their new language and then to try out communicating their ideas with a partner before sharing with the whole class. In effect, the language and content are "recycled" at least three times.

Be the Expert

1. The teacher selects a task that can be accomplished by dividing it into parts and then putting the parts together to accomplish the whole. For example, the teacher might have students read parts of a long chapter and then share the information.

2. Students number off in their groups. All students with the same number are assigned the same part of the task. These students may move into "expert" groups to complete their tasks and become authorities.

3. Students then return to their home groups to share their parts of the task and to accomplish their task as a whole.

Peer Tutoring

Assign a more proficient bilingual English speaker to help an English language learner. Give the pair a task to accomplish, so they have a need to communicate. For example, the more proficient student might read to ELL student, highlight key passages in the text, and/or paraphrase difficult material.

Guidelines for Group Work

Teachers should follow these guidelines to conduct successful group work activities (FLDOE, 2003):

1. *Plan for positive interdependence and individual accountability.* Many teachers object to group work, because they feel that one or two students end up doing all the work. A way to avoid this is to assign roles to group members and then rotate roles throughout the activity or project. Another way to avoid an unfair division of work is to design group activities that foster both positive interdependence and individual accountability. Students achieve *positive interdependence* when they rely on one another in positive ways to complete

a task. *Individual accountability* is accomplished when each student participates according to the designated group work rules and roles. To help ensure that students achieve individual accountability, they can complete an evaluation form, similar to that in Figure 7.2. The form should include statements that address both what the student did individually and how well the group worked together.

2. *Teach and model activities before asking students to do them.* Teachers should provide explicit instruction in how to work together and then **model** those behaviors, as well. They might also conduct a role-play about the "do's and don'ts" of cooperative learning situations. Groups should start with simple tasks and then evaluate and improve their work process. As stated earlier, cooperative learning rules should be posted on the wall in the classroom, so that students are continually reminded of the purpose and expectations of group work. Every group member should contribute one response to each problem or question. In addition, each member should perform his or her role without complaining, behave respectfully, be a good listener, and solve the problem within the time allowed.

3. *Vary grouping strategies.* Groups should be formed depending on the purpose of the activity. In most cases, teachers will want to form heterogeneous groups of ELLs and non-ELLs, so the ELLs can learn from the native English speakers. Teachers should also pair ELLs with native English speakers who are not struggling with the curriculum. In certain cases, homogeneous groups might be formed. For example, all-ELL groups are appropriate when the teacher can individualize instruction for the group and when students can use their native language to aid understanding. In any type of group, students should rotate roles to avoid having anyone do the same task repeatedly.

4. *Recognize and reward effective group work.* Teachers should give special recognition or points to groups who demonstrate effective or improved work processes. To evaluate students' work, teachers might have them complete a version of the Group Work Evaluation Form (see Figure 7.2) and award points for honest responses about individual and member contributions to completing the task. A version of the evaluation form could be condensed to a one-half or even one-quarter sheet of paper. Questions and comments about

This teacher is checking group members' comprehension and providing feedback about their work. Cooperative learning activities provide an opportunity to address individual students' questions and check on-task behavior.

the group's performance might be on one side of the paper, and questions and comments about the individual's performance might be on the other side. Completing this type of form will help students reflect on their participation in cooperative learning. Moreover, if students know their group work will be evaluated and rewarded, they may be more industrious and more cooperative in doing the activity. With all cooperative learning work, the importance of classroom management cannot be overemphasized.

Activities for Group Work

Pass the Poster

In this activity, the teacher creates posters by writing one or two different questions on each of several sheets of large chart paper—one poster per group of three or four students. Each group receives a poster, and each member of the group has a marker.

The teacher gives students just a few minutes to discuss and write down answers to the questions. Then the teacher announces "Time to pass the poster," and groups exchange posters. If students have been sitting for some time, the teacher might say "Time for each group to move to the next poster." For example, group A might move to group B's poster, group B might move to group C's poster, and so on.

After exchanging posters, each group reads the new questions and answers and then adds answers of their own. Then the groups exchange posters again. This process continues until the groups have worked on all the posters and have their original posters back.

The completed posters are displayed on the walls of the classroom. Students can do a "gallery walk" by reviewing all the posters, reading the questions and answers, and recording what they think is the best answer to each question. Each student hands in his or her written responses to the teacher.

Text Quests

A *Text Quest* is an excellent tool for helping students find information in their textbooks. In sum, it guides students through the reading by asking a series of specific questions that identify key points and features of the text (see Figure 7.6). This is a low-anxiety assignment and exercises the metacognitive skill of knowing how and where to find information.

A *Text Quest* can be used as an anticipatory or initiating activity by having ELLs review the next chapter or section in their textbook. Doing so also fosters a mindset for learning the new information the teacher will introduce. The first few times students do a *Text Quest*, they might work in pairs; once they have experience using this tool, they can work independently. This assignment is a valid form of assessment to include in students' **portfolios**.

Give One, Get One

In the *Give One, Get One* activity, students share vocabulary words they have identified from their reading from prior knowledge. To begin, the teacher distributes sheets of paper and has students draw pictures of the topic that will be covered. Next, the teacher directs each student to fold the piece of paper in half the long way, forming two columns. On the blank side of the paper, at

Figure 7.6 Sample *Text Quest*

Name _____ Date _____

Chapter _____

Complete the quest!

1. What is the title of the chapter?

2. How many years are represented on the *time line* on page 104?

3. What are the men doing in the *picture* on page 106? What is the caption?

4. What does the *pen-and-ink icon* on page 107 symbolize?

5. What is the *heading* on page 102?

6. What is the *subheading* on page 102?

7. In the *margin* on page 105, there are two key terms. What are they?

8. Where can you find the definitions of those two terms? Write the definitions.

9. Find the *graphic* on page 108. What is the title of this graphic?

10. On page 107, write the phrase at the bottom of the page that is in *bold print*.

11. What is one question you might find on a test about this chapter?

12. A *citation* is a quotation from another source. On page 110, what is the citation?

13. On what page will you find a *map* of Egypt?

14. Look on page 111, paragraph 2. What does the prefix *milli* mean, as used in the word *millimeter*?

15. Use the *Index* to find the formula for energy. Write down the formula and the page number on which it can be found.

16. Refer to the Review Questions at the end of the chapter. Answer question 5, and provide the page number on which you found the answer.

---

the top of the left column, the student writes "Give One," and at the top of the right column, he or she writes "Get One."

In the "Give One" column, each student writes five to seven words that describe the picture he or she drew on the front of the paper. Then students move around the room and review other students' lists, getting words they did not have on their lists and giving words others did not have on their lists. After completing this review, students come back to form a large group and discuss their words, identifying them as verbs, nouns, adjectives, and adverbs.

This activity can be extended to composing sentences that use the student-generated vocabulary. It works well in any content area.

Academic Vocabulary Posters

In a course entitled ESOL Reading in Content (GADOE, 2009), one of the weekly activities is to create academic vocabulary posters using newsprint. Rolls of newsprint are inexpensive, last for a long time, and are ideal for group projects.

To prepare for this activity, the teacher writes on the board a master list of vocabulary words from whatever content area is being emphasized that week. Working in groups of four, students select four words from the list. Each group is to select unique words, so that all the groups have different vocabulary.

Next, each group takes a sheet of paper and divides it into four equal sections. Students write one word at the top of each section. Together, students look up the definition of each word and then write it below the word. Students also add an illustration of each word. After the poster has been completed, one designated group member presents it to the whole class.

In defining each word, students should recognize that it may have more than one definition. They must choose the correct definition of the word as it relates to the content area they are studying. For example, if the word *mixture* is being used as a chemistry term, then the definition must be "a substance containing two or more elements or compounds that still retain their separate physical and chemical properties," not "the ingredients in a recipe."

Figure 7.7 is an example of an academic vocabulary poster that a group of ELLs created using social studies terms in a world geography course. The students made the poster as a study tool to help them prepare for a test in that class. The four vocabulary words are *equator, volcano, immigration,* and *urban.* The different handwriting used for each word reflects the fact that each student in the group contributed to the poster. The aerial view used in illustrating the term *urban* also indicates the unique perspective contributed by each student.

What's the Script?

The *What's the Script?* activity involves the use of video clips. To prepare for the activity, the teacher previews and selects segments of a video that relate to the topic being taught. Each segment should be short (less than five minutes) but include enough information for students to make sense of the dialogue and determine the scenario that is likely taking place.

To conduct the activity, the teacher plays the video segment *without sound* for students.

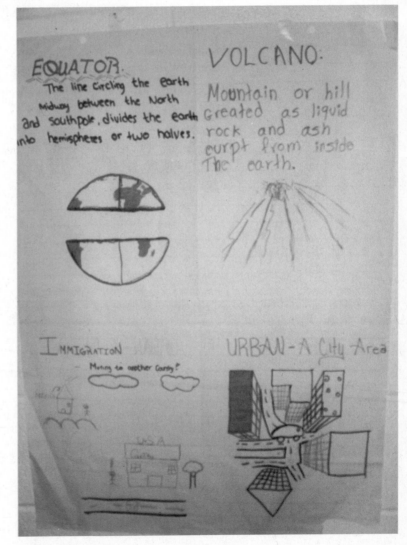

Figure 7.7 Sample Academic Vocabulary Poster

Working with partners or in small groups, students deduce what is being said and what is happening in the scene. They then create a possible dialogue, which can be shared with the large group.

This activity requires the use of higher-level thinking skills and is highly motivating for ELLs. It is an excellent initiating or concluding activity for a topic or unit of study.

Accountable Talk

This is a questioning strategy that dovetails well with cooperative structures such as the activities described in this chapter. As groups and group representatives begin to respond in those cooperative learning settings, the opportunity for extended questions can be presented in the form of "accountable talk" (DPS, 2009). Here are some examples:

- Keeping the channels open: "What did she just say?" Teacher makes sure students understand that every student is responsible for hearing and remembering each student's contribution by having another student repeat something just said.

- Linking contributions: "Who wants to add . . . ? Teacher encourages students to invest in the discussion by having others add on to what was just said.

- Pressing for accuracy: "Where can we find that"? Teacher is pressing for correct facts.

Conducting these kinds of interaction can keep the focus on the topic and culminate the activity by creating a shared understanding of the information. This can help build self-esteem by providing an environment that promotes risk taking.

References

Daniels, H. (2001). *Literature circles: Voice and choice in the student-centered classroom.* York, ME: Stenhouse.

Denver Public Schools. (2009). Cooperative structures and accountable talk. In-service teacher training provided to teachers at a local school on November 20, 2009.

Florida Department of Education (FLDOE), Center for Applied Linguistics, Sunbelt Office. (2003). *Enriching content classes for secondary ESOL students.* Tallahassee, FL: Author.

Georgia Department of Education (GADOE). (2009). Georgia Department of Education Title III ESOL Resource Guide. Retrieved on October 16, 2008 from www.doe.k12.ga.us/DMGetDocument.aspx/2009-10%20Title%20III%20ESOL%20Resource%20Guide%20073109.pdf?p=6CC6799F8C1371F6E3A23FF57AB6E574361E3610E66D5BB042BD6AB13082A4D5&Type=D

Keefe, M. R. (2006). *The impact of training secondary teachers to adapt content to empower English for speakers of other languages.* Unpublished dissertation, Nova Southeastern University, North Miami Beach, FL.

Kendall, J. (2006). Small group instruction for English language learners. *Principal Leadership, 6,* 28–31.

Kenfield, K. (2003). *The basics of sheltered instruction.* Materials distributed at a workshop presented in Orlando, FL.

Koutselini, M. (2008). Teacher misconceptions and understanding of cooperative learning: An intervention study. *Journal of Classroom Interaction, 43*(2), 34–44.

Schaetzel, K. (2003, July/August). Creating congenial classrooms. *ESL Magazine,* 26–27.

Chapter 8

Technology, Multiliteracy Instruction, and ELLs

Despite the communications power of the computer and cell phones, and all the applications available on these devices today, nothing can replace human interaction and capability when it comes to learning a new skill. As Gerstner, the CEO of IBM, believes, "Computers are magnificent tools for the realization of our dreams, but no machine can replace the human spark of spirit, compassion, love, and understanding" (www.pcsndreams.com/Pages/TechQuotes1.htm). No technology can replace the safe, motivating, challenging, and community-like environment that a good teacher fosters in the classroom.

Technology is vital for participation in the social, political and economical life in the United States. Therefore, schools must provide students familiarity with computer technology and related skills, in order for them to be successful both in and outside the classroom. In K–12 schools, we are experiencing exponential growth in the use of technology so much so that governments and organizations are highly motivated to dedicate substantial funds to enhance instruction through the use of technology.

Benefits of Technology in the Classroom

The use of technology in the classroom has several benefits. It promotes active engagement with language and content through authentic, demanding activities that are interdisciplinary in nature. Moreover, as ELLs search for information in a hyperlinked setting, they have increased exposure to language and content information. Used as a tool for learning, technology supports and promotes the acquisition of multiliteracies.

Ten education and linguistics experts known as the New London Group, affiliated with universities from Australia, United Kingdom, and the United States, met in New London, New Hampshire, to discuss and present a theoretical overview of the connections between the changing social environment facing students and teachers and a new approach to literacy pedagogy that they call *multiliteracies*. ***Multiliteracies*** is a term that is used to describe two important arguments regarding emerging cultural, institutional, and global order, which is the multiplicity of communications channels and media, and the increasing saliency of cultural and linguistic diversity (Cazden et al., 1996).

In 1996, the New London Group reported that developing multiliteracy requires the following:

1. Engagement in meaningful tasks that demonstrate the use of real tools for real purposes

2. Engagement with multiple forms of communication and text, made possible by electronic technologies

3. Participation in collaborative learning environments

Other researchers have supported these recommendations, adding that technologically based literacy instruction must include opportunities for critical inquiry and problem solving, cooperation and collaboration, interdisciplinary exploration, **scaffolding** of instruction, and shifting of control from teacher to student (Chatel, 2002; Leu, 2000; Stepp-Greany, 2002). In addition, research has supported the use of electronic technologies with English language learners (ELLs) to help them acquire the linguistic, social, and technological skills needed for success in the digital age (Chatel, 2002).

The use of technology also increases students' motivation to learn and results in students spending more time on task. Research has shown that behavior problems decrease in classrooms when students are using computers (Chatel, 2002).

Teachers can use technology to facilitate collaboration in the classroom. Technology is not a dehumanizing element but in fact brings together students and teachers. Research on teachers' flexibility in adapting technology in their classroom indicates that there is no one system or method for doing so (Chatel, 2002).

Technology has become a bridge for ELLs in K–12 classrooms. From a theoretical perspective, the richness of lessons can be seen as students use a variety of hypertext documents, access visual and audio information, and communicate in both their first languages (L1s) and English.

Research has shown that reading hypertext facilitates students' acquisition of knowledge by providing easy access to multiple references or screens on related topics and juxtaposing a variety of ideas and information (Egbert, 2002). In addition, reading hypertext allows students an easy and flexible means of exploring those ideas without flipping through multiple pages of a traditional textbook. As students explore hyperlinks and listen to new information to gather ideas for their assignment, they are actively engaged in a process of acquiring and creating knowledge. These students' acquisition of knowledge is further supported by the use of photographs, diagrams, charts, and other types of graphics, which help to strengthen understanding of abstract concepts.

Thematic Curricular Approach

Give the **text-heavy** nature of most content area textbooks, teachers of ELLs must teach reading and **academic language** along with the topics of their content areas. This reality is compounded by the fact that most students at the **secondary level** have a daily schedule that includes a math class, a science class, and a language arts class.

To address these challenges, the **thematic approach** to curriculum planning is optimal. Such planning begins with collaboration among colleagues to coordinate the teaching of lessons on the same topic at the same time. For example, suppose the current topic in social studies is the American Revolution. During the time this topic is studied, the science class will conduct lessons on experiments from that period of history; the math class will work on word problems, graphs, or problem solving involving people, places, and events from that period; and the language arts class will read and write about literature written about or during the American Revolution.

With the thematic approach, the same vocabulary and academic language are reinforced across the content areas, as ELLs move from class to class.

Students' achievement improves when teachers plan together, have discussions on individual students' performance, and coordinate thematic units.

The thematic approach can be built into the regular calendar of the school curriculum, thereby integrating the content areas across all grade levels. Teachers can plan the calendar to include such features as "Word of the Week," "Quote of the Week," "Topic of the Week," and/or "Strategy of the Week."

Developing a Thematic Unit

Using this *ACEES* book as part of a teacher-training course, groups of participants can develop a thematic unit that incorporates the content areas. One group can create a math lesson, another a language arts lesson, another a social studies lesson, and another a science lesson.

The suggested theme for the unit is humans' relationship with the environment, as portrayed in the following poem written in 1854 by Chief Seathl (Seattle), a well-known leader of the Native American Suquamish people:

We are part of the earth, and it is part of us.

Perfumed flowers are our sisters, the rivers, the deer, the horse, the great eagle—these are our brothers.

The air shares its spirit with all the life it supports.

We must give them the kindness you would give any brother.

All things are connected—all belong to the same family.

We must teach the children the earth is our mother, so that they will respect the land.

Whatever befalls the earth, befalls the sons of the earth.

This we know.

Man did not weave the web of life, he is merely a strand in it.

Whatever he does to the web, he does to himself.

Participants can refer to the websites listed in Table 8.1 for activities that fit the topic of environmentalism and can be incorporated into a thematic unit. When completed, this unit can be shared with other teachers and used as an example of the thematic approach to a topic.

Computer Software for English Language Learning

Any classroom with ELLs should provide English language software programs, which are indispensable tools for students learning English. These programs are a means by which teachers can fairly evaluate students' English language learning and English language goals.

Useful programs for ELLs include the following:

■ *Rosetta Stone* (www.rosettastone.com): This program provides activities for students with little or no English experience. As students work through the various levels, they will find that the exercises become progressively more difficult. Exercises are provided in the content areas. The high-quality photographs in this program reflect a diversity of people from all over the world and all walks of life. A student management system allows teachers to evaluate students' progress and assess their performance equitably by comparing

Table 8.1 Online Resources for Planning Thematic Unit

Website URL	Resource Provided
http://calm.indiana.edu	Free chemistry-learning tool for students
http://rubistar.4teachers.org/index.php	Rubric maker for any content area
www.brainpop.com	Variety of content area activities
www.breakingnewsenglish.com	Ready-to-use lesson plans and podcasts
www.colorincolorado.org	ELL guides, toolkits, podcasts, and videos
www.daveseslcafe.com	ELL activities and ideas
www.edhelper.com	Activities and organizers
www.elladvocates.org	ELL research-based policies
www.eslgold.net	Teaching and learning activities
www.esl.net	ELL activities
www.freeology.com	Graphic organizers and journal topics
www.newseum.org/todaysfrontpages/flash/	Click on continent, then city, has headline news from that city that day
www.google.com/ig	Free word translations (including in Arabic)
www.imaginationcubed.com	Free website for writing and drawing
www.lexiles.com	Information/book suggestions appropriate for individual reading ability
www.makebeliefscomix.com	Creating comic strips
www.manythings.org	Interesting word games, slang, and proverbs
www.math.hmc.edu/funfacts	Algebra, geometry, and other math fun facts
www.ncela.gwu.edu	Lesson plans and activities
www.nclrc.org/essentials	Essentials of language teaching
www.pdictionary.com	Picture dictionary
www.puzzlemaker.com	Puzzles, cryptograms, and word games
www.remember.org	Information about the Holocaust
www.teachingtolerance.org	Multicultural education
www.teachervision.com	Graphic organizers
www.tesol.org	Research, resources, activities, and videos
www.untiedstreaming.com	Videos on 4,000 topics
www.yourdictionary.com	Multiple language dictionary
http://tell.fll.purdue.edu/JapanProj//FLClipart	Small icons to describe words

grades of individual students' progress, not against native English speakers. This system also makes it easy to schedule individual students' curricula. Rosetta Stone Version 3 is accessible through the Internet.

■ *Open Book* (www.openbookenglish.com): This English language learning program is different from the Rosetta Stone program because it has a variety of lesson presentations, such as graphs and charts. The Open Book program also has a helpful feature that provides instruction in oral pronunciation. Like Rosetta Stone, Open Book has a student management system. Open Book is very useful with secondary-level students.

This student is using an online program for English language learning. As she looks at a picture, she keyboards the words she hears through the headphones about the picture.

- *Read 180* (http://teacher.scholastic.com/products/read180/) is a proven program that produces quantifiable learning gains among struggling readers whose reading achievement is below proficient. This program, designed to extend classroom instruction, uses a teaching system that provides a clear instructional path, integrated professional development, and resources for assessing students and differentiating instruction. Read 180 contains multicultural content and promotes active participation of ELLs. It provides support in Spanish, Cantonese, Haitian **Creole**, Hmong, and Vietnamese.

- *Inspiration Software* (www.inspiration.com) is one of the leading publishers of visual thinking and learning tools for students in grades K–12. The Inspiration company facilitates visual learning through the use of webs, brainstorming, concept maps, and the like. The symbols, templates, and example files in the program were designed specifically for diagramming, outlining, flowcharting, knowledge mapping, brainstorming, systems thinking, and multimedia design. Inspiration is intended for use with students in grades 6 through 12 in the content areas of language arts, science, math, social studies, and history.

- *CORE* (www.educationaltools.org/core/) is based on the differentiated instruction approach, which tailors teaching to students of different abilities. This program delivers the curriculum via multiple learning styles, engaging auditory, visual, and kinesthetic learners, as well as low-level readers. Demonstrations for high school math and science can be found online at www.edtools.org/core.

- *STAR Reading Program* (www.renlearn.com/sr/) was designed to determine a student's reading ability. Students' reading levels are assessed in less than 30 minutes, and accurate, reliable, norm-referenced reading scores are provided, including grade equivalents, percentile ranks, and normal curve equivalents.

This program is well suited to the response to intervention (RTI) approach, because it provides the necessary individualized practice and progress monitoring. It is also an excellent tool for determining students' pre- and post-progress in reading comprehension and English proficiency. Teachers can track students' growth in reading achievement across time, facilitating the kind of analysis recommended by state and federal standards. The National Center on Student Progress Monitoring has found the STAR program to meet its evaluation criteria for scientifically based progress-monitoring tools.

Technology-Based Activities

Digital Storytelling

A *digital story* is a three- to five-minute videolike digital production. The student writes a story, revises it to produce a short script, and then records it. Photos and other images can be inserted into the story, and music can be added, as well.

Teachers can devote one or two class sessions to teach students how to use the software needed to create a digital story. Several free, easy-to-use programs are available, including Photo Story 3 from Microsoft and iMovie from Apple/Macintosh.

This activity involves ELLs in all aspects of language: reading, writing, speaking, and listening. To create a digital story, students write a narrative, edit their writing, read and record the story, listen to the recording, and then edit and possibly rerecord it. Students tend to perfect their language in speaking and presentation.

Creating a digital story is a motivating and effective way for ELLs students to experience the English language. As described by Ohler (2007), a student's digital story contains a number of artifacts for assessing literacy, and can literally be a portfolio unto itself of great depth and breadth. Students' poems, tales, and short essays can reveal their feelings about **culture** and events in their lives or their hopes and dreams for the future. Creating digital stories also helps ELLs understand the power that storytelling holds for sharing across cultures.

With the Push of a Button

A teacher asked ninth-grade students to name the fraction that represented the shady area on a grid displayed on a PowerPoint slide. Within a few seconds, the teacher knew which of the students knew the answer without a single student raising his or her hand. The students had entered their answers into a handheld remote electronic-response system, giving the teacher instant feedback (Manzo 2009).

Good teachers know when they ask a question, it is usually the higher-functioning students who answer. This system uses interactive technology to promote a risk-free environment for all students to participate and encourages students to stay actively engaged in lessons (Manzo, 2009).

Podcasting

A *podcast* is a multimedia broadcast that is provided over the Internet and downloaded on a personal computer or listening device. Used in the classroom, podcasting is innovative and effective and applicable to any content area. Podcasting offers limitless opportunities for ELLs, from accessing free, premade podcasts to creating their own and perhaps teaching fellow students to create them, too. "How to" tutorials for creating podcasts can be found online via any search engine.

Podcasting can be used to create an electronic pen pal program. The ePals website (www.epals.com) boasts that it is the largest global community of connected classrooms. Students can safely connect, collaborate, and learn using the protected email and blog providers for schools and districts. Teachers should get parents' permissions before having students work on these kinds of projects.

Integrating Technology with Content

Imagine this scenario (Egbert, 2002): In a **mainstream classroom,** students are beginning a unit on the Vietnam War. Teams of four students are assigned to explore the political, historical, social, and demographic aspects of the war by conducting library and web-based research, discussing and synthesizing the information, and presenting a report supported by a PowerPoint presentation to the rest of the class. Through this work, students develop a broad definition of war and a personal understanding of its contexts and effects.

Like many U.S. classrooms, this one has 23 students—5 of whom speak a first language other than English and several more with different levels of English proficiency. One of the ELLs emigrated from Haiti and another from Korea. Even though both can write in English at slightly below grade level, the teacher is concerned that they may have difficulty with or be embarrassed by participating in the oral segment of the project. The teacher therefore adapts the project for these two ELLs. They will participate in the written part of the research project but be excused from the oral presentation. In addition, the teacher groups these students with two native English speakers who have shown a willingness to help others in class.

The other three ELLs are from Central America and speak Spanish or a dialect of Spanish as their L1. One of these students is proficient at communicating orally in English, but his reading ability is considerably below grade level. The remaining two Hispanic students, both from Guatemala, have limited English language proficiency and have had little classroom experience. The teacher groups these three Hispanic students with a bilingual student, so they can help each other with the reading and the oral part of the project. In sum, by grouping the ELLs with stronger English speakers, the ELLs will be able to work on their academic language skills while also learning cultural and social content about the Vietnam War.

Before addressing the issues involved in a classroom like the one just described, teachers must answer the following questions:

- How can ELLs' language and content learning be facilitated while they work on tasks such as gathering, discussing, and presenting data?

- What classroom conditions support ELLs' language and content learning?

- What technology supports ELLs' language and content learning? How can technology support or enhance the existing classroom conditions? (Egbert, 2002).

Egbert (2002) has identified eight conditions that support ELLs' content and language learning, along with examples of the technology that supports those conditions:

1. Social **interaction** (email, telecollaborative projects, online discussions)

2. Authentic audiences (web page development, oral presentations)

3. Authentic tasks (email, word processing, spreadsheets)

4. Exposure and production (multimedia presentations)

5. Appropriate time and feedback (email, online discussion groups and chat rooms)

6. Intentional cognition (HTML, word processing)

7. Optimal stress (computer-based testing, multimedia)

8. Learner control (WebQuests)

Role-playing also encourages active learning by providing opportunities for ELLs to interact with native English speakers, use a variety of media, and promote a range of sources of feedback and prompting.

In the scenario about the Vietnam War project, students will gather, discuss, transform, and present information about the war, which will meet some of the learning conditions. For example, student teams will be created to support interaction (condition 1) and authentic audiences (condition 2). Those teams will use technology by creating PowerPoint (Microsoft) or Keystone (Apple) slides, importing video clips and clip art, and hyperlinking to various websites (condition 4). Doing so will allow learners some autonomy in deciding how to gather data (condition 8).

Working in small groups, students will assume roles such as secretary, team leader, researcher, and data collector. Playing different roles and using different tools gives ELLs choices and helps them develop the skills needed to complete different tasks.

Before students start their projects, the teacher should provide a thorough review of how to explore websites and build a presentation. Here are other guidelines for ensuring successful student projects:

- Content-based websites, which can be easily accessed by ELLs, provide both textual and graphic exposure to materials.

- Students can experiment with forms of data collection and representation, including maps, tables, and photographs in addition to text. Students can use their maps, graphs, and email messages to support their input to fellow group members.

- Students also can present their findings in a number of forms, including both visual and textual (such as a narrative).

- Dual-language dictionaries and translation websites can be used to assist ELLs in understanding the main concepts of the topic, focusing on the project, and not getting lost in language and content.

- Students can be taught to use the advanced "Search" or "Find" feature available with most search engines. Using this feature, students can reduce the amount of extraneous information they find yet still be exposed to the content-based information and academic language they need.

■ Learners should be encouraged to interact with authentic sources and audiences, as provided. For instance, in using email, students can plan what they want to say and take time to form a clear response (Egbert, 2002).

Following these guidelines will help students acquire tools, strategies, and information they can use in future projects.

English language learners can record their interactions with group members using the tools provided at websites Call Graph (www.callgraph.biz) and Audacity (http://audacity.sourceforge.net). Another option is for the group secretary or recorder to type notes using a word-processing program and printing out the transcript for everyone in the group. This not only provides a view of students' progress and a lasting record of their interactions, but it also supplies documentation for ELLs to use to check their comprehension of group decisions.

In preparing written reports, students identify and fix errors using the spellchecker, thesaurus, and other features of the word-processing software. Students who need extra feedback on their written work can submit their papers or questions to an online writing lab or clinic.

The use of *graphic organizers,* such as the *Sentence Opening Sheet* (SOS) (refer back to Figures 5.11 and 5.12), will help students prepare and edit information for their presentations. They can then transfer the information they gather and organize to a PowerPoint or Keystone presentation. Following this procedure also gives ELLs the opportunity to practice their speeches and perfect their pronunciations of new words. To reduce the anxiety of making a speech or live report, students' presentations might be videotaped, rather than presented live (Keefe, 2008). Group members can prepare a graphic organizer or bulleted list of the information audience members will hear during the group's presentation.

For a project such as the one about the Vietnam War, as described in the scenario, each group will cover a different aspect of the topic. To learn about the topic in full, all students must be attentive during the other groups'

*E*nglish language learners should have access to a classroom computer lab of laptops with wireless Internet capability, which students can take to their desks, and a wireless printer.

presentations. After the presentations have been completed, students can offer feedback in the form of questions and comments written on a poster. Using this approach gives learners time to understand questions and ideas and to form concise, accurate answers to the issues they are exploring in this project (Egbert, 2002). Developing **rubrics** for the different aspects of the project, as well as an overall project rubric, will also guide students as they are creating their project.

In addition to participating in the group project, individual learners might create narratives using a bookmaking or writing program. They might also create electronic posters reflecting their personal views on the subject. By using technological tools in completing their projects, ELLs will be able to focus on the content and format of their responses, providing a form of **alternative assessment**.

There is no guarantee that all students will learn with optimal outcomes just because technology was employed to support the conditions for content and language learning. However, teachers can make sure to provide opportunities that support different students' learning styles and other diverse needs. As students gain confidence with the language, content, and tools, they will also meet many of the standards for technology, language, and content.

Creating Optimal Learning Conditions

The conditions that contribute to achievement also can provide a foundation for meeting the National Educational Technology Standards for Students (NETS•S) (ISTE, 2008) and PK–12 English as a second language (ESL) standards. The eight conditions that support language and content learning are briefly explained here in terms of the related technology standards (Egbert, 2002):

1. *Social interaction:* Learners have opportunities to interact socially and negotiate meaning. Communication technologies, such as email and online chats, can support social interaction and content learning beyond the students' classroom. For example, as noted earlier, online pen pals can be used to create a global community of classrooms, allowing both teachers and students to link with partners in other cultures and countries for correspondence and other project exchanges. (NETS•S 4)

2. *Authentic audiences:* Learners interact in the target language with an authentic audience. Communicating in English with a genuinely interested audience is important to fostering ELLs' social interaction. To ensure the audience has a stake in the presentation or report that students are presenting, the teacher can provide an evaluation sheet with which audience members provide feedback. Completing an evaluation also engages the audience in higher-level thinking skills. (NETS•S 3 & 4)

3. *Authentic tasks:* Learners are involved in authentic tasks, which are tasks perceived to be of use outside school because they parallel or replicate real-world functions or needs. Learning skills related to the use of technology is authentic for many students, regardless of content, because they perceive these skills to be necessary to their lives beyond the classroom. In addition, completing authentic tasks influences all of the other conditions for learning. (NETS•S 3 & 4)

4. *Exposure and production:* Learners are exposed to and encouraged to use varied and creative language. Not all students can demonstrate their knowledge and experiences in the same way. Many students, for instance, have

experienced test anxiety. This may be especially true for students from diverse educational, linguistic, and cultural backgrounds. The use of multimedia can provide diverse opportunities for both exposure to and production of language and content. Content-based multimedia programs can present information to students through a variety of modes, such as still graphics, movies, text, and sound. (NETS•S 3, 4 & 5)

5. *Appropriate time and feedback:* Learners have an appropriate amount of time and receive constructive feedback. Individual students work at various speeds and require different amounts of guidance for specific tasks. Communicating electronically with outside sources, such as online writing labs, can relieve some of the teacher's burden of providing feedback. Doing so also helps students work at their own pace by giving them time to form questions and responses. Computer adaptive tests also allow students to work at their own pace and provide another kind of feedback about their progress and achievement. (NETS•S 3)

6. *Intentional cognition:* Learners are guided to focus on the learning process. This focus benefits ELLs, in particular, because they are often told what to learn but not how to learn it (Keefe, 2008). Providing a variety of technologies—such as hypertext, search engines, and word-processing programs—can demonstrate to learners that there are many sources of information and many ways to learn (Egbert, 2002). (NETS•S 5 & 6)

7. *Optimal stress:* Learners work in an atmosphere with an ideal level of stress or anxiety. The amount of pressure under which students learn most effectively varies for each individual. English language learners should feel comfortable enough to take risks with English yet not become bored with simple-minded tasks and exercises. Computer programs and online resources that allow students to develop open-ended, creative responses, such as the Young Voices Foundation, Mentoring Young Writers (www.youngvoicesfoundation.org), provide an appropriate level of pressure by allowing for a variety of responses using multimedia. (NETS•S 3)

8. *Learner control:* Learner autonomy is supported. Many teachers put ELLs on a rigid schedule, pushing them to complete a given amount of work in a given amount of time. Instead, teachers should consider giving students' control over some aspects of their learning. This approach can facilitate instruction for ELLs with different levels of language proficiency and with different interests and learning styles.

By taking advantage of available technology, teachers can direct ELLs to choose both topics and the resources they will use to investigate those topics, to create their own presentations, and even to choose what tasks they will do and when. Language learning and content area WebQuests (http://webquest.org/index.php) are structured yet creative activities that give students decision-making power. Students can choose their roles within the WebQuest, decide which sources of information to use, and even design the format of the final product. Students' personal investment in the project tends to result in high-quality outcomes.

References

Cazden, C., Cope, B., Faircloth, N., Gee, J., et al. (1996). A pedagogy of multiliteracies: Designing social futures. *Harvard Educational Review, 66*(1), 60–93.

Chatel, R. (2002). New technology, new literacy: Creating a bridge for English language learners. *New England Reading Association Journal, 38*(3), 45–49.

Egbert, J. (2002). A project for everyone: English-language-learners and technology in content area classrooms. *Learning and Leading with Technology, 29*(8), 36–41.

International Society for Technology in Education (ISTE). (2008). National Educational Technology Standards (NETS). Retrieved October 16, 2008, from www.iste.org/AM/Template.cfm?Section=NETS

Keefe, M. R. (Producer/Researcher). (2008). *Voices of immigrant ELL high school students* [Video]. Martin County School District, Florida, TV Production Classes.

Leu, Donald J. (2000). Literacy and Technology: Deictic Consequences for Literacy Education in an Information Age. In M. Kamil, P. Mosenthal, D. Pearson & R. Barr (Eds.), *Handbook of Reading Research, 3,* 743–770. Mahwah, New Jersey: Lawrence Erlbaum Associates.

Manzo, J. J. (2009). Instant class feedback with the push of a button. *Education Week* (Spring/Summer supp), 14.

Ohler, J. (2007). *Digital storytelling in the classroom: New media pathways to literacy, learning and creativity.* Thousand Oaks, CA: Corwin Press.

Stepp-Greany, J. (2002). Student perceptions of language learning in a technological environment: Implications for the new millennium. *Language Learning & Technology, 6*(1).

Chapter 9

Cross-Cultural Dimensions

The world in which you were born is just one reality. Other cultures are not failed attempts at being you. They are unique manifestations of the human spirit.

—*Wade Davis*

Culture is a way of life. It is the context in which we think, feel, and relate to others. Larson and Smalley (1972) describe culture as a blueprint that guides the behavior of people in a community and is incubated in family life. It governs people's behavior in groups and makes them sensitive to matters of status. It also helps people to know what others expect of them and what will happen if they do not meet others' expectations. Culture helps people to know how far they can go as individuals and what responsibilities they have to the group.

Culture can be defined as "the ideas, customs, skills, arts and tools that characterize a given group of people in a certain period of time." Culture is more than the sum of its parts, however. The fact that every society has a culture reflects the need for culture to fulfill certain biological and psychological needs in human beings (Richard-Amato & Snow, 1992). The mental constructs that enable humans to survive comprise the way of life known as "culture."

People tend to perceive reality within the context of their own culture. Moreover, they tend to believe that their reality is the only correct perception. However, what appears to one person to be an objective perception of an idea, individual, or custom can, in many ways, seem unnatural or strange to someone from another culture.

For teachers to provide a classroom environment that reflects and embraces multicultural education, they must recognize their own heritages, acknowledge and try to overcome their own prejudices, and, most importantly, adopt attitudes to implement a transformative approach to students and instruction. Teachers must be willing to reduce the cultural biases found in educational materials, be able to conduct discussions of a controversial nature, provide multiple perspectives on events and ideas, and tolerate divergent thinking on issues.

Valuing Cultural Diversity

According to Boynton (2003), adults transmit their culture to their children in both conscious and unconscious ways. Parents, consciously and unconsciously, teach their children things such as language, manners, religion, and family history. Children also gain knowledge of their culture without conscious awareness, such as ideas of personal beauty and means of nonverbal communication. Through the transmission of culture, children define themselves and their identities.

Children's beliefs derive from their ethnic and family backgrounds, but they are also shaped by the experiences children have in school and the larger society. For example, if a culture values the well-being of the group over that of the individual, then children in that culture will usually be more comfortable in cooperative, rather than competitive, settings. And if those children are placed in competitive situations, as they often are in American schools, they will likely not understand why they feel uneasy. They will either adjust to the competitive situation or fail to perform in a way satisfactory to the teacher.

Language minority students experience the conflict of two cultures and must find a personal accommodation. The process of accommodation is highly individual, and each person's adjustment will be unique. Students who do not find a comfortable accommodation may become alienated from both their native culture and American culture. Language minority children start school with positive attitudes about their native culture. However, when the culture of the school conflicts with what they have learned at home, they may reject their native culture in an effort to find comfort in school. On some level, these students feel that accepting the culture represented by the school will ensure that the school culture will accept them (Boynton, 2003). But in fact, they are usually still seen as different from the norm—as "those ESL kids."

In today's world, which is characterized by an ever-expanding capitalist, high-tech, computerized, global market, the traditional demands of language learning are much less relevant. Today, language skills are sociopolitically acceptable as symbolic capital in situated social practices of a given community, whether at schools, workplaces, laboratories, shopping malls, or on the streets of any city (Ajayi, 2006).

Given this environment, teachers should encourage students to maintain and use their first languages (L1s) regularly as they acquire a second language (L2). Being bilingual, rather than monolingual, will give English language learners (ELLs) an advantage in business of any kind. Becoming bilingual will also help ELLs gain access to the social practices of the communities to which they want to belong. This concept has major implications for language teaching, as teachers have the opportunity to teach students to engage critically in the analysis and reconstruction of discourses and texts (Ajaya, 2006; Luke, 2000).

Multicultural Education

Mounting evidence indicates that **multicultural education** makes schooling more relevant and effective for Latino American, Native American, African American, and Asian American students (Gay, 2004). Banks and Banks (1995) define *multicultural education* as:

> [A] field of study and an emerging discipline whose major aim is to create equal educational opportunities for students from diverse racial, ethnic, social-class, and cultural groups. One of its important goals is to help all students to acquire the knowledge, attitudes, and skills needed to function effectively in a pluralistic democratic society and to interact, negotiate, and communicate with peoples from diverse groups in order to create a civic and moral community that works for the common good. (xi)

Students perform more successfully on all levels when there is greater congruence between their cultural backgrounds and school experiences such as task interest, effort, academic achievement, and feelings of personal efficacy or social accountability.

Research has validated several theoretical assertions in multicultural education:

1. That culture, ethnicity, and education are interrelated

2. That different students need different instructional strategies to improve their achievement

3. That explicit engagement with ethnic, linguistic, racial, and cultural diversity in classrooms facilitates, rather than obstructs, academic performance

4. That making educational opportunities equal for ethnically and linguistically diverse students is contingent on pluralistic curriculum content and instructional strategies that are culturally responsive (Ajayi, 2006; Banks, 2006; Gay, 2004; Luke, 2000; Reeves, 2006)

Multicultural education has the potential to genuinely desegregate U.S. education, fulfilling the promise of equity made by the *Brown v. Board of Education* (1954) case and the No Child Left Behind (NCLB) Act. Considering the political climate surrounding immigration and so-called English-only programs, the perspectives of multicultural education are seen as a threat to the status quo. This threat provokes resistance and results in the reentrenchment of attitudes, behaviors, and practices that violate policies of racial and ethnic inclusion and equity (Gay, 2004).

Multicultural education is a product of the United States context and represents the highest democratic ideals. Increasing philosophical and pedagogical clarity, depth, coherency, complexity, and practicality have all been evident in the development of multicultural education. Moreover, it will continue to evolve over time, so that it can keep pace with the changing demographics of the schools it was created to represent and serve.

As the challenge to better educate underachieving students intensifies and diversity among students expands, the need for multicultural education will grow exponentially. Multicultural education may be the solution to problems that currently appear insolvable: closing the achievement gap; revitalizing faith and trust in the promises of equity and justice; building education systems that reflect the diverse cultural, ethnic, racial, and social contributions that forge society; and providing better opportunities for all students (Gay, 2004).

Twenty-first-century classrooms have students from many cultures who speak many languages.

Thoughts of James Banks

In discussing cultural and cross-cultural issues in education, it is useful to examine what pioneer researcher of multicultural education Dr. James Banks (2006) has described as the *multicultural ideology*. The multicultural theorist thinks that the cultural pluralist exaggerates the importance of the ethnic group in the socialization of the individual and that the **assimilationist** greatly understates the role of cultural and ethnic groups in Western societies. The multicultural theorist sees neither separatism, as the pluralist does, nor total integration, as the assimilationist does, as ideal societal goals. Rather, the multicultural theorist envisions an open society in which individuals from diverse cultural, ethnic, language, and social class groups have equal opportunities to function and participate. In an open society, individuals can take full advantage of the opportunities and rewards within all societal, economic, and political institutions without regard to their ancestry or ethnic identity.

Traditionally powerless and marginalized groups, such as Puerto Ricans and African Americans, must participate in shaping educational policy in order for reforms related to ethnic diversity to become institutionalized within the U.S. educational system. The groups that exercise power in the U.S. educational establishment design and run the schools, so that they reflect their ideas, assumptions, values, and perspectives. Assimilationists, who control much of the popular culture and public opinion, often see pluralism as a threat to the survival of the United States.

Ways must be found for marginalized ethnic groups to gain power in education and to participate in decision making that will affect the education of their youths. Only when this occurs will the multicultural ideology become institutionalized within education, making education legitimate from the perspectives of the diverse groups that make up the U.S. population. For that institutionalization to occur, the dominant mainstream groups must share power with the less powerful groups (Banks, 2006).

Effective multicultural teachers have a clarified understanding of their own cultural heritage, do not hesitate to discuss controversial information with students, and they allow divergent thinking on a topic, rather than taking the textbook view. They welcome discussion from multiple perspectives and help students develop the skill of respectfully disagreeing with others.

Banks's five dimensions of multicultural education are identified in Table 9.1.

Common Vocabulary for Cross-Cultural Issues

The terms defined in this section provide a common vocabulary and thus a foundation for discussing cross-cultural issues (ADL, 1998; Banks, 2001). By acknowledging that elements in society are prejudicial and recognizing that people and systems are biased, teachers can better understand the difficult and sometimes hostile environment that ELLs face. By realizing these prejudices, teachers can mitigate the negative effects of that bias in their instruction, materials, and resources.

- **Acculturation** occurs when individuals adapt effectively to the mainstream culture. This concept should be distinguished from *enculturation*, the process through which individuals learn the patterns of their own culture. To

Table 9.1 Banks' Dimensions of Multicultural Education

Dimension	Description
1. An empowering school culture and social structure	Grouping and labeling practices, sports, disproportionality in achievement, and interaction between staff and students across ethnic/racial lines must be examined to create a school culture that empowers all stakeholders and students from diverse racial, ethnic, language, and cultural groups.
2. Knowledge construction process	This relates to the extent that teachers help students to understand, investigate, and determine how the implicit cultural assumptions, frames of references, perspectives and biases within a discipline/content area, influence the ways in which knowledge is constructed within it.
3. Equity pedagogy	By using a variety of teaching styles that are consistent with the wide range of learning styles with various cultural and ethnic groups, teachers provide equity pedagogy when they modify their instruction to facilitate the academic achievement of diverse groups of students.
4. Content integration	This deals with the extent that teachers imbed examples, persons, and contributions from a variety of cultures, races, and ethnic groups within content to illustrate key concepts, principles, generalizations, and theories in their discipline/subject area.
5. Prejudice reduction	This concept focuses on the characteristics of students' racial attitudes and how tolerance can be fostered by teaching methods and materials, and the level of discussion dealing with controversial issues through divergent interpretations.

Source: Banks, 2006. CULTURAL DIVERSITY AND EDUCATION: FOUNDATIONS, CURRICULUM AND TEACHING (Fifth Edition). Boston: Allyn and Bacon, page 5.

acculturate is to adapt a second culture without necessarily giving up one's first culture. Acculturation is an additive process, in which an individual's right to participate in her or his own heritage is preserved (Diaz-Rico & Weed, 2006).

■ **Assimilation** occurs when members of an ethnic group are absorbed into the dominant culture and their culture gradually disappears in the process. Cultural assimilation is the process by which individuals adopt the behaviors, values, beliefs, and ways of life of the dominant culture.

■ **Biculturalism** is the state of functioning successfully in two cultures. Bicultural individuals have learned to function in two distinct sociocultural environments: that of their native culture and that of the dominant culture of the society in which they live. These individuals can mediate between the dominant discourse of educational institutions and the realities they face as members of subordinate cultures (ADL, 1998; Banks, 2001).

■ **Classism** is the tendency to view people according to their socioeconomic status in terms of upper, middle, or lower class. Discrimination is often rooted in classism.

■ **Culture** is an interdependent system of valued traditional and current knowledge and conceptions, embodied in behaviors and artifacts, within a society. Culture evolves to give meaning to its definitions of present and future problems relative to its existence (Banks, 2001).

- **Ethnocentrism** is the tendency to evaluate other ethnic groups according to the values and standards of one's own and often believing that one's own culture is superior to others.

- **Pluralism** occurs when minority and ethnic groups and their advocates assert that they have a right, if not a responsibility, to maintain valued elements of their ethnic cultures. Pluralists believe that the coexistence of multicultural traditions within a single society provides a variety of alternatives that enrich life in the United States. Pluralism is the condition in which members of diverse cultural groups have equal opportunities for success, in which cultural similarities and differences are valued, and in which students are provided cultural alternatives (ADL, 1998; Banks, 2001).

- **Prejudice** is an adverse judgment or opinion formed before receiving or without knowledge or examination of the facts. Prejudice is a preference, idea, act, or state of holding unreasonable, preconceived judgments or convictions. It is the irrational suspicion or hatred of people from a particular group, race, or religion.

- **Ableism** is the tendency to discriminate according to an individual's disability.

- **Ageism** is the tendency to discriminate according to an individual's age.

- **Sexism** is the tendency to discriminate according to an individual's sex or sexual orientation.

Being aware of the meanings of these terms can assist teachers in reviewing content materials. Sharing these concepts with students will help them understand that the classroom environment is characterized by tolerance and encourages risk taking in discussing controversial issues. In addition, sharing these concepts demonstrates to students that the teacher promotes open-minded thinking and deals with issues equitably.

Stereotyping

Addressing **stereotyping** is essential in any multicultural curriculum. In striving for harmony and tolerance in the classroom, it is helpful for both teachers and students to consider their own biases and prejudices. The way to becoming a more just society becomes clearer when it is understood how stereotyping promotes forms of discrimination.

The Anti-Defamation League (ADL) has created entire curriculums on how teachers can achieve better tolerance and harmony in the classrooms. The ADL's World of Difference Institute (ADL, 1998) discusses how stereotyping is applied to racial, religious, ethnic, gender, sexual orientation, and other groups and how it can become a part of prejudice and discrimination.

Here is how the ADL describes the stages or process of stereotyping:

- Stereotyping is a frequent part of people's thinking. It represents a shorthand way people process information about individuals (e.g., dumb blondes, dumb jocks).

- When people meet others, they are predisposed to focus on certain qualities and ignore other qualities. The qualities people focus on are *salient attributes*.

- People make generalizations about others on the basis of their salient attributes. Some of the generalizations are accurate, but many are false.

- Stereotyping involves making false generalizations about individuals on the basis of believing that the group to which they belong is homogeneous with regard to a wide range of traits. This kind of thinking ignores individual differences in group members.

- Stereotypes are resilient. Even when people meet others who do not fit the stereotype, they do not change their opinion. They ignore, misperceive, or forget examples that do not fit the generalization. Sometimes, people make an exception of someone who does not fill their preconceived notion, but the stereotype remains intact (e.g., the articulate athlete; the competent, unemotional woman; the sensitive man).

Stereotyping is not only a personal process, but it is also a social phenomenon. Attributes of race and ethnicity, religion, gender and sexual orientation, and physical and mental ability are all made salient in U.S. society. Even so, generalizations based on these attributes are generally false. People who belong to the same, say, racial or ethnic group are far too diverse in other ways to make accurate generalizations about all or most of them.

Society produces stereotypes, but individuals and the institutions they create act on those stereotypes. Stereotyping can turn into a form of differential treatment: discrimination. Stereotyping leads to discrimination according to this three-step process:

1. By creating high-saliency categories

2. By making false generalizations about the group, thus creating stereotypes

3. By treating people differently based on false assumptions, which is discrimination

When a group of people is discussed as a whole, everyone within the group might possibly be stereotyped. The generalizations made about a particular ethnic group ultimately provide erroneous information, rather than clarify the situation.

Elements of Surface and Deep Culture

Every cultural group has undergone and continues to undergo the processes of acculturation and assimilation. However, every cultural group maintains certain customs that are unique to it. These customs and practices become associated with the group until it is difficult to think of one without the other.

Elements of *surface culture* include the tangible things related to a group of people. Surface culture includes foods, holidays, arts, folklore, history, and personalities.

Elements of *deep culture* include the feelings and attitudes people learn by being members of particular groups. Each culture stipulates certain behaviors and mores to follow in particular situations and promotes particular attitudes. Deep culture includes courtship and marriage, ethics and values, gestures and kinetics, rewards and privileges, sex roles, space and proxemics, grooming, and rights and duties.

It is beneficial for teachers to understand that all of these elements contribute to the belief systems of students and their families. In approaching ELLs, consideration of and respect for these elements may help to foster positive student–teacher relationships and enhance communication with parents and guardians.

$\int$ome Differences among Cultural Groups

All individuals have their own learning channels and different educational experiences. Many factors—such as culture, religion, family beliefs, and health—contribute to the development of students and are reflected by students' cognitive behavior in the classroom (Zainuddin, Morales-Jones, Yahya, & Ariza, 2002).

Many elements of students' native cultures collide with elements of American culture, creating miscommunication and misunderstanding in the classroom. Teachers' own cultural beliefs often clash with students' cultural beliefs, thus preventing learning. Conflicts can occur because the customs and beliefs of students from other cultures do not fit the norms of the mainstream American classroom.

These misunderstandings may be rooted in teachers' lack of knowledge and understanding of the different cultural values students bring to the classroom. For instance, culturally based learning styles vary from student to student, and instruction must be designed to complement student preferences, gradually providing experiences for them to function appropriately in different academic situations (Ariza, 2006).

Teachers should consider differences among other cultures relative to U.S. culture in their effort to provide the optimal learning environment for all students. The following sections describe other cultures in abbreviated, general terms. The discussion includes Hispanic and Latino American, Native American, Haitian American, Asian American, Indian (sub-Asian continent) American, and Middle Eastern American cultures (Ariza, 2006). These truncated descriptions should not be perceived as stereotypes.

Hispanic and Latino American Culture

- Even though many ELLs speak Spanish, their native cultures vary greatly. For instance, there are significant differences between the Cuban and Mexican cultures.

- Independence is not seen as a positive value. Rather, family obligations and interdependence are valued, and family members strongly support one another.

- Members of extended families often live in the same home.

- Spanish speakers maintain physical closeness while talking with one another.

- Affection is displayed openly.

- Affluence is projected through the quality of clothing and possessions.

- Latinos often comment on one another's flaws and physical appearance and correct each other's mistakes.

- The concept of time is relative, not fixed, and so punctuality is not expected.

- Catholicism is the dominant religion, and spiritualism is also popular. Political functions are generally not connected with religion.

- Parents from many Hispanic countries are not involved with their children's day-to-day school operations and do not interact directly with the schools. Even so, these parents should not be judged as disinterested or uncaring.

- Students do well in *cooperative learning* groups and informal class discussions. They tend to share answers and do well with personalized rewards.

- Students who attended school in their native countries are accustomed to wearing uniforms. Also, at the **secondary level,** students are used to having teachers move from room to room, rather than having students move from class to class. Teachers move from one class to another in Asian, Central American, and South American classrooms (Keefe, 2008).

Native American Culture

- There are hundreds of different tribal groups, each with its own traditions, governance, mythology, and so on.

- Native American students typically have visual and holistic learning styles.

- In many households, problems are corrected through discussion and applying rules of wisdom, not yelling.

- Schools on reservations are generally circular, with the rooms leading to an atrium or fire circle, and each room exits to the outside, providing an entrance to nature. Computers are found in classrooms and labs, since many schools receive additional funds from Native American casinos.

- Teachers watch students carefully to identify their natural talents and abilities and then teach them occupations within the tribe.

- Good manners are extremely important. Native Americans are generally not rude or belligerent; they may seem introverted.

- Like most children, Native American children like to be outside. They believe everything has a spirit and may feel they are keepers of the earth and sky.

- People are believed to be responsible for their own actions, rather than allowed to place blame on good or evil. Balance and harmony are important to the community.

- A person is held in high esteem for his or her generosity; therefore, students may give away their school supplies.

- Each individual has a unique experience and is expected to share it with the tribe, which translates into the classroom.

Haitian American Culture

- Haitian Americans proudly proclaim they were the first blacks to gain freedom from slavery.

- Religious practices are complex and traditionally Catholic. Many Haitians have become fundamentalist Christians. Some are exclusively Vodouists, which combines African religious beliefs with Catholic rituals, symbols, saints, and prayers.

- During illness or crisis, religion plays a major role in Haitian life. Folk or spiritual healing and prayer may be the only option to heal disease available to these people, whose daily lives are shaped by a lack of basic health care, such as clean water, antibiotics, and prenatal care.

- Many can recall the shame and indignity that resulted in the 1980s from the misconception that Haitians had AIDS.

- Haitians usually live with their extended family members. Children can be disciplined using corporal punishment.

- Haitian culture has a vibrant and rich oral tradition. Stories, proverbs, and riddles reflect a clever use of oral expression.

- Many have witnessed much violence in their homeland.

- The educational system in Haiti was modeled after the traditional French system, with a rigorous, classical curriculum. Receiving an education remains an elusive goal for most citizens.

Asian American Culture

- Many Asian Americans follow the values taught by Confucianism, which include harmony with the family and community, hard work, and a strong emphasis on education.

- The stereotype of Asians as the model minority is rooted in this heavy emphasis on education and academic success, as well as family integrity. Teachers who assume these students are high achievers may unintentionally neglect them.

- Students place a lot of pressure on themselves to excel academically and thus avoid bringing shame to the family.

- Students are not usually comfortable speaking out or drawing attention to themselves; they may be hesitant and shy.

- Being chastised can be particularly distressing (Keefe, 2008).

- Listening, rather than speaking, and speaking softly and behaving modestly are valued.

- Many Asian customs and holidays come from Buddhism, and events are based on different calendars.

- Asian languages are very different from English, in that certain sounds in English do not exist in Asian languages. Given this, Asian students may have great difficulty with oral expression. Asian written languages are created with characters, rather than letters, and some are written in columns.

Indian American Culture

- India's macroculture is traditionalist and rests on freedom of religion, spirituality, and belief in the family as an institution.

- Religion is clearly present in art, devotional music, fashion, housing, décor, festivals, marriage, business, and the environment.

- Traditionally, Indian culture regarded getting an education as a holy duty linked to religion.

- The Hindu goddess Saraswati, the goddess of knowledge, is widely revered and worshipped.

- Respect for all elders is sacred.

- Male children are favored, and more males are educated than females.

- Arranged marriages are still prevalent.

- Parental involvement in the schools is the norm, with teachers and parents working together to ensure children's academic success.

- Over 1,600 minor languages are spoken in India, but English is widely spoken, as well.

- Students are dedicated to the pursuit of education and strongly attached to their families back home. Changing entrenched family values and social beliefs is difficult, as is true of most cultures.

- Students have an innate sense of "looking out for younger ones."

Middle Eastern American Culture

- Many Middle Eastern cultures, particularly those of Islamic faith, are at present misunderstood and experiencing discrimination and negative profiling.

- Behavior is dictated by society, as opposed to individual beliefs.

- Middle Eastern society is paternalistic and authoritative, and elders play an important role. Parents must always be obeyed, and students will study what their parents want them to study.

- Same-sex relationships are very close, and openly opposite-sex relationships are not socially appropriate.

- Special preparation of food is necessary to observe Islamic and Judaic law.

- In Islamic cultures, modesty in dress is expected of females and males. Undressing in front of others—even others of the same sex—is discouraged. Middle Eastern students may feel uncomfortable changing before and after physical education classes.

- Both the Arabic and Hebrew languages are written from right to left.

- Muslims pray five times a day. Saluting the flag or saying the Pledge of Allegiance may be considered offensive, as it seems irreverent to God.

- Islamic law prefers segregation by gender. Therefore, dating and dancing are discouraged, and cross-gender touching is not appropriate in most Muslim societies.

- Middle Eastern students in U.S. classrooms may be uncomfortable with cooperative learning arrangements.

- The American instructional practices of encouraging self-exploration and self-expression and posing peer-learning situations may make Middle Eastern students wonder when *real* teaching begins.

It would be impossible for teachers to know and understand all the nuances of the diverse cultures represented in their classrooms. Nonetheless, teachers must make an effort to understand some of those aspects of culture that affect classroom interactions and activities. Conflicts can be mitigated by creating a tolerant atmosphere and by not forcing students to behave in ways contrary to their backgrounds. In addition, when teachers validate the languages and customs of ELLs, they provide opportunities for native English speakers to learn about those other cultures. Doing so heightens students' curiosity about and interest in others who are not like them. All of these developments lead to greater multicultural harmony and tolerance, not only in classrooms and schools but also in neighborhoods and communities.

Individualist versus Collectivist Perspectives

An **individualist perspective** among students is the norm in many U.S. classrooms. Among world cultures, a **collectivist perspective** to culture is often found among Native Americans, Hispanic and Latino Americans, African Americans, and Asian Americans (Greenfield, Raeff, & Quiroz, 1996). African American culture has been described as more collectivist than the dominant U.S. culture in terms of family orientation and kinship. Yet it is more individualistic than many other cultures in terms of its emphasis on individual achievement.

Individualism and collectivism are often invisible to the people who live within cultures aligned with these perspectives. For example, members of a collectivist culture probably go about their daily business without consciously thinking "I'm helping my brother with his homework, because we have a network of interdependent relationships within my collectivist culture." Similarly, a member of an individualist culture likely does not stop to reflect, "I am striving to get all A's in my classes, because in my individualist culture, we value personal achievement over all else" (Brown, 2002, 23).

When students with a collectivist orientation are forced to conform to individualistic modes of learning, they face a cultural mismatch. The result is often frustration and failure for teachers, students, and families.

See Table 9.2 for a comparison/contrast of individualist and collectivist perspectives in the realm of education. Use the information to answer the following questions:

- What elements of the individualist perspective make sense to you?

- What elements of the collectivist perspective make sense to you?

- Elaborate on some of the expectations of students, and explain why you agree or disagree with them as an educator. What factors from your own cultural background might influence your opinions?

- What kinds of conflicts might occur in a classroom because of these different cultural perspectives? How might you deal with such conflicts?

- What might you do in your classroom to allow for cultural values to be shared?

Multiple Perspectives Activities

Looking at an issue from **multiple perspectives** fosters the notion that most situations are not all black and white, right or wrong, good or bad. Teachers who allow students to discuss issues that may be controversial promote critical thinking among students. In such discussions, the challenge for teachers is to remain unbiased and act as a moderator, and circulate with a clipboard to record student comments and reply to group questions. The rules that apply to working in cooperative learning groups can apply to discussions such as these.

This section presents a series of activities that explore two perspectives on the same topic or issue. Three topics or issues are identified: (1) establishing English as the official language of the United States, (2) instituting a program for clean alternative energy (LWV, 2006), and (3) events in the year 1492 (Jameson, 1998a).

Table 9.2 Individualist versus Collectivist Perspectives in Education

Individualist	Collectivist
Student should work independently and get his own work done.	Student should be helpful and cooperate with his peers, giving assistance when needed.
Giving help to others may be considered cheating.	Helping is not considered cheating.
Student should be praised frequently.	Student should not be singled out for praise in front of peers.
The positive should be emphasized whenever possible.	Positive feedback should be stated in terms of student's ability to help family or community.
Student should attain intellectual skills in school: education is schooling.	Student should learn appropriate social behaviors and intellectual skills; education is upbringing.
Student should engage in discussion and argument in order to learn to think critically.	Student should be quiet and respectful in class because he will learn more this way.
Property belongs to individuals, and others must ask to borrow or share it.	Most property is communal and not considered the domain of an individual.
Teacher manages behavior indirectly or emphasizes student self-control.	Teacher has primary authority for managing behavior but also expects peers to guide each other's behavior.
Parent is integrally involved with student's academic progress.	Parent believes that it is the teacher's role to provide academic instruction to student.

Source: The Education Alliance at Brown University, 2002, www.alliance.brown.edu/pubs/diversity_kit/. Reprinted with permission of the Education Alliance at Brown University.

To conduct these activities, six groups should be formed. Each group should get a posterboard on which one perspective about one topic has been written. If this book is being used with preservice or seasoned teachers as participants, each group should develop a lesson plan around their perspective, which will include ELL instructional strategies and **alternative assessments.** Each group should later share their plan with the whole group. Others outside each group can be solicited for additional suggestions for the lesson plans.

English as the Official Language

Perspective 1

The pro side of this topic supports making English the official, or common, language of the United States. The main reason many Americans would prefer to have an official language is to unite the country. As President Theodore Roosevelt said, "We have room for but one language here, and that is the English language." Establishing a national language would encourage immigrants who do not speak it to learn it, and that would bring the country together.

Others in support of establishing English as the official language argue that it would simplify and expedite matters in education, government, and business and that it would ease communication and racial conflicts. Still others, including several prominent politicians, claim that knowing how to speak English is one of the keys to success in the United States.

Perspective 2

The con side of establishing a national language is that it would destroy the unique cultures of various groups in the United States, which is a nation of immigrants. Having an official language would, in fact, obscure cultural identities and discourage immigrants whose native language is not English. Other arguments on the con side are that having a multilingual country would better protect public health and public safety, promote tourism, handle emergencies, and administer justice.

People against implementing an official language point out that doing so would not necessarily increase the number of Americans who can speak English. Moreover, people who do not speak English would not be any less American than those who do. Critics of the idea also note that English-only laws are politically incorrect and biased against immigrants.

Additionally, many feel that having multiple languages spoken throughout the country makes it interesting, diplomatic, and worldly. In addition, there are clear advantages to being bilingual, particularly in this global world.

A final argument is that passing an English-only law would resolve a heated topic within the government but does nothing to solve the real conflicts that go on within the country.

Program for Clean Alternative Energy

Background

California is the third-largest oil-producing state, and virtually all of the oil produced in California is delivered to California refineries. Yet, California still imports 42 percent of their oil from foreign countries. California oil producers pay the state corporate income tax on profits, pay a regulatory fee but not an extraction tax. In 2006, a referendum called Proposal 87 was put on the state ballot with the goal of changing that. The funds generated by the extraction tax the oil producers paid would be designated for research and development of alternative, more efficient energy solutions, as well as training and education (League of Women Voters, 2006).

Perspective 1

In support of Proposition 87, consideration for the fact that several other states, such as Alaska, Louisiana, and Texas, pay billions of drilling fees, whereas oil producers in California do not. California consumes more oil and Californians are among those who pay the highest gas prices in the United States. Proposition 87 would prohibit oil companies from passing the added tax on to consumers, and has incentives for consumers to purchase fuel-efficient cars. With this law in place, oil producers would be encouraged to develop less polluting ways to produce cleaner energy. In addition to these concerns, air pollution from gas emissions and health issues, such as very high rates of asthma and lung diseases, are very negative by-products facing Californians, and cannot be overlooked in this discussion. Organizations that supported the proposition were Americans for Energy Independence, The Foundation for

Taxpayer and Consumer Rights, Natural Resources Defense Council, and the Union of Concerned Scientists. Students can be asked if the proposition won or was defeated. (Proposition 87 was defeated 45.3% to 54.7%.)

Perspective 2

In opposition to Proposition 87, consideration for the billions of dollars worth of bonds that could be sold, and possibly force a state bailout, at the taxpayers expense. Bonds are debt obligations, and are issued by state government. The money from the sale of the bonds is used for financing projects, such as Proposition 87. This law would involve spending billions to fund 50 political appointees, who are not required to produce results or be accountable to taxpayers. This proposition if passed does not require the generated funds to be spent in California, which would boost the state's economy. Lastly, Proposition 87 is not the way to advance needed energy alternatives. Some of the opponents of this proposition were the Association of Energy Service Companies, Automobile Club of Southern California, the California Chamber of Commerce, and the California Trucking Association.

The Year 1492

Perspective 1

For Spanish Jews and Muslims, the year 1492 meant the Inquisition: religious persecution, death and torture, and being driven out of Spain, their country for hundreds of years. My name is Mara Ibn-Isak, and I will remember 1492. I am 16 years old. I live in Cordova, Spain, but not for long. Soon I will have to leave here and go somewhere else. I am looking at every corner of my house so that I can remember. This house and the land have been in my family for over 500 years. Life was good for all of us, Christians, Jews, and Moors, who lived peacefully together. We produced great art, music, and philosophy. Business and trade was good too. On the Christian holy day of Ash Wednesday in 1391, a mob broke into the Jewish quarter of our neighbor city of Seville and demanded that all Jews convert to Christianity. Four thousand people were killed. Our homes and synagogues were burned. Due to the fear that they would be burned or killed, many Jews outwardly became Christian but secretly they practiced their Jewish faith.

Ferdinand and Isabella wanted to get rid of all the Muslims and Jews in Spain, so they got the church to help them. Taxes were levied on Jews, and 14,000 families became bankrupt and others were ransomed as slaves.

In March of this year, 1492, the king and queen decreed that by July 30 not a single Jew was to remain in Spain. All of our property became property of the crown or the church. My father says we will go to Fez, Morocco and start again. Will anyone understand my language? My mother says that when she bakes her "pan de casa" our house will be the same. My father and all our family will have to work hard to build a new life, and our Jewish community will be dispersed throughout Africa, Europe, and the New World. I will remember July of 1492 and tell my children about this, so generations will know that year as a very bad year for Mara Ibn-Isak.

Perspective 2

- Approximately 13,000 BC: first known human beings live in the Caribbean.

- Approximately 8 BC: the Taino "men of good" people arrive in the region. With great care for the earth, the Tainos are able to feed millions of people, no one goes hungry. They play sports, recite poetry, are great inventors and travel from island to island. One Spanish priest reported that he never saw two Tainos fighting.

- 1450: There may be as many as 70 to 100 million people living in what will one day be called the Americas. They are of many nationalities, with perhaps 2,000 different languages.

- August 3, 1492: Columbus departs from Palos instead of the port of Cadiz, which is filled with ships taking some 8,000 Jews into exile as result of the Inquisition.

- October 12, 1492: The ships arrive at the island, Guanahana, where Columbus takes possession of the island for Ferdinand and Isabella. Columbus receives presents from the people he encounters and gives them some red caps, glass beads, and "many other things of little value." The first thing he tries to ask the people is "if they have gold."

- October 14: Columbus's thoughts turn to slavery. "When your highness so commands, they [the Indians] can be carried off to Castile or held captive in the island itself, since with 50 men they would be all kept in subjection and forced to do whatever may be wished."

- December 25: Columbus's ship the Santa Maria hits rocks of Espanola. He is forced to abandon it. The Taino cacique [leader] Guacanagari weeps when he hears of the shipwreck. Tainos help unload the ship "without the loss of a shoestring."

- January 13, 1493: First reported skirmish between the Spaniards and Indians. After landing on an island to trade for bows, Columbus writes that many Indians prepared "to assault the Christians and capture them."

- February 15: Columbus returns [to Spain] with relatively little value. In a letter written aboard ship, Columbus lies, saying on Espanola there are many spices and great mines of gold and other metals.

- September 25: Columbus's second voyage begins. Some of the money to finance the voyage comes from wealth taken from Spanish Jews.

- Early February 1494: Columbus sends 12 of the 17 ships back to Spain for supplies. Several dozen Indian slaves are taken aboard, men, women, and children, he writes. He justifies this by writing that they are cannibals and thus, slavery will more readily "secure the welfare of their souls." Spanish priest Bartolome de las Casas, later was known to have written that claims of cannibalism are used to "excuse violence, cruelty, plunder and slaughter committed against the Indians every day."

- February 1495: Columbus must be desperate to prove that his enterprise can be profitable. He rounds up 1,600 Tainos, who are chained and taken to ships to be sent to Spain as slaves.

- 1495: Columbus establishes the tribute system. Every Taino, 14 or older, is required to fill a hawk's bill full of gold every 3 months. The Spaniards cut the hands off of those who do not comply. As de las Casas writes, "The tribute is impossible and intolerable." Columbus will soon replace the tribute system with outright slavery.

- May 20, 1506: Columbus dies in Valladolid, Spain.

■ 1542: Bartolome de las Casas writes that a mere 200 Tainos still live in Espanola. Some scholar recently estimated more than 3 million Tainos lived there when Columbus first arrived.

The issues explored in these activities relate to the social studies (events of the year 1492), science (alternative energy), and the language arts (English-only policy). For each activity, students are allowed to discuss and defend their perspectives, exercise problem-solving skills, and reach a consensus diplomatically within the group.

Stereotyping Activity

This activity illustrates how people stereotype others by the way they look (for instance, their facial features and how they dress) and the way they speak and interact (FLDOE, 2003). This activity should be done in small groups.

Using a form such as that shown in Figure 9.1, each member of the group writes down three memorable, unusual related experiences. Two of them should be true experiences, and one of them should be false. Next, group members take turns reading aloud their experiences. As each member listens, he or she selects the experience believed to be false and writes why. The person reading his or experiences then reveals which one is false. This procedure is completed with each member of the group.

As a class, students should discuss the strategies they used to determine what was true or false about each person. This discussion can lead to an analysis of the stereotypical thinking everyone has done at one time or another in making judgments and creating predispositions about people based on factors such as the cars they drive, the jobs they do, the houses and neighborhoods in which they live, and so on.

My Experiences

Experience 1 _____

Experience 2 _____

Experience 3 _____

Others' False Experiences

Person A _____

Person B _____

Person C _____

Figure 9.1 Form for Stereotyping Activity

Source: Jameson, 1998b.

This activity can be used with middle or high school students to **build background** knowledge and to elicit what they know about a topic. The directions might be changed as follows:

> Write down two things that you know about a topic, and make up a third statement. Then share your statements with your group members to see if they can determine which one is false.

A version calling for two facts and one opinion about a topic could also be created. Teachers may want to change "experience(s)" to "what I know about this topic."

Taking a Stand Activity

This activity can be done with teachers participating in a training course. Content area teachers might also conduct this activity with students, replacing the following statements with statements relating to the lesson topic.

In an area inside or outside the classroom, the teacher or trainer draws a line on the floor or the ground, or places a strip of colored tape on it that extends from one end of the area to the other. At one end of the line, the teacher places a sign that says "I SUPPORT," and at the other end, he or she places a sign that says "I DO NOT SUPPORT."

The teacher or trainer tells participants that this is a silent activity (ADL, 1998). He or she will read aloud each statement, and participants will decide whether they support or do not support it. Then each participant will walk to that area of the line nearest the sign that reflects his or her thoughts on that statement. Anyone who feels neutral about the statement should stand in the middle of the line.

The purpose of this activity is for participants to affirm their feelings about an issue. They are to follow their own minds on the issue and not pay attention to where others are standing.

The following statements can be modified according to the topic/lesson objective or audience/participants. Statements can be deleted or added:

- I believe the official language of the United States should be English.

- I accept interracial dating.

- I think U.S. immigration policies should be more restrictive.

- Individual school districts should decide their policy on school prayer.

- My parents' generation is more respectful of racial and religious differences than my generation.

- I feel comfortable when in the company of people of different faiths, such as Jews, Buddhists, Muslims, and Christians.

- The multimedia organizations in the United States deliver a fair and accurate account of the news.

- I would accept and feel comfortable with a gay or homosexual child.

- Everyone should have the right to free speech, including members of hate groups.

- Implementing a multicultural education program should be mandatory in all schools, grades K–12.

After completing the exercise, students should discuss which statements they had the most difficulty in terms of deciding where to stand. They should also discuss whether anyone felt uncomfortable with the exercise and why.

Cultural Vignette Activity

Working in groups, students will simulate a teacher and student conducting an interactive journal writing activity (Jameson, 1998b). Each group will be assigned one of the five vignettes that follows:

1. The student is a 12-year-old girl from a Mexican family. The mother, who speaks no English, is extremely modest. The mother has to go to a physician for an embarrassing problem. The daughter has to accompany her mother into the examining room and translate the ensuing discussion with the physician. The experience is upsetting to the girl, and she writes about it in her interactive journal.

2. The student is a 15-year-old Korean immigrant girl. At school she appears to have lots of friends, especially among the girls. However, she is not invited to any of the parties the students have. At school dances, no boy ever asks her to dance. She feels physically unattractive and rejected and writes about this in her interactive journal.

3. A 13-year-old Miccosukee Indian boy has been invited to a special summer program for gifted students. However, if he goes he will miss the Green Corn Dance, which is one of the most important events in his traditional religious calendar. His family does not want him to go, but the school guidance counselor (Anglo American) sees this as a marvelous opportunity. The student has tremendous respect for his family and an excellent relationship with the guidance counselor. The student does not know what to do and writes about the problem in his interactive journal.

4. A 17-year-old Puerto Rican boy is confused about finding a social group in which he feels accepted. Physically, the boy has beige skin and dark brown, slightly curly hair. His mother has very dark skin, and her hair is black and curly. His father has light brown, straight hair and fair skin. In Puerto Rico, his was not an unusual family. However, in the United States, people seem to consider him and his mother black and his father white. People seem to be disapproving of what they consider an "interracial" marriage. This boy does not have a sense of himself as "black" or as "white," nor does he feel as though he belongs to a different racial group from his dad. At school the white kids tell him he is black and the black kids say that he thinks he is white. The boy writes about this in his interactive journal.

5. Annette is a 14-year-old Haitian girl who has recently arrived in the United States. In Haiti, she attended school and was educated in French. However, upon coming to the United States, she was placed in a bilingual Haitian Creole class. She speaks Haitian Creole but does not know how to read and write it. She speaks, reads, and writes French fluently but neither speaks nor understands English. The students in her school often tease the children who are Haitian, so Annette wants to be in an English class so that no one will know she is Haitian. She says it is a waste of time for her to be in the bilingual class, since she cannot read or write Haitian Creole. She is very upset about the situation and writes about it in her interactive journal.

After being assigned a scenario, each group will first consider the journal entry from the student's perspective. Then, the group will respond as a teacher to the student's entry. Group members should keep in mind that each student is unique and that the purpose of the activity is not necessarily to solve a problem but rather to help the student feel some degree of comfort with two cultures.

Each group's responses can be discussed, and suggestions from members outside each group can be shared. This kind of activity can be done in content area classrooms, with groups of students exploring different solutions by discussing how they would react to content-specific concepts and situations.

A video entitled *A Place at the Table,* created by the Southern Poverty Law Center (www.teachingtolerance.org), explores different cultures that exist in U.S. society through student testimonials. Depicted in the video are several young adults from different cultures who discuss the difficulties of race and culture they encounter with other teens. The video is appropriate for middle and high school students. Accompanying it are lesson plans and suggestions for extended activities.

References

Ajayi, L. (2006). Multiple voices, multiple realities: Self-defined images of self among adolescent Hispanic English language learners. *Education, 126*(3), 468–480.

Anti-Defamation League (ADL). (1998). *A classroom of difference.* New York: World of Difference Institute.

Ariza, E. (2006). *Not for ESOL teachers.* New York: Pearson.

Banks, J., & Banks, C. (Ed.). (1995). *Handbook of research on multicultural education.* San Francisco: Jossey-Bass.

Banks, J. (2001). *Cultural diversity and education: Foundations, curriculum, and teaching* (4th ed.). Boston: Allyn & Bacon.

Banks, J. (2006). *Cultural diversity and education: Foundations, curriculum, and teaching* (5th ed.). Boston: Allyn & Bacon.

Boynton, S. (2003). *Enriching content classes for secondary ESOL students.* Tallahassee, FL: Department of Education, Center for Applied Linguistics, Sunbelt Office.

Brown University LAB. (2002). *The Diversity Kit: An Introductory Resource for Social Change in Education.* Providence, RI: Education Alliance.

Diaz-Rico, L., & Weed, K. (2006). *The cross-cultural, language, and academic development handbook.* New York: Pearson.

Florida Department of Education (FLDOE), Center for Applied Linguistics, Sunbelt Office. (2003). *Enriching content classes for secondary ESOL students.* Tallahassee: Author.

Gay, G. (2004). The importance of multicultural education. *Educational Leadership, 61*(4), 30–35.

Greenfield, P. M., Raeff, C., & Quiroz, B. (1996). Cultural values in learning and education. In B. Williams (Ed.), *Closing the achievement gap: A vision for changing beliefs and practices* (pp. 37–55). Alexandria, VA: Association for Supervision and Curriculum Development.

Jameson, J. H. (1998a). *Enriching content classes for secondary ESOL students: Study guide* (pp. 184–185). Washington, DC & McHenry, IL: Center for Applied Linguistics and Delta Systems, Inc.

Jameson, J. H. (1998b). *Enriching content classes for secondary ESOL students: Study guide* (p. 60). Washington, DC & McHenry, IL: Center for Applied Linguistics and Delta Systems, Inc.

Keefe, M. R. (Producer/Researcher). (2008). *Voices of immigrant ELL high school students* [Video]. Martin County School District, Florida, TV Production Classes.

Larson, D., & Smalley, W. (1972). *Becoming bilingual: A guide to language learning.* New Canaan, CT: Practical Anthropology.

Luke, A. (2000). Critical literacy in Australia: A matter of context and standpoint. *Journal of Adolescent and Adult Literacy, 43*(5), 448–460.

Reeves, J. (2006). Secondary teacher attitudes toward including English-language learners in mainstream classrooms. *Journal of Educational Research, 99*(3), 131–142.

Richard-Amato, P., & Snow, M. (1992). *The multicultural classroom.* White Plains, NY: Longman.

Southern Poverty Law Center. (2002). A place at the table [Video]. Freedom's Main Line. *Teaching Tolerance.* (free material available from the Center)

Zainuddin, H., Morales-Jones, C., Yahya, N., & Ariza, E. (2002). *Fundamentals of teaching English to speakers of other languages in K–12 mainstream classrooms.* Dubuque, IA: Kendall/Hunt.

Chapter 10

Parent-Teacher Communication,
Students with Abilities,
Professional Collaboration,
and Final Thoughts

*S*ince changes are going on anyway, the great thing is to learn enough about them, so that we will be able to lay hold of them, and turn them in the direction of our desires.

—*John Dewey*

"Lost in translation" is an expression used in social, economical, political, and educational circles to indicate a breakdown in communication. Communicating with students and parents whose home language is not the language of instruction poses many obstacles. Not only the literal, word-for-word translation of language is problematic, but so are the pragmatics of the language, such as what language to use in different settings, how to enter a conversation, and what words are acceptable in one **culture** versus another (Keefe, 2008). In education, teachers and language **facilitators** sometimes encounter words in English that have no accurate translations in another language. And because the dominant language in the United States is English, most states do not provide high-stakes tests in other languages. Therefore, learning English **academic language** must be the instructional priority for English language learners (ELLs) to achieve success.

In the last chapter, the discussion examined some of the differences among students' native cultures and how cultural diversity can work positively to foster tolerance and ultimately acceptance in the classroom. For this to happen, teachers must do some introspection of their own attitudes and expressions and acknowledge that they have prejudices. This is one of the most pivotal challenges facing teachers in the twenty-first century classroom. Only when teachers confront their own biases will they be able to transform their psychological, emotional, and intellectual beings and instill compassion and understanding in their students.

With this in mind, consider the following excerpt from William Ayers's (1994) book *To Teach: The Journey of a Teacher*. The excerpt contains a letter written by a Native American mother to a teacher at the beginning of a school year. After reading the letter, think about your reaction to the views the mother expresses here:

A Mother's Letter

Before you take charge of the classroom that contains my child, please ask yourself why you are going to teach Indian children. What are your expectations? . . . Write down and examine all the information and opinions you possess about Indians. What are the stereotypes and untested assumptions that you bring with you into the classroom? How many negative attitudes towards Indians will you put before my child? Too many teachers, unfortunately, seem to see their role as rescuer. My child does not need to be rescued; he does not consider being Indian a misfortune. He has a culture, probably older than yours; he has meaningful values and a rich and varied, experiential background. . . . [Don't] say anything that implies to him that it is less than satisfactory. Like most Indian children his age, he is competent. He can dress himself, prepare a meal for himself, clean up afterwards, and care for a younger child. He knows his Reserve, all of which is his home, like the back of his hand. He is not accustomed to having to ask permission to do the ordinary things that are part of normal living. He is seldom forbidden to do anything, usually the consequences of an action are explained to him, and he is allowed to decide for himself whether or not to act. [He has developed] . . . his skills and confidence in his own capabilities. Didactic teaching will be an alien experience for him. He has been taught . . . that courtesy is an essential part of human conduct, and rudeness is any action that makes another person feel stupid or foolish. Do not mistake his patient courtesy for indifference or passivity. He doesn't speak standard English, but he is in no way "linguistically handicapped." . . . Indian children communicate very well, both among themselves and with other Indians. They speak "functional" English, very effectively augmented by their fluency in the silent language, the subtle, unspoken communication of facial expressions, gestures, body movement and the use of personal space. . . . [O]ur children are skillful interpreters of the silent language. They will know your feelings and attitudes with unerring precision, no matter how carefully you arrange your smile or modulate your voice. They will learn in your classroom, because children learn involuntarily. What they will learn will depend upon you. Will you help my child to learn to read, or will you teach him that he has a reading problem? Will you help him develop problem-solving skills, or will you teach him that school is where you try to guess what answer the teacher wants? Will he learn that his sense of his own value and dignity is valid, or will he learn that he must forever be apologetic and "trying harder" because he isn't white? Can you help him acquire the intellectual skills he needs without, at the same time, imposing your values on top of those he already has? Respect my child. He is a person. He has a right to be himself.

In reading "A Mother's Letter" (Ayers, 1994), you become aware of the concern the mother has for her son, and you sense that she has had some negative experiences with non–Native American teachers. She reveals some of the educational values of her culture by reminding the teacher that teaching in a didactic, patronizing manner is both presumptuous and discourteous. The mother informs the teacher that Native American children are skillful at reading facial expressions. The mother also points out that even if the teacher does not actually vocalize negativity, her students will understand her unspoken meaning. They are not "linguistically handicapped," after all. The mother ends the letter with a series of provocative questions that are surely intended to prompt some reflection on the part of the teacher. The mother hopes the teacher will abandon the preconceived notion that because her son is Native American, he will struggle with learning. The mother also pleads with the teacher to treat her son with the respect that all students deserve.

In terms of cultural diversity and conflict, the new millennium does not appear much different from the last century or centuries before. Clashes between people of different religions and beliefs continue, and armed struggles between governments and other factions still exist. These conflicts help shape individuals' bigoted attitudes and prejudicial perspectives toward others who are unlike them.

Teachers are not immune from having similar feelings. Recognizing one's own biases is the first step toward becoming a more open-minded, tolerant individual. It is not easy to identify and acknowledge one's prejudices and then to orient one's philosophy to be healthy and more accepting of differences. The importance of doing so becomes more apparent, however, as teachers experience the diversity of classrooms today. Therefore, teachers' ability to adapt their approach and embrace this diversity is crucial for the success of all students.

Communicating with Parents

"A Mother's Letter" (Ayers, 1994) was written by a Native American mother in the early 1990s, but it could just as well have been written by a Muslim, Jewish, or Asian mother today. As the level of cultural diversity increases in U.S. schools, teachers may encounter more parents expressing themselves, as this mother did, for the purpose of ensuring that there is a fundamental understanding between a student's home and school. Teachers may also encounter parents of ELLs who do not understand what is expected of them in U.S. schools or do not know how to become involved in school activities. In some cultures, the unspoken norm is that it is the teacher's job to educate the student. Participation from the parents shows disrespect for the teacher's expertise (Sobel & Kugler, 2007).

What are some of the factors that make communicating with parents a challenge? First of all, some parents of ELLs understand little or no English. In addition, they may have struggled in their homeland and had limited experience with school. These experiences may cause parents to undervalue education, particularly in comparison to how native-born Americans value education. Americans place immense value on the degree of education one has; it may ultimately determine the socioeconomic status that he or she can achieve in life. The parents of new immigrant students tend to work day in and day out to provide their families with shelter, food and clothing, basic amenities, a stable life, and perhaps a chance of a better future. They see their role in their children's education as making sure their children listen to their teachers, follow the teachers' directions, and do the homework their teachers assign (Fu, 2004). However, making ends meet takes all these parents' energy and time.

Some of the jobs held by parents of ELLs are in the services industries, may be labor intensive, and involve exposure to outside elements of weather during all seasons. Many of these jobs require starting very early in the morning or late at night. Parents with jobs such as these will likely find it difficult to attend school meetings and other functions. Some parents of ELLs are undocumented immigrants and thus unable to open a bank account, get a driver's license, or have the documents necessary to secure standard housing. In many cases, these people live in a rural environment, which is a good distance from the school. For these parents, transportation to school functions can be difficult if a bus or mass transportation is not available. And if students miss the bus ride to school, they will likely be absent the entire day. Even if students' parents do drive and are home during the day, they may not have the funds for fuel to travel the distance to school.

All of these factors certainly contribute to making parental communication problematic. Yet one of the more obvious challenges in communicating with parents is the language barrier. In any school district in any state, up to 100 or more different languages and dialects may be spoken. Families of ELLs are found all across the country. They are not just limited to New York, California, Texas, Florida, and the border states, as in the past.

So, how can schools overcome these barriers and do a better job of addressing the issues emphasized in the No Child Left Behind (NCLB) Act? At the district level, administrators can hire specialists—experts in ELL programs—to assist principals and assistant principals at school sites. Schools can provide language facilitators and translations of important information that parents need to know. Individual schools can also encourage their school advisory counsels (SACs) to recruit **language minority** members in the community to participate on them. Schools may even use funds to transport parents to important meetings (Smith, Coggins, & Cardoso, 2008). Schools must demonstrate a positive, welcoming tone not just in the classroom but also at the registration desk, where parents first encounter school personnel. All of these ideas, when put in place, create a welcoming environment and validate the various cultures and ethnicities that are represented in our schools.

The most critical element in effective parental communication is likely the classroom teacher. His or her direct, daily contact with children and ability to create an equitable atmosphere in the classroom can increase the degree of parental involvement and provide opportunities to influence parents in placing a higher value on education.

Students with Abilities

Schools must avoid placing ELLs in special education programs on the basis of criteria that essentially measure and evaluate their English language skills (GaDOE, 2009). When tested in English, students who were born outside the United States and cannot use English well are often unable to demonstrate how skilled they really are in the content areas. Because of their lack of English language proficiency, these students are often placed in special education. Conversely, schools must ensure that ELLs are not improperly excluded from participation in special education because of their limited English proficiency.

By considering both ELLs' language and cultural backgrounds and their need for special education, schools can take steps to ensure that all students receive an appropriate education. Those steps are as follow (GaDOE, 2009):

1. When an ELL does not demonstrate progress in a course and the teacher has exhausted the best practices in ELL instruction, the teacher will alert the ELL instructor/case manager, who will provide forms for documenting intervention.

2. After the teacher has attempted and documented intervention, taken anecdotal notes of the ELL's behaviors, and made consistent language **accommodations** and after the student's academic performance within a nine-week grading period has declined, the ELL contact will refer the student to a **response to intervention (RTI) team**.

3. The language assessment committee develops further interventions. If deemed appropriate, the ELL may be referred for a special education evaluation to determine if he or she qualifies as a "student with abilities" under the

Individuals with Disabilities Education Act (IDEA). If so, the student may be served through the special education program. Depending on the extent of the student's disability, the content area teacher, ELL teacher, and special education teacher may work collaboratively to meet the needs of the student.

An ELL who is experiencing learning or behavioral problems in a particular instructional setting may be referred to the RTI team at any time. A student should be referred whenever it is suspected that something beyond language is acting as a barrier to his or her academic achievement. English language learners must be given access to all the same opportunities and services that other students receive.

The information in Table 10.1 can be used to provide guidance for effectively determining whether a student has a language difference or a language disorder. In making this determination, teachers should build a file of documentation to support the need for testing and seek the professional assistance of qualified personnel, such as a speech language pathologist.

Table 10.1 Differences between Students with Language Differences and Language Disorders

Characteristic	Students with Language Differences	Students with Language Disorders
Communicative Skills	Has normal language learning potential	May exhibit speech/language disorders in areas of articulation, voice, fluency, or receptive and expressive language
	Communicative use of English is reduced	
	May be misdiagnosed as having speech and language disorder	May not always achieve communicative competence in first or secondary language
	Home language is impacted	
	Demonstrates interlanguage variables in voice and/or articulation	
	Uses social language to function in society	
Language Skills	Home language is appropriate while English skills are being acquired	May exhibit needs in understanding and expression, including vocabulary and word finding, following directions, forming sentences, and pragmatics in either first and/or second language
	Nonverbal communication skills are appropriate (e.g., eye contact, response to speaker, clarification of response)	
	May not know specific vocabulary but may be familiar with item or concept	Degree of disorder varies, depending on processing skills and cognitive level
	Use of correct syntax is in highly transitional stage that follows similar patterns of normal language development	Difficulties in first language and/or English cannot be attributed to first language loss due to length of time in English-speaking schools
	May pass through predictable periods (i.e., silent period, speech emergence, etc.)	
Sensory Functioning	Usually normal	May have auditory- and/or visual-processing difficulties
		May have vision and/or hearing loss of varying degrees, even with use of glasses or hearing aids

(continued on next page)

Table 10.1 Differences between Students with Language Differences and Language Disorders (continued)

Characteristic	Students with Language Differences	Students with Language Disorders
Health	No significant health characteristics but consider developmental factors in cultural context	May have history of risk infancy, ear infections or hearing problems, sleep or eating disturbances, incontinence, and family incidence of learning problems May have seizures or other health-related conditions that impact learning
Cognitive Abilities	Although problems may be apparent, cognitive abilities are usually normal Students usually score better on nonverbal sections of cognitive tests	Depending on disability, cognition may be significantly affected (mild to profound intellectual disability) or may be average to above
Academic Functioning	Normal language learning potential Apparent problems due to culturally determined learning style, different perceptual strategies, or lack of schooling in home country	Below grade-level performance (15-point discrepancy between ability and achievement) may not be calculable for an ELL student. Factors in addition to numerical discrepancy must be considered and may include inability to make progress in second language acquisition; difficulty retaining academic information in spite of a variety of interventions; history of and reasons for difficulty in schools in home country, etc. Depending on disability or disabilities, academic deficiencies may vary from difficulties in specific skills to pervasive academic difficulties across all skill levels Students may have psychological processing deficits related to disability that significantly impact acquisition, retrieval, and application of information taught

Source: GaDOE, 2009

Providing for Newcomers

When ELLs register for school for the first time, many come with records and course grades from schools in their home countries. When provided with this information, many school districts struggle with how best to award credits, and many guidance departments need training on how to evaluate transcripts. Guidelines for evaluating high school transcripts have been published by the National Association of Foreign Student Advisors (NAFSA): Association of International Educators (Zehr, 2009) and the National Association of Credential Evaluation Services (NACES, 2009). Recognizing the work ELLs have done in their native countries is one step that schools can take to support them in earning a high school diploma.

Conducting routine activities and being well organized will help ELLs navigate the classroom more efficiently. Students will quickly learn where to find information and what and when certain activities will be done. Learning these things will also help ELLs understand how they can fulfill teachers' expectations.

The optimal classroom arrangement allows for many opportunities for interactive activities, and the seating is clustered for **cooperative learning** group work. Having a designated area—such as a table or group of desks, preferably somewhat close to the teacher's desk—provides space where ELLs, buddies, and facilitators can work together. Weekly assignments, schedules, and materials should be displayed in this area. Items might include the following:

- Tape recorder/CD player and earphones
- Computer(s) with English language learning software and headphones
- Plenty of well-illustrated magazines from which to cut pictures and letters
- Classroom library of books and newsprint in different languages
- Storage for **portfolio** file folders
- Scissors, paper, pencils, colored pencils
- Student-made recordings of reading selections from textbooks
- Picture dictionaries
- Index cards for vocabulary words
- Modified text passages
- Word puzzles with content vocabulary terms
- Picture books
- Posters of survival words and **cognates** in different languages
- Journals

Another area in the classroom should be dedicated to creating a word wall of vocabulary terms with which students are working in the weekly lesson. Word walls are commonly used at the elementary level, but they are very effective at the **secondary level,** as well. The teacher should have a more advanced student prepare the word wall. It should include posters, photographs, and drawings that reflect ELLs' diverse countries, cultures, and ethnicities. These kinds of displays validate ELLs and create a comfortable environment for them.

Classroom items can also be labeled in different languages. Translations can be found for terms on several websites, including www.google.com/language_tools, www.freetranslation.com, and http://babelfish.yahoo.com/translate_txt.

Providing areas like these will make ELLs feel welcome and create a low-anxiety environment, which will be beneficial to students' acquiring English. Doing so also demonstrates to ELLs that the teacher cares about their learning, considers it important for them to be engaged in the content, and views them as an integral part of the class.

Professional Collaboration

Members of professional learning communities emphasize a shared vision, parent–teacher communication, and teacher collaboration in developing the best practices and programs for all students, including ELLs. When teachers share successful ideas, practices, and instructional techniques with each other, student performance improves (DuFour, 2004).

According to Barth (2006), good schools have replaced classrooms in isolation and adversarial relationships among adults with congenial and collegial relationships. Effective meetings begin with one or two participants sharing something important or useful that they have recently learned. A teacher new to the school, for instance, might explain how students were evaluated in his or her previous workplace. Once the exchange of so-called craft knowledge becomes sanctioned in this way, educators no longer feel pretentious or in violation of a taboo by sharing their insights. A new taboo against withholding knowledge and insights eventually replaces the old one. Over time, the disclosure of craft knowledge becomes embedded in the culture of the school or school system.

In fact, the existence of a collegial culture in which professionals talk about practice, share craft knowledge, and observe and support one another's success is a precondition for strengthening teacher practice and improving schools. Unless these factors are in place, it will not be possible to bring about meaningful improvement, staff or curriculum development, teacher leadership, student appraisal, team teaching, parent involvement, or sustained change.

Empowerment, recognition, satisfaction, and success in the work of educators will never emerge from "going it alone" as a masterful teacher, principal, or student—no matter how accomplished one is. These outcomes come only from being an active participant in a masterful group of colleagues.

Final Thoughts

Given the rapid increase in the number of ELLs in U.S. schools, many teachers are finding more and more students in their classrooms who have to master content area matter in a language they are still learning. Postponing content instruction until ELLs master English to sufficiently keep pace with their English-speaking peers often results in these students' underachievement and dropping out of school.

The complaint heard in many secondary educational settings is that "these students don't even have basic English skills, and here they are in the middle school where they are supposed to read chapter books and novels and do literature study. I am an English teacher; I should be teaching literature, not the ABCs" (Fu, 2004, p. 8). The content of this book will provide some solutions, as it has illuminated many techniques, approaches, and tools that can be used to provide optimal learning opportunities not only for ELLs but also for struggling native speakers of English. As teachers well know, high school graduation rates can always be improved.

This student is choosing a book to read from the teacher's supplementary classroom library of multicultural stories and stories in different languages.

The philosophy underlying the integration of instruction in language and the content areas is that the responsibility for a child's education is shared among all teachers. Integrating language and content involves incorporating content area material into language classes, modifying expectations for language use, and adapting content materials to provide comprehensible input not only for ELLs but all students in content area classes.

As this discussion of best practices for ELLs at the secondary level continues, it is important to reemphasize that **contextualizing** lessons is indisputability linked to improving ELLs' academic performance (Keefe, 2006). When information is presented through a variety of sources—such as video streaming, pictures, real items, cartoons, and demonstrations—ELLs understand concepts better and therefore improve their mastery of content.

How can instructors provide effective instruction to their English language learners? They can do the following:

- Examine content materials to determine what skills ELLs must have to understand concepts, and then adapt texts and other written materials.

- Identify key words and terms, limiting the number of new academic vocabulary words.

- Establish and maintain routines, always listing and reviewing instructions step by step.

- Use **modeling** to show students the processes you want to see them follow.

- Teach study and metacognitive skills by using graphic organizers, charts, graphs, mapping, *Text Quests*, outlines, and portfolios.

- Provide plenty of visual and graphic depictions of concepts.
- Provide opportunities for cooperative learning daily.
- Use **alternative assessments** and portfolios.

If this text is being used for a teacher-training course, the course can conclude by viewing the video *Passion and Persistence,* by Richard DuFour. This is a short, seven-minute, reading video without photos or animation, but it delivers a powerful message for teachers, administrators, and all stakeholders in education.

Teachers not only need but deserve to develop processes and pedagogical practices that will build on ELLs' languages and cultures, not take way from them. Through a sociopolitical lens, educational leaders must develop a greater understanding of and response to the policy implications that create inequities in the education of ELLs (Kaplan & Rodriguez, 2008). Educational leaders must also redefine the concept of a highly qualified teacher by moving beyond content knowledge and incorporating process, pedagogy, and policy engagement to be educationally responsive to the needs of ELLs.

The most challenging aspect of professional development in the area of day-to-day, effective ELL instruction is adjusting teaching styles and abandoning traditional approaches to instruction. Teachers' resistance to change is a significant barrier to improving instructional methods. By embracing different perspectives, appreciating diversity, and adopting nontraditional teaching techniques, teachers will see student performance improve.

References

Ayers, W. (1994). *To teach: The journey of a teacher*. New York: Teachers College Press.

Barth, R. (2006). Improving relationships within the schoolhouse. *Educational Leadership*. Retrieved July 20, 2007, from www.ascd.org

DuFour, R. (2004). Professional learning communities. *Educational Leadership*. Retrieved July 18, 2006, from www.ascd.org

DuFour, R. (Producer). (2002). *Passion and persistence* [Video]. How to Develop a Professional Learning Community. Retrieved on September 21, 2008, from www.solution-tree.com/Public/Media.aspx?ShowDetail=true&ProductID=VIF067

Fu, D. (2004). Teaching ELL students in regular classrooms at the secondary level. *Voices from the Middle, 11*(4), 8–15.

Georgia Department of Education (GaDOE). (2009). *Georgia Department of Education Title III Resource Guide 2009–2010*. Retrieved on September 21, 2009, from www.doe.k12.ga.us/DMGetDocument.aspx/2009-10%20Title%20III%20ESOL%20Resource%20Guide%20073109.pdf?p=6CC6799F8C1371F6E3A23FF57AB6E574361E3610E66D5BB042BD6AB13082A4D5&Type=D

Kaplan, K., & Rodriguez, J. (2008). The preparation of highly qualified teachers for English language learners: Educational responsiveness for unmet needs. *Equity and Excellence in Education, 41*(3), 372–387.

Keefe, M. R. (2006). *The impact of training secondary teachers to adapt content to empower English for speakers of other languages*. Unpublished dissertation, Nova Southeastern University, North Miami Beach, FL.

Keefe, M. R. (Producer/Researcher). (2008). *Voices of immigrant ELL high school students*. TV Production Classes, Martin County School District, Florida.

National Association of Credential Evaluation Services (NACES). (2009). The Standard of Excellence. Retrieved on September 1, 2009 from www.naces.org/aboutnaces.htm

Smith, J., Coggins, C., & Cardoso, J. (2008). Best practices for English language learners in Massachsetts: Five years after the question 2 mandate. *Equity and Excellence in Education, 41*(3), 293–310.

Sobel, A., & Kugler, E. (2007). Building partnerships with immigrant parents. *Educational Leadership, 64*(6), 62–66.

Zehr, M. A. (2009). High school credits for ELLs still a challenge. *Education Week, 28*(19), 12–14.

Glossary

Ableism   Discrimination based on an individual's disability.

Academic language   A complex form of language generally acquired in a classroom setting; focuses on abstract topics and uses specialized vocabulary and complex sentence structures.

Academic language proficiency   The level of language ability with which a student can use advanced reading and writing skills; usually takes four to six years to develop in a second language.

Accommodations   Allowances given to ELLs during tests, including extra time, having directions read aloud, or reading the test in the student's first language.

Acculturation   The process of adapting effectively to the mainstream culture; to be distinguished from enculturation, the process through which individuals learn the patterns of their own culture. To acculturate is to adapt a second culture without necessarily giving up one's first culture. Acculturation is an additive process, in which individuals preserve the right to participate in their own heritage.

Acquisition versus learning hypothesis   Stephen Krashen's theory that there are two distinct ways of developing ability in a second language: Language acquisition is a subconscious process of absorbing language, and language learning is a formal, conscious process involving grammar and rules. Acquisition is the most important process.

Adequate yearly progress (AYP)   A benchmark used to guide schools in assisting all students to reach certain goals and standards; established by the No Child Left Behind (NCLB) Act of 2001.

Affective filter hypothesis   The theory that a mental block, caused by affective or emotional factors, can prevent input from reaching the student's language acquisition device (the LAD suggested by Chomsky).

Ageism   Discrimination based on an individual's age.

Alternative assessment   Authentic testing and assessment settings that show what students can do, not what they cannot; encourages student responsibility and accommodates varying student interests, learning styles, backgrounds, and language levels.

Analytical rubric   An assessment device in which the requirements of an assignment are indicated by numbers or points that correspond to the key aspects or features of the assignment; for instance, the student will earn 4 points if the project includes the requisite four features.

Assimilation   The process by which members of an ethnic group are absorbed into the dominant culture, effectively giving up the elements of their own culture. Cultural assimilation is the process by which individuals adopt the behaviors, values, beliefs, and lifestyles of the dominant culture.

Assimilationist   A member of an ethnic group who becomes absorbed into the dominant culture and whose home culture gradually disappears; also someone who supports the process of assimilation.

Basic Interpersonal Communication Skills (BICS)   Language skills that are needed in social situations. ELLs use these skills when they are on the playground, in the lunch room, on the school bus, at parties, playing sports and talking on the telephone, and are not very demanding cognitively.

Biculturalism   The state of being able to function successfully in two cultures: that of one's native country and that of the dominant society in which one lives. Bicultural individuals can mediate between the dominant discourse of educational institutions and the realities they face as members of subordinate cultures.

Bloom's taxonomy   A hierarchy of thinking skills in which knowledge is considered the lowest level and evaluation, the highest level; created by Benjamin Bloom.

Bottom-up strategies   Text-based listening approaches in which the listener relies on the language in the message he or she hears.

Bridging   Laying a foundation for understanding by tapping students' prior knowledge.

Building background   Conducting activities that help students learn those concepts and ideas that are necessary for understanding new information.

Classism   Discrimination based on an individual's socioeconomic status, such as upper, middle, or lower class.

Cognates   Words in English that are similar to words in a student's first language.

Cognitive academic language learning approach (CALLA)   An approach in which transitional instruction is provided from a standard ELL or bilingual program to a grade-level content area classroom.

Cognitive academic language proficiency (CALP) Formal academic learning, which includes listening, speaking, reading, and writing about subject area content material, and is the level of language learning essential for students to succeed in school and pass high-stakes tests.

Cognitive demand The level of difficulty that a topic or type of content poses for the ELL.

Collectivist perspective A cultural orientation characterized by supporting the family, giving assistance when needed, owning property communally, and guiding one another's behavior.

Comprehensibility The level of conceptual understanding a student must have to process and absorb a given concept; must be presented in a format that students can understand, regardless of their first language.

Contextual support The clues provided to a speaker or listener that assist in conveying the meaning of the language.

Contextualize To create sensory experiences through the use of manipulatives, videos, pictures, and type for the purpose of making language more accessible.

Cooperative learning An approach in which students are grouped together to solve problems, complete projects, and so on; is most effective when students have certain roles and follow certain rules of engagement.

Creole (pronounced "Kree-ohl") A dialect of French spoken among Haitians.

Cryptograms Vocabulary puzzle in which salient vocabulary terms are encrypted.

Culturally biased The characteristic of test items or instructional materials that require students to have specific cultural experiences or background knowledge to complete them successfully; culturally biased materials depict ethnic groups in limited and stereotypical ways.

Culture The ideas, customs, skills, arts and tools that characterize a given group of people in a certain period of time.

Cummins' quadrants James Cummins's characterization of language based on levels of contextual support and cognitive demand. Quadrant I represents the language that is easiest to master. It is characterized by a high degree of contextual support—that is, a lot of visual clues and realia to aid understanding—and a low degree of cognitive demand. Quadrant IV represents language with a high degree of difficulty. Not only are the contextual clues greatly reduced, as in lectures and textbooks, but the topics addressed by the language are unfamiliar and pose a greater cognitive challenge. Quadrants II and III are intermediary areas between Quadrant I and Quadrant IV.

Customized dictionaries Student-created vocabulary lists in which words are translated without the use of definitions; to be used during testing settings.

Dialogue journal A type of journal in which the student and teacher exchange communication about a topic or issue, each responding to the other's journal entry; can be used to elicit discussion of a more personal nature from the student.

Directed reading thinking activities (DRTA) Activities conducted with small groups of students that include previewing, predicting, reading, checking, and summarizing.

Educative A type of scoring criteria that helps students understand how they can learn and perform in a particular content area.

Ethnocentrism The belief that one's own culture is superior to that of others; results in the tendency to evaluate members of other cultures according to the values and standards of one's own culture.

Evaluative A type of scoring criteria that indicates ways to design instruction that fits individual students' needs.

Experiential activities Activities conducted at all stages of second language acquisition that includes playing games, solving problems in groups, making crafts and models, taking field trips, and role playing.

Facilitator A person who interprets information in a language that is not the dominant language of instruction.

First language (L1) The primary language a person heard and spoke at home, and in which a person thinks, sometimes referred to as the *home language, heritage language,* or *native language.*

Fluency The quality of spoken language that is free flowing and devoid of grammatical and syntactical errors.

Formative A type of scoring criteria that provides information about a student's strengths and weaknesses; obtained from assessments conducted in an informal setting, such as a weekly test.

Grammatical interference Elements of one's first language that are different from those of the second language and thus interfere with the correctness of speech in the second language.

Graphic organizers Visual tools, such as charts and webs, that students use to record and organize information in advance of applying it in some kind of discussion or project; can be used to help lighten the linguistic load of text in a textbook or to help students organize their thoughts on paper.

Heterogeneous grouping A grouping strategy in which students of different languages and academic levels are assigned to work together.

High-stakes tests Tests students must take and earn a certain score to matriculate to the next grade level or earn a passing score in all components to gain a standard high school diploma.

Higher-order thinking skills The skills necessary to respond to information and questions of evaluation, synthesis, and analysis. *Refer to* Bloom's taxonomy.

Holistic rubric An assessment device in which the requirements of an assignment are described and evaluated along various levels of quality or ability; for instance, the highest level might be described as "proficient" and the lowest level as "limited."

Homogeneous grouping   A grouping strategy in which students of the same language and academic levels are assigned to work together.

Individuals with Disabilities Education Act (IDEA)   A law ensuring services to children with disabilities throughout the nation. IDEA governs how states and public agencies provide early intervention, special education, and related services to eligible infants, toddlers, children and youth with disabilities.

Individualist perspective   A cultural orientation characterized by the value of individuals working independently, thinking critically, and practicing self-control.

Information gap   The situation in which participants in a conversation or discussion have different sets of information; to bridge the gap, participants may have to clarify their own meaning or ask for confirmation of their own understanding. Information Gap activities involve students in reconciling such differences in information to solve a problem or complete a picture or puzzle.

Input hypothesis   Stephen Krashen's theory that people acquire language in only one way: by understanding messages received via the comprehensible input of information.

Interaction   Cooperative and peer learning activities that allow for the negotiation of language meaning within given content.

Jigsaw   A form of Information Gap activity in which groups of students cooperate to arrange pieces of information into a whole picture or complete story.

Language acquisition device (LAD)   The device or region of the brain that facilitates learning symbolic language, as proposed by Noam Chomsky.

Language focus lesson   Lesson that specifically targets the vocabulary and terms that apply to the topic being studied, and that students will encounter within the lesson and activities.

Language minority   Individuals whose first language is not the language of the dominant culture and thus not the language of instruction.

Mainstream classes   Content area classrooms in which instruction is provided in English, with no extra language support.

Modeling   Behavior in which teachers perform clear examples of what students are to learn and do, whether independently or in a group.

Modifications   Adaptations made to tests and testing situations that include simplifying the language, reading the questions aloud, using word banks, providing matching exercises, allowing students to respond orally, and following a dual-grading system (i.e., giving one grade for content and another for structure).

Monitor hypothesis   Stephen Krashen's theory that conscious learning and the outcome of grammar instruction serve only as a monitor or editor for ELLs; similar to Chomsky's theory of the language acquisition device.

Morpheme   The smallest unit of meaning in a language.

Multicultural education   A field of study and an emerging discipline; the major aim is to create equal educational opportunities for students from diverse racial, ethnic, social-class, and cultural groups. One of its important goals is to help all students to acquire the knowledge, attitudes, and skills needed to function effectively in a pluralistic democratic society and to interact, negotiate, and communicate with people from diverse groups in order to create a civic and moral community that works for the common good.

Multicultural ideology   The vision of an open society in which individuals from diverse cultural, ethnic, language, and socioeconomic groups have equal opportunities to function and participate.

Multiliteracies   A term that is used to describe two important arguments regarding emerging cultural, institutional, and global order, which is the multiplicity of communications channels and media, and the increasing saliency of cultural and linguistic diversity.

Multiple perspectives   The ability to look at an issue from several different viewpoints without claiming any one of them to be good or bad, right or wrong, and so on.

Natural order hypothesis   Stephen Krashen's theory that a person acquires, not learns, the grammatical structures of a language in a predictable order.

No Child Left Behind Act (NCLB)   The federal law, passed in 2001, that mandates higher standards for programs for low-level socioeconomic and ELL students, in particular, but also for all students in grades PK–12; results are generally measured through the use of high-stakes testing.

Oral proficiency   The degree to how well someone can speak and articulate responses.

Phonics   The correspondence between sounds and letters in learning a language.

Phonology   The sound system of a language.

Pluralism   The state in which minority and ethnic groups and their advocates assert that they have a right, if not a responsibility, to maintain valued elements of their ethnic cultures. In a pluralistic society, members of diverse cultural groups have equal opportunities for success, cultural similarities and differences are valued, and students are provided cultural alternatives.

Portfolios   Collections of student work that represent a selection of performances over a certain period of time; students are involved in selecting, evaluating, and organizing the work.

Positive interdependence   The condition that is fostered when students work with partners or in groups to solve problems; when practiced regularly, it promotes field independence among individual students in testing situations.

Prejudice   An adverse judgment or opinion formed before receiving or without knowledge or examination of the facts; involves the irrational suspicion or hatred of people from a particular group, race, or religion.

Print-rich environment   A classroom that is characterized by the presence of ample print materials in varied appealing genres, ranging from posters and maps to books.

Process writing   An approach to writing instruction in which a composition is completed in stages such as prewriting or planning, drafting or writing, and editing or revising; allows students to make a variety of mistakes, recognize these mistakes either on their own or with a peer, correct these mistakes, and continue to write.

Reciprocal teaching   An instructional strategy in which pairs of students question each other while engaged in problem solving.

Response to Intervention (RTI) team   A specified group of individuals, including teachers, administrators and counselors, at a school site who are designated to discuss individual student issues and behavior, and who make a decision about optimal programming for that student.

Revoicing   An instructional strategy in which the teacher repeats some or all of what a student just said, modeling a more fully realized version of the statement.

Role-playing   Activities in which students assume character or roles and dramatize a given situation for an audience.

Rubric   An assessment tool that informs students of the expectations of an assignment before they begin work on the assignment; also used to evaluate the depth, breadth, creativity, detail, and completeness of the completed assignment.

Scaffolding   An instructional strategy in which students are provided the encouragement, support, and language assistance needed to reach higher levels of comprehension; uses supportive activities to help students perform beyond their current level of competence.

Schedule of balanced instruction (SBI)   An instructional model in which a class or course are divided into short time periods for students to do a variety of tasks.

Schema building   An instructional strategy in which new information is woven into or related to existing knowledge or structures of meaning; involves activities such as previewing the text, reading the summary first, chunking information on a graphic organizer, and so on.

Second language (L2)   The language a person is attempting to acquire and/or the language in which the person is immersed.

Secondary level   Students or schools in grades 6 through 12.

Sexism   Discrimination based on an individual's gender or sexual orientation.

Sheltered instruction   A nontraditional approach to instruction that includes the use of many visuals, graphic organizers, vocabulary games, cooperative learning settings, and so on.

Sheltered instruction observation protocol (SIOP)   A model of lesson planning and instructional delivery comprised of 30 instructional strategies that are grouped into 8 components.

Silent period   The length of time ELLs may not respond verbally to content materials or oral questioning while they are in the preproductive stage of second language acquisition.

Social language   The common, daily language used in social situations; it is simple in structure and usually accompanied by contextual support.

Specially designed academic instruction in English (SDAIE)   An instructional approach in which traditional strategies are adapted; access to content area knowledge is provided through language development and other instructional modifications.

Stereotyping   The process of making a generalization about an entire group of people based on the salient characteristics of the group; a stereotype is rooted in the assumption that the group to which someone belongs is homogeneous with regard to a wide range of traits.

Summative   A type of scoring criteria that provides information about a student's knowledge.

Syntax   The structure and organization of a language.

Text heavy   The quality of a text that is linguistically and conceptually dense; characterizes many content area textbooks.

Text Quest   An activity in which students find specific information in a content area textbook; develops familiarity with the text and the ability to know where to find information. *Text Quests* can be done independently or with partners or groups.

Text re-presentation   An instructional strategy in which students demonstrate their understanding of a concept by transforming content from one genre to another.

Thematic approach   An instructional approach in which teachers in different content areas collaborate and organize instruction to cover the same topic and the same time.

Top-down strategies   Listener-based listening approaches that tap students' background knowledge of the topic.

Unconscious marginalization   Behavior in which teachers unintentionally or unknowingly ignore or demean students—for instance, by limiting their interaction with the teacher or other students.

Zone of proximal development   A concept introduced by Lev Vygotsky that suggests that what learners can do with assistance today, they can do independently tomorrow; advocates instruction in which content becomes increasingly more challenging but is supplemented with support and encouragement.

Acronyms in ELL Education

A wide variety of acronyms are used in the area of ELL education. Below are some of the most common, presented in alphabetical order:

ELLs	English language learners
ESL	English as a second language
ESOL	English for speakers of other languages
FES	Full English speaker
IEP	Intensive English program
L1	First language
L2	Second language
LCDS	Linguistically and culturally diverse students
LEP	Limited English proficient or language-enriched pupil
LES	Limited English speaker
LF	Limited, former (being monitored for two years after exit from a program)
LMS	Language minority student
LN	An active ELL not being served
LP	Pending testing
LY	Limited, yes (active in current ESOL program)
LZ	A former ELL no longer being monitored
NES	Non-English speaker

Schedule of Balanced Instruction (SBI)

Here are two working models for conducting activities that maximize the class schedule:

Total class time: 90 minutes

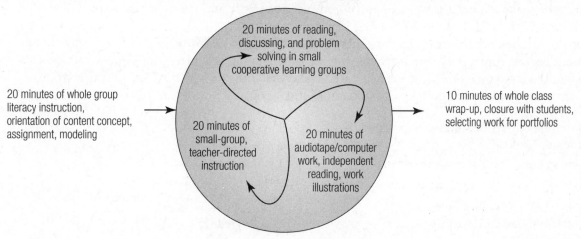

20 minutes of whole group literacy instruction, orientation of content concept, assignment, modeling

20 minutes of reading, discussing, and problem solving in small cooperative learning groups

20 minutes of small-group, teacher-directed instruction

20 minutes of audiotape/computer work, independent reading, work illustrations

10 minutes of whole class wrap-up, closure with students, selecting work for portfolios

Total class time: 55–60 minutes

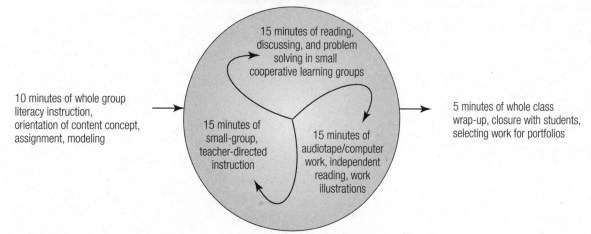

10 minutes of whole group literacy instruction, orientation of content concept, assignment, modeling

15 minutes of reading, discussing, and problem solving in small cooperative learning groups

15 minutes of small-group, teacher-directed instruction

15 minutes of audiotape/computer work, independent reading, work illustrations

5 minutes of whole class wrap-up, closure with students, selecting work for portfolios

Documentation of ELL Strategies

In this appendix, ELL strategies are grouped according to modality, such as oral, reading, writing, modifications, adaptations, visuals, reinforcement, comprehension checks, and vocabulary development. Teachers can use these modalities to code activities in their lesson plans as they incorporate these different teaching tools into their daily practice (NSU, 2007).

Teachers may want to print this list on a colored piece of paper and then use that same color of type when they write "ELL" codes, identifying ELL activities during the lesson. This makes it very convenient for the teacher, administrators, and others to identify when and how ELL strategies are being implemented. For example, if a lesson includes the use of a graphic organizer, the teacher can indicate "8e" or when the lesson includes student-generated test items indicate "7f" or "1d" in the lesson plan, if the student activity is reducing nonessential details, and so on.

1. Modifies appropriate instructional program to meet the needs of ELLs by:
   a. teaching concrete first and then abstract.
   b. relating to students' experiences.
   c. using visual representations.
   d. reducing nonessential details.
   e. checking word choice and sentence order.
   f. developing necessary background knowledge.
   g. using media materials and manipulatives to explain content.

2. Uses "pre-" activities:
   a. Jigsaw
   b. language games
   c. demonstrations
   d. songs and raps

3. Uses oral strategies:
   a. props
   b. chunking
   c. reading aloud
   d. modeling
   e. storytelling

4. Identifies and selects appropriate materials:
   a. multimedia
   b. English language learning software
   c. video streaming
   d. native language support

5. Cultivates academic vocabulary by:
   a. explaining terms in words students know.
   b. using pictures.
   c. using realia to illustrate new words.
   d. using individual card files.
   e. playing Word Bingo.
   f. conducting the ABCs of a Topic activity.
   g. creating a word wall.

6. Uses writing strategies:
   a. process writing
   b. the *Into-through-Beyond* activity
   c. journal writing
   d. shared writing
   e. graphic organizers for writing

7. Reinforces study skills by using:
   a. graphs/charts.
   b. rubrics.
   c. Venn diagrams.
   d. underlining.
   e. highlighting.
   f. student-generated test items.

8. Modifies content area instruction by using:
   a. *Text Quests*.
   b. highlighting of main points.
   c. paraphrasing.
   d. related vocabulary content organizers.
   e. picture/page number graphic organizers.

9. Addresses language learning through:
   a. the thematic approach.
   b. semantic webbing.
   c. pairs/partners work.
   d. maps/illustrations
   e. the *Pass the Poster* activity.
   f. cooperative learning groups.

10. Implements thinking skills:
    a. predicting
    b. observing
    c. categorizing
    d. sequencing
    e. summarizing
    f. classifying
    g. reporting techniques

11. Uses specific classroom management techniques to enhance comprehensibility:
    a. establishing simple class rules with visual cues
    b. checking for comprehension of rules
    c. providing positive feedback
    d. utilizing the buddy system

12. Provides forms of alternative assessment for ELLs:
    a. drawings
    b. interviews
    c. rubrics
    d. demonstrations
    e. oral tests
    f. games
    g. portfolios
    h. group projects
    i. checklists
    j. open book quizzes

13. Uses reading strategies:
    a. graphic organizers
    b. guided reading
    c. self-questioning
    d. read-alouds
    e. skimming
    f. summarizing
    g. reading summaries
    h. question–answer responses

14. Builds and checks comprehension using:
    a. learning logs
    b. dialogue journals
    c. role-playing
    d. "writing strip" stories
    e. cloze activities
    f. experiments
    g. illustrations
    h. writing headlines

15. Adapts content area tests to the appropriate level of ELLs' language development: preproductive, early production, speech emergence, and intermediate fluency.

16. Uses displays, pictures, reading materials/classroom library, wall hangings, and instructional activities to address cultural diversity and encourage tolerance.

Source: Palm Beach County School District, www.palmbeach.k12.fl.us/Multicultural/ESOLCurriculumDocs

English/Spanish Cognates

This list can be enlarged and placed on the classroom wall.

All Content

predict	predecir
connect	conectar
describe	describer
analyze	analizar
compare	comparer
contrast	contrastar
respond	responder
infer	inferior
conclude	concluir
evaluate	evaluar
paraphrase	parafrasear
demonstrate	demonstrar
differentiate	diferenciar
classify	clasificar
simplify	simplificar
resolve	resolver
respect	respetar
appeal	apelar
declare	declarer

Science

classification	clasificacion
reproduce	reproducir
hypothesis	hipotesis
cycle	ciclo
metamorphosis	metamorfosis
insect	insecto
photosynthesis	fotosintesis
rodent	roedor
membrane	membrane
extinct	extinto

Math

number	numero
multiplication	multiplicacion
division	dividion
fractions	fracciones
problem	problema
numerator	numerador
denominator	denominador
difference	diferencia
sum	suma
equal	igual
reciprocal	reciproco
parallel	paralelo

Social Studies

democracy	democracia
republic	republica
constitution	constitucion
federation	federacion
United Nations	NacionesUnidos
United States	EstadosUnidos
civility	civilidad
vote	votar
congress	congreso
legislature	legislatura
presidency	presidencia
reform	reformar
annexation	anexion
public sector	sector publico

Geography

transportation	transpotacion
city	ciudad
state	estado
nation	nacion
region	region
continent	continente
hemisphere	hemisfero
globe	globo
desert	desierto
mountains	montanas
peninsulas	peninsulas
islands	islas
lakes	lagos
rivers	rios
gulfs	golfos
oceans	ceanos
poles	polares
latitude	latitude
longitude	longitude

Legal Foundations for ELL Instruction

The following court cases and legislative acts are arranged in chronological order, from oldest to most recent:

Brown v. Board of Education of Topeka (1954)—This was a landmark decision of the United States Supreme Court that declared state laws establishing separate public schools for black and white students denied black children equal educational opportunities. The decision overturned earlier rulings going back to *Plessy v. Ferguson* in 1896. Handed down on May 17, 1954, the Warren Court's unanimous (9–0) decision stated that "separate educational facilities are inherently unequal" (http://brownvboard.org/summary/).

Title VI of the Civil Rights Act (1964)—A federal law that stated that non-English speakers are entitled to equal education opportunities (www.justice.gov/crt/cor/coord/titlevi.php).

Lau v. Nichols (1974)—A U.S. Supreme Court decision about English language use in the schools. In the case, a group of Chinese students in San Francisco sued the school district, claiming they were denied access to a meaningful education because they could not understand the all-English instruction. The students claimed that this was a violation of the Civil Rights Act, which prohibits discrimination on the basis of race, color, or national origin. The Court found for the plaintiffs but did not specify a remedy for their complaint. Instead, the Court noted that several solutions were possible, including native language instruction and ESOL classes. Following the decision, several states enacted legislation mandating service for ELLs (www.pbs.org/beyondbrown/brownpdfs/launichols.pdf).

Equal Educational Opportunities Act (1974)—This act is currently the strongest federal protection for the educational rights of ELLs. Section 1703 requires state educational agencies (SEAs) and school districts to take action to overcome language barriers that impede English Language Learner (ELL) students from participating equally in school districts' educational programs (http://www.justice.gov/crt/edo/ellpage.php).

Castaneda v. Pichard (1981)—In this case, the Fifth Circuit Court of Appeals formulated a test to determine whether school districts are complying with the Equal Educational Opportunities Act (1974). The three-part test includes the following criteria:

1. *Theory:* The school must pursue a program based on an educational theory recognized as valid or at least as a legitimate experimental strategy.
2. *Practice:* The school must actually implement the program by providing the instructional

practices, resources, and personnel necessary to transfer theory to reality.

3. *Results:* The school must not persist in a program that fails to produce results (www.alliance. brown.edu/tdl/policy/pol_rsrc_crtlg.shtml).

Plyler v. Doe (1982)—A U.S. Supreme Court decision that stated that undocumented children and young adults have the same right to attend public schools as U.S. citizens. Schools cannot refuse to enroll or educate children based on their parents' illegal entry into the United States. Schools may not require students or parents to disclose or document their immigration status or make inquiries that may expose their undocumented status. In addition, public schools may not require Social Security numbers or "green cards" from students as a condition of admission. Students without Social Security numbers should be assigned numbers generated by the school (www.americanpatrol.com/REFERENCE/PlylerVDoeSummary.html).

No Child Left Behind (NCLB) Act of 2001—This act provides for strong accountability for the education of all children and for certain provisions specific to limited English proficient students, especially under Titles I and III of the Act. NCLB also provides funds to states and local schools and universities to carry out the intent of the Act (www.alliance.brown.edu/tdl/policy/pol_rsrc_crtlg.shtml).

References

American Patrol. *Plyler vs. Doe 1982: A summary.* Retrieved on October 16, 2008, from www.americanpatrol.com/REFERENCE/PlylerVDoeSummary.html

Brown Foundation. *Brown v. Board of Education about the case.* Retrieved on October 16, 2008, from http://brownvboard.org/summary/

Public Broadcasting System. *Beyond Brown pursuing the promise.* Retrieved on October 16, 2008, from www.pbs.org/beyondbrown/brownpdfs/launichols.pdf

Teaching Diverse Learners. *Policy legal provisions for the education of English language learners.* Retrieved on October 16, 2008, from www.alliance.brown.edu/tdl/policy/pol_rsrc_crtlg.shtml

U.S. Department of Justice. Civil Rights Division. *Discrimination Against English Language Learner Students.* Retrieved on October 16, 2008, from www.justice.gov/crt/edo/ellpage.php

U.S. Department of Justice. *Title VI of the Civil Rights Act of 1964.* Retrieved on October 16, 2008, from www.justice.gov/crt/cor/coord/titlevi.php

Index